WITHDRAWN

WALKING NORTH
WITH KEATS

Pencil sketch of John Keats, by Charles Armitage Brown.

WALKING NORTH WITH KEATS

Carol Kyros Walker

Yale University Press

New Haven and London

1992

For Norman, enough of a Scot to rejoice in my long walk.

Published with assistance from the
Charles S. Brooks Fund.

Designed by John Nicoll
Set in Linotron Ehrhardt
by Best-set Typesetter Ltd., Hong Kong
Printed in Hong Kong by Kwong Fat Offset Printing Co. Ltd.

Library of Congress Cataloging-in-Publication Data

Walker, Carol Kyros, 1934–
Walking north with Keats / Carol Kyros Walker.
p.   cm.
Includes bibliographical references and index.
ISBN 0-300-04824-6 (alk. paper)
1. Keats, John, 1795–1821—Journeys—England, Northern.   2. Keats,
John, 1795–1821—Journeys—Scotland.   3. Keats, John, 1795–1821—
Correspondence.   4. Poets, English—19th century—Correspondence.
5. Scotland—Description and travel—1801–1900.   6. England,
Northern—Description and travel.   7. Walking—England, Northern.
8. Walking—Scotland.   I. Title.
PR4836.W27   1992
821'.7—dc20
[B]
                                          91-25635
                                          CIP

CONTENTS

PREFACE

This book had its very simple beginning when I was travelling south, not north, with Keats in England in the winter of 1978 to photograph some of the places he had visited on the Isle of Wight. It was a brief indulgence, growing out of my study of photography and a much longer concern with Keats. I sent a few casual photographs, along with a narrative about my solitary adventure to the south and amusing captions for the photographs (such as "Beauty is Truth" for one of the buildings in Shanklin where Keats and Brown had stayed that now housed a hair salon), to my friend the Keats scholar Jack Stillinger. He responded with a suggestion which struck home so effectively that I could not afterwards remember when it had not seemed imperative to follow it—to photograph the walking tour Keats took with Brown in the summer of 1818 and then make a book of it.

For three successive summers, in 1979, 1980, and 1981, I followed the tour alone, making my photographic study. My route had been clarified by Nelson Bushnell, an American scholar who made the journey almost entirely on foot in 1931 (with a follow-up visit in 1935 to correct his error of having gone up the wrong side of Loch Ness). A veteran of World War I, Bushnell was conditioned to footing it. He pieced together all the evidence left by Keats and Brown in their letters and a journal, tested it out on his walk, and produced *A Walk after John Keats*, published in 1936. The book was an anecdotal, witty, engaging work that did the job of documenting and confirming the 1818 tour while it entertained with Bushnell's adventures. His scholarship, much of it relegated to an appendix, his map, and his itinerary were invaluable in my own pursuit and are much in evidence in my book.

Bushnell's pioneering freed me to concentrate on the photography. I resolved to keep my visual experiences as responsive to the landscape as possible, not to impose an interpretation on what I found. To that end, I attempted to simulate the circumstances and conditions Keats found, arriving at a given place as close as possible to the same day of the year Keats had been there and photographing at the same time of day he had experienced a particular view. If Keats ate dinner before his walk to see the Druid Circle, I did too; if he wrote a poem about Ailsa Craig in the evening, I found it in my Nikon then.

I did, of course, have to make concessions to the modern world and to the weather. Many of the old coaching roads Keats trod with his friend Brown are now major highways, so it made sense for me to rent an English Ford, pack my camera equipment into it, and drive a crowded motorway to a place where I could get out and walk. But even then there were surprises. The lush, colorful pilgrimage from Bowness to Ambleside that filled the journals of Keats, Brown, and even Bushnell turned out to be the A591 of today, heavily traveled in July by automobiles, caravans, and lorries. The rain never let up when I first attempted to climb Skiddaw, so I had to try again a year later. I couldn't (and wouldn't if I could) take a small boat with two old men singing ballads from Portpatrick, Scotland, to Donaghadee, Ireland; the impersonal Sealink ferry served my queasy stomach better. A military guard stopped me to search my bags as I went from zone to zone in central Belfast, and once as I was photographing I found my lens filled with the camouflage pattern of a uniform. Keats had seen poverty but not rifles and barbed-wire fences. It took two trips to Belfast to bag just a few shots. And I made three separate journeys to Mull before I triumphed over vague directions to find Derry-na-cullen, a ruin no one on the island could understand my wanting to see, much less photograph.

But the instances in which I was indeed able to recapture Keats's history were so many that I could stake my creative energies upon them. There were places, even in the tourist-dominated Lake District, where I experienced such perfect solitude and sensed such strange remoteness that I knew my work as a photographer would reveal Keats's story. This was more frequently the case as I travelled north, where my guides often were not poets, scholars, or cartographers, but those who had the Gaelic, as they say in Scotland. Increasingly I noticed that the more attention I paid to time, the more I experienced timelessness.

"I have a feeling that the setting of Keats's walk has changed more in the half century since my book than it did in the century between him and me," Bushnell wrote to me in the early stages of my work (letter, December 31, 1978). When I thought of the time I got caught in what threatened to be an eternal orbit in a British roundabout, a road construction that the pre-motoring travellers from 1818 through the 1930s never had to cope with, I agreed. Then again, I remembered my solitary, rather risky hike through bogs and over rocky paths on the Isle of Mull, and took exception.

The physical world of the walking tour as I experienced it had a prevailing quality of harshness, which I recognized to some extent as I travelled and photographed, but appreciated more fully as I began to process the film, examine the proofsheets, reexperience what I had seen, and slowly build the body of photographs that are now a part of this book. Keats's letters about his trip tend to make light of the genuine severity of the landscape he crossed, climbed, and responded to emotionally. As I tried to reconcile the generally upbeat tone of his letters with what I identified as a gothic experience, I came to understand that metaphor and fact lead to different conclusions. The walking tour celebrated the conjunction of melancholy and joy, pleasure and pain that would be found in his poetry. At the same time, however, it led to the terrible deterioration of Keats's health.

My photography responds to these perceptions. I have intended it not to be merely documentary but to express a Keatsian sensibility. Buildings and ruins are sometimes shown from the perspective of someone short looking up, to show how Keats, who was conscious of his lack of height, might have felt when he encountered a large structure. I have emphasized images of pairs of men, reiterating male companionship and friendship. One of the strongest interpretations available through the photographs is somatic. Keats's health, which was tested to the limits by the strenuous walking tour, is a central issue. The severe, damp conditions of the Isle of Mull and the taxing, mist-enshrouded ascent of Ben Nevis, for example, are stressed in the photography. Just as Keats and Brown cite the sore throat contracted on the Isle of Mull as the cause of Keats's having to return to England prematurely, so do I cite all that is dark and portentous in the environment of the journey, prefiguring it early in the photographic retracing of the tour and referring to it far less obliquely at the end with skull and crossbone tombstones at Beauly Priory, night imagery at Inverness, and desolation at the narrows of Cromarty Firth. The sheer wetness of the walking tour points up the irony of the inscription Keats composed for his own tombstone in Rome three years later: "Here lies one whose name was writ in water."

While travelling to do the photography for the Keats tour I also visited libraries, the most fascinating of which were in Liverpool, Carlisle, Belfast, Ayr, and Glasgow. I examined newspapers published in the areas in which Keats travelled for the approximate dates he was there. This research bore significant fruit, which turns up in the introduction of my book, where I develop a picture of how the world appeared to local reporters when Keats passed through.

Beyond establishing a setting for the tour, the introduction is meant to provide the general reader with an understanding of Keats's circumstances when he walked north with Brown. Much of what Keats is famous for comes after the 1818 trip, and Brown figured importantly in his life after the tour. The biographical background I offer on Keats, his family, and Brown up to the time of the walk north should be regarded as basic, however, and the reader who wishes to go much beyond the summer of 1818 or do detective work on Keatsian data should turn to three excellent biographies that came out in the 1960s: two by American scholars, Walter Jackson Bate and Aileen Ward, and the third by a British scholar and poet, Robert Gittings. Reading these books comparatively one finds, for example, disagreement about Georgiana's age, the Keats children's inheritance, and the character of George.

Keats's letters are represented with all his idiosyncrasies of spelling and punctuation intact. If Keats writes "recollo-lections" we respect his rendering of the word. Perhaps we ought to consider whether somewhere in his subconscious Keats might have been playing with a songlike "recall o" plus "collection," because word play and ballads figure so wonderfully in what he wrote on his travells. Also, Keats produced his travel letters and poems at times and in places not at all conducive to the physical act of writing—in a smoke-filled shepherd's hut or on the top of a mountain, after hours of strenuous clambering (and sometimes without daylight). Of course, some of the vagaries of spelling, grammar, and punctuation are simply consistent with his overall habit of writing as if a dam had broken and stylistic formalities were inadequate to guide the flow.

ACKNOWLEDGMENTS

I am grateful to several people and institutions who invited me to present my walking tour project as an illustrated lecture before it became a book. Ben Harris McClary arranged for me to present the work at Middle Georgia College in 1979 and 1984. Carl Woodring, whom I had come to know through his National Endowment for the Humanities Summer Seminar at Columbia University in 1977, added to his many professional gestures in support of my subsequent work the introduction of my Keats project, and me, to the Keats-Shelley Association of America at its annual meeting in 1981. Frank Farrell, director of the Free Shakespeare theatre, made my walk north part of the Keats Festival he arranged in Chicago in 1983.

The National Endowment for the Humanities, through its Summer Seminars program, made it possible for me to give an illustrated lecture at the University of California, Berkeley, in 1984 and at Yale University in 1989. My fellow seminarians, particularly at Yale, must be thanked for the rightness and gusto of their responses. Frances Ferguson, directing the Berkeley seminar, nourished my writing on travel literature. And had Paul Fry, at Yale, not sent me in exactly the right direction, I might not be enjoying the reality of publication now. In turn, I am grateful to the NEH for making these academic associations possible.

From beginning to end I am indebted to Jack Stillinger of the University of Illinois at Urbana-Champaign, who gave valuable counsel over the long haul, remembering and forgetting at just the right times that I had been his student. His close reading of my manuscript resulted in many significant improvements and corrections; the dispatch with which he answered my questions reduced many uncertainties. I wish to thank Stuart Sperry of the University of Indiana for his endorsement of the work as a whole and for thoughtful and useful comments on the introduction. Ellen Graham ushered the work through publication with elegant authority. Susan Laity brought about countless refinements as manuscript editor. John Nicoll contributed expert editing and design to the making of the book. Carole Harmel taught me photography and critiqued the early images of the walking tour. My husband and colleague Norman Walker provided instant intelligent reaction to my ideas and style. John Shields of Illinois State University cast a critical eye upon my introduction and stimulated thought about it. Of the many renowned Keats scholars of the past whose work paved the way for mine the one I must acknowledge especially is Hyder Edward Rollins, on whose editing of Keats's letters I have depended. Family and close friends who gave encouragement all along should know I continue to be thankful.

Stanley Pilling, F.S.A. Scot., of the District Museum, Stranraer, Scotland, helped me with questions of local history. Janet Smith, of the Liverpool Record Office, Brown, Picton and Hornby Libraries, provided assistance critical to my research on the passage of the George Keatses from Liverpool. I appreciate as well the assistance I received from A. E. Truckell, of the Dumfries Museum, the Observatory; R. Gillespie, the Mitchell Library, Glasgow; Allan Leach, Director of Library Services, Carnegie Library, Ayr; Eveline Barron of the *Inverness Courier*; John Killen, Deputy Librarian, Linen Hall Library, Belfast; and E. R. Wilkinson, Local History Librarian, Carlisle Library. In America I enjoyed the resources and special services of the Houghton Library, the Pierpont Morgan Library, Bancroft Library of the University of California, the University of Illinois Library, Newberry Library, the Regenstein Library of the University of Chicago Library, the Chicago Public Library, the State Library of Pennsylvania, the Yale Center for British Art, Sterling Memorial Library of Yale University, the National Archives and Records Administration, and the Library of Congress.

Christina M. Gee, Curator of Keats House, Hampstead, facilitated my use of materials in the Keats Memorial Library. Her assistant, Roberta Davis, gave prompt attention to my recent correspondence. It was thanks to Dr. Stephen Gill and Dr. Peter Lavery of the Dove Cottage Library, Grasmere, that I was able to photograph the mantlepiece in the dining room at Rydal Mount, and I gladly acknowledge the courtesy they extended me.

A portion of a personal letter to me from Nelson Bushnell is reproduced with the permission of the author. The letter from Stanley Pilling is quoted by courtesy of Wigtown District Museum Service. All poetry by John Keats is reprinted by permission of the publishers from *The Poems of John Keats*, Jack Stillinger, editor, Cambridge, Mass.: The Belknap Press

INTRODUCTION

A Time to Travel

Reports issued regularly and discreetly from newspapers throughout the land that the aged King George III, living in seclusion, blind and mad, had suffered further debilitation. "His lower extremities, it is said, have become affected with paralysis," wrote the *Inverness Journal* on August 7, 1818. His wife, the queen, was dying. A crotchety Napoleon Bonaparte, living in exile on St. Helena, wanted to relocate on the island. "He had become extremely fractious and uneasy, and appeared perfectly unhappy," one read in the *Belfast News Letter* on July 7. In a distant new country James Monroe had been president for one year, and government land was attracting overseas speculators and developers to the prairies of Illinois, which was assured of becoming the twenty-first state of the United States before the year was out. England had been at peace with America and France since 1815. Travellers following an itinerary from London to the northernmost point in Scotland with a side trip to Ireland found that veterans of one campaign or another since 1793 turned up in odd places with their lives at loose ends.

The British economy was weak. America was receiving two hundred immigrants a day, many of them from Great Britain. The shipping industry in Liverpool was exploding, and among sailors a rumour that the Americans had built a steamship, the *Savannah*, capable of crossing the Atlantic in record time stirred anxieties about jobs. Travel literature—books and articles—proliferated. In the late spring of this year of 1818 Parliament had been dissolved so that a general election could take place. Passions were high; cabbages and mud were flung; one candidate was horsewhipped. In so many ways and for so many people in England it was a time of movement and change. The poet whose travels are the subject of this book was one of those people.

John Keats was twenty-two years old when he accepted the invitation of his friend Charles Brown, thirty-one and a writer as well, to undertake a walking tour of roughly two thousand miles through northern England and Scotland, with a diversion to northern Ireland. They were to leave in late June, wend their way along a generally coastal route that would take them to the inner Hebrides, and finish up some three months later at John

o' Groats at the northern extremity of Scotland, returning to London by a different way. The starting point would be Lancaster. In April Keats wrote to his friend Benjamin Robert Haydon:

> I purpose within a Month to put my knapsack at my back and make a pedestrian tour through the North of England, and part of Scotland—to make a sort of Prologue to the Life I intend to pursue—that is to write, to study and to see all of Europe at the lowest expence. I will clamber through the Clouds and exist. I will get such an accumulation of stupendous recollolections that as I walk through the suburbs of London I may not see them—I will stand upon Mount Blanc and remember this coming Summer when I intend to straddle ben Lomond—with my Soul! (*Letters*, 1, 264)

This was a poet writing to a painter about a commitment to his art. But Keats never lived to stand upon Mont Blanc, for he died of consumption at the age of twenty-five. In fact, he did not even complete the walking tour. He caught a severe sore throat on the Isle of Mull and had to turn back on August 7. The price of this lively journey was Keats's health and span of life. But he did straddle mountains with his soul that summer, and generations of literary critics and ordinary readers have recognized that the most important part of the "Prologue" he outlined was brilliantly realized a year later, in his poetry of 1819.

For a poet, Scotland in 1818 held the allures of remoteness, mythical Celtic bards, Gaelic songs, rugged landscape, and primitive communities. Scottish songs were sold and sung everywhere in England. Beethoven had visited Scotland and set its native songs to music; his Scottish publisher George Thompson was getting out a collection that very year. *Frankenstein, or the Modern Prometheus* had just come out in March, and Mary Shelley chose an Orkney island, in northern Scotland, as the faraway setting in which Victor Frankenstein, under duress, set up a second laboratory to produce a female mate for his creature. The characters and plots of Sir Walter Scott's novels figured in daily conversation. From time to time since 1797 J. M. W. Turner had been visiting Scotland; he would visit again in November 1818, and he was on his way to becoming Scott's illustrator. For Keats there was the special awareness that William Wordsworth had made Scottish tours, as had Robert Burns, and that he and Brown were to visit the homes of both the living English and the dead Scots poets on this trip.

Keats was not the only member of his family with dramatic travel plans. His brother George, the second oldest in the family, had decided to emigrate to the frontiers of America with his new wife. Keats and Brown organized their departure from London to correspond with these startling plans. They would all four—Keats, Brown, George, and George's bride, Georgiana—take a coach from London for Liverpool on June 22. Keats and Brown would spend one night there, leave the George Keatses, who were to sail for either Philadelphia or Baltimore (they were not certain which) as soon as possible, and take another coach to Lancaster, the official starting point of their travels on foot.

The logistics would seem simple enough, but everything that touched one of his siblings had a profound effect on John Keats. Though he travelled with few worldly goods that summer, he carried with him the acute awareness that a drama was playing itself out in the lives of his family. The Keats children had been orphaned at a young age, and an extraordinary closeness developed among them. John, the oldest, felt responsible for his two brothers, George and Tom, and for the youngest in the family, his only sister, Fanny.

Keats's father, Thomas Keats, had managed a livery stable. He died suddenly, when John was eight, as a consequence of being thrown from his horse. His mother, Frances, had remarried, but not wisely, and the children were placed in the care of their maternal grandparents, Alice and John Jennings. When Keats was fourteen his mother, who had come back to live with her parents, died of consumption, which was to become known as the family illness. The boy's grief was intense. Since Mrs. Jennings survived her husband, the responsibility fell upon her to ensure that after her own demise the grandchildren would receive supervision, an annual income, and an inheritance as each came of age. Accordingly, she appointed two trustees, only one of whom, her old friend Richard Abbey, ultimately played an active role in guiding the lives or controlling the financial affairs of the four Keats children. Married with one adopted daughter, Abbey was foremost a businessman—a senior partner in a wholesale tea business in London. Keats never had anything good to say about Abbey.

Tom for a short time and George for a longer period worked in Abbey's business after leaving the excellent school in Enfield that all the Keats boys attended. They lived above Abbey's counting house while Abbey lived in a comfortable home outside the city. John was apprenticed to a surgeon, Thomas Hammond of Edmonton, for five years, from the time he was fourteen years and eight months. He subsequently entered Guy's Hospital in London as a student, progressed to being a dresser to surgeons, and finally, in the summer of his twentieth year, passed exams that qualified him to practice as a physician, a surgeon, or an apothecary. But from that point on, except for a desperate financial period when he toyed with the idea of becoming a ship's surgeon on an Indiaman, Keats went in a literary direction.

Now, in the late spring of 1818, Tom, eighteen years old, was dying of consumption. George Keats had nursed him for more than a year—actually since 1816, when Tom had had to leave Abbey's counting house because of poor health. He had rallied a bit in April, giving George the encouragement to go ahead with plans for his own future. Then, in early May, Tom had a severe hemorrhage. It would have been all too clear to his medically informed brother John what that signified. Why, then, did Keats leave Tom alone in the house on Well Walk in Hampstead with only the landlord and his wife and a few friends to look in on him? The most reasonable explanation is that Tom wanted Keats to have the experience of that walking tour to the north and convinced him that his condition had stabilized and that he was feeling well enough to be on his own for a while. Tom understood Keats better than anyone in England, according to George; he no doubt practiced some deception in his poet-brother's interest.

The youngest member of the family, Fanny, turned fifteen on June 3, but she was still under Abbey's guardianship, and Abbey bent every effort to prevent Keats from seeing her. She had been given a traditional education in a girls' school and when not in the school lived with the Abbeys in their home in Walthamstow. Fanny's experiences of growing up, her sense of well being (or lack of it), and even her view of Keats family affairs could not be entirely clear to her brother, for with the imposed distance between them he could not enjoy a spontaneous exchange of worries and joys or plumb her thoughts as he did those of Tom and George. Fanny saved Keats's letters, fortunately for posterity, and Keats must have sensed that if he could not participate directly in her life, he could at least touch her with his written words.

On June 10 he wrote to his friend Benjamin Bailey: "I have two Brothers one is driven by the 'burden of Society' to America the other, with an exquisite love of Life, is in a lingering state—My Love for my Brothers from the early loss of our parents and even for earlier Misfortunes has grown into a affection 'passing the Love of Women'—... I have a Sister too and may not follow them, either to America or to the Grave—" (*Letters*, 1, 293). The "Sister" is not Fanny, but George's new wife, Georgiana, whom Keats readily embraced as a family member and perhaps as a substitute for the real sister whose company he had been denied. His love for his brothers would have been evident to anyone who read his first collection of work, *Poems* (1817). "To My Brother George" is the title of a sonnet and an epistle, both written at Margate in August 1816. "But what, without the social thought of thee, / Would be the wonders of the sky and sea?" the sonnet concludes. The epistle is a kind of dream vision in which Keats achieves greatness in both his present life and posterity. The epistle ends with two curiously prophetic images: a ship sailing out to sea and the gesture of blowing a farewell kiss to George. On Tom's seventeenth birthday, November 18, 1816, Keats composed another sonnet, "To My Brothers," in which he rejoices that the day has passed so "smoothly" and wishes that the brothers might have many evenings in which to "calmly try / What are this world's true joys,—ere the great voice, / From its fair face, shall bid our spirits fly." Keats's concern over separation and loss had clearly been a part of his relationship with his brothers for some time. In December 1816 Keats composed a sonnet for the girl who was to become his sister-in-law, Georgiana Augusta Wylie, entitled "To G. A. W." and offering one of the few descriptions we have of Georgiana's face: "Nymph of the downward smile, and sidelong glance."

The Keats brothers had been receiving sixty pounds a year annual income from Abbey. As first John and then George came of age, each received an inheritance from their grandmother's estate. For reasons that are not entirely clear, however, the Keats children did not know that there was also an inheritance from their grandfather's estate due them as they came of age that remained in Chancery. Abbey, as their guardian, should have known about it; but if he did, he did not inform the Keats children. George had turned twenty-one on February 28, 1818, and could certainly have used his entire share to start a new life in America with Georgiana. The poet had turned twenty-one on October 31, 1816, and could have

used his portion to launch his writing career—or at least to feel comfortable in the attempt. Instead, Keats assumed that a livelihood as well as a name had to come of his writing soon. His need for a well-defined "Prologue" must have been intensified by the sense that he would have to produce an income, especially since George, who was the practical one among them, was leaving, and Tom would never be able to work. Fortunately, in June 1818 Abbey credited five hundred pounds to Keats's account.

In the months before the walking tour, Keats's life could have been weighed in Dickens's best-of-times worst-of-times scales. Since Christmas, to use an arbitrary marker, Keats had been moving among stimulating people and meeting major figures in literary and art circles. In that period alone the names of Wordsworth, Percy Bysshe Shelley, Mary Shelley, Leigh Hunt, Benjamin Robert Haydon, John Hamilton Reynolds, Thomas Jefferson Hogg, Thomas Love Peacock, Crabb Robinson, William Godwin, and Charles Lamb could be linked with his. He accepted invitations to dinner parties, attended performances at Covent Garden and Drury Lane, haunted Hazlitt's celebrated lectures on the English poets, viewed exhibitions at the Royal Academy, read a great deal of Shakespeare, and most important, wrote. In March he went south to the coastal town of Teignmouth, in Devonshire, where George had taken Tom in the hope that the change would improve his health. There he walked, composed (the epistle beginning, "Dear Reynolds, as last night I lay in bed," for example), corresponded with his publisher, announced his plans to travel north with Brown, and worked through a kind of meditation growing out of his understanding of Wordsworth's "Tintern Abbey"—the extended metaphor beginning, "I compare human life to a large Mansion of Many Apartments." In early May he and Tom returned to their upstairs apartment in Hampstead.

The work that dominated this period was a long (four thousand lines), ambitious poem that began "A thing of beauty is a joy forever," a starkly simple line with unimagined mnemonic power. *Endymion*, the first draft of which had been completed the previous November, was revised, copied, proofread, and sent off to be published by one of London's best houses, Taylor and Hessey.

But *Endymion* also belongs to the counterweight of the Dickensian scales. Before he left on the walking tour Keats had a warning of sorts that his new work would be not be reviewed objectively by at least one critic: John Gibson

Lockhart, who since October 1817 had been attacking Leigh Hunt and a group of literary figures who gathered around him, to whom collectively Lockhart gave the somewhat disparaging label "The Cockney School." Lockhart's invective was aired in four numbers of *Blackwood's Magazine*, an influential, politically conservative Scottish publication. The first two specifically assailed Hunt (his poem "Rimini," his liberal politics, his friends, and even the way he parted his hair), who was supposed to be the founder and prophet of the Cockney School. At the head of each article, however, came an epigram, a short satirical poem in which Keats's name appeared with Hunt's. Here the reader learned that the forthcoming criticism was going to "talk" (in the indefinite future) about Keats, "The Muses' son of promise; and of what feats / He yet may do." In May 1818 Lockhart came out with a third assault on Hunt, this time casting aspersions at Keats in the process, calling him an "infatuated bardling" (197) for having composed a poem ("Written on the Day That Mr. Leigh Hunt Left Prison") in his friend's honor. By now there could be no doubt in Keats's mind that in the larger literary world there was a stigma attached to admiring Hunt.

Keats may have sensed that *Endymion* would fall victim to a Cockney School attack. In the preface of the poem he expressed the hope that a critic "will leave me alone, with the conviction that there is not a fiercer hell than the failure in a great object." A full-blown hostile review of *Endymion* appeared in *Blackwood's* in August and must have greeted him soon after his return from Scotland. It was followed by yet another, in the same vein, by John Wilson Croker in the September issue of the *Quarterly Review*. Lockhart's attack particularly raised the indignation of the friends of Keats, in his own time and for years to come, for it was not so much about the poetry as about the poet, his friends, his associates, and his lack of social and familial status. It called him "only a boy of petty abilities" and concluded with the unkindest advice of all: "It is a better and a wiser thing to be a starved apothecary than a starved poet; so back to the shop Mr John, back to 'plasters, pills, and ointment boxes'" (*Blackwood's*, August 1818, 524).

It was fortunate Keats did not see the threats in the first three Cockney School articles fully realized before he left on his journey. He could not leave related concerns behind entirely, however. In the Lake District, where the Westmorland election was in full swing, he would have to think about the significance of Hunt and his political connections again.

Fitness

Keats's health up to the time of the walking tour, compared to that of his friends, was unexceptional but noteworthy. He had paid attention to significant symptoms, as a person well trained in medicine knew he should, and he had consulted a physician when necessary. On June 6, less than two weeks before he was to begin his travels, he wrote to his friend Joseph Severn, "The Doctor says I mustn't go out" (*Letters*, 1, 291). Whatever threatened his health then seems to have been related to the rainy two months he had just spent in Teignmouth with Tom and to their return journey by coach, which had been a horrendous trip. "Lord what a Journey I had and what a relief at the end of it—I'm sure I could not have stood it many more days," he had written to Marian and Sarah Jeffrey two days earlier (1, 291). By June 10 he was still unsure about his ability to travel north. "I am not certain whether I shall be able to go my Journey on account of my Brother Tom and a little indisposition of my own," he wrote Benjamin Bailey (1, 293). But by June 21 he had bounced back and was writing to his publisher, Taylor, "Au revoir! God keep us all well.—I start tomorrow morning" (1, 295).

The early letters of the walking tour allude to fatigue, but rather boastfully and quite in proportion to the effort he and Brown expended in walking so many miles a day and their almost ascetic practice of denying themselves breakfast until they had put in some walking time. In the first letters to Tom and to George and Georgiana he offers assurances of his own health—"I am well in health," and "God send you both as good Health as I have now." Not until the end of the Hebrides part of the tour did he acknowledge a sore throat and recognize the need to stay in Oban for a few days before undertaking the next leg of the journey, the climb of Ben Nevis.

The place of origin of the sore throat is the Isle of Mull, where Keats "caught a violent cold . . . , which far from leaving him, has become worse," according to Brown in his letter to C. W. Dilke, Sr. (Letter 13).[1] Keats concurred in this assessment, for as soon as he returned to London he wrote to his sister, Fanny, that he had "a bad sore throat from a cold I caught in the island of Mull" (*Letters*, 1, 364). But in his *Life of John Keats*, written years later, Brown speaks more generally of the causes for Keats's illness: "For some time he had been annoyed by a slight inflammation in the throat, occasioned by rainy days, fatigue, privation, and, I am afraid, in one instance, by damp sheets" (52).[2] There had indeed been much rain to contend with. They had been "emprisoned awhile by the weather" in Ballantrae, and before reaching Oban they had had to walk fifteen miles "in a soaking rain." As well, Keats had visited two cities where an epidemic of typhus was raging. Belfast issued regular reports from its Fever Hospital, and Glasgow was about to establish such a hospital.

Some Keats scholars believe that in tending Tom, who was mortally infected with tuberculosis before the walking tour began, Keats developed the infection. But this argument is melodramatic and medically unsound. Once exposed to the bacilli of the disease one does not necessarily contract it; normally the immune system will check it. In Keats's case it seems far more likely that he contracted the disease after the walking tour, when his resistance to infection had given way. We know that Keats and Brown had not been receiving adequate nutrition to maintain health, for their letters bemoan a diet consisting primarily of eggs and oat cakes in Scotland. The Isle of Mull, then, is appropriately cited as the place where the threshold of Keats's resistance was crossed.

Keats paid attention to what his body was telling him when he decided to rest in Oban. He did not complain but in an interestingly detached way remained vigilant of his symptoms. After climbing Ben Nevis he thought his throat was "in a fair way of getting quite well," as he told Tom, but three days later he was forced to reverse his report: "My Sore throat is not quite well and I intend stopping here [in Inverness] a few days" (Letter 11). He deferred to an Inverness physician's judgment that he was "too thin and fevered to proceed on our journey" (Letter 13). This seems to be the second of two consultations with a physician since the flare-up of the throat, for Brown in his biography implies that an agreement was reached before they came to Inverness: "It was prudently resolved, with the assistance of medical advice, that if, when we reached Inverness, he should not be much better, he should part from me, and proceed from the port of Cromarty to London by sea" (Life of Keats, 52).

The walking tour proved critical in the somatic profile of Keats. His condition was never quite the same afterward. His defenses were permanently down.

Keats's Travelling Companion

Keats could not have been more fortunate in his companion than he was in Charles Armitage Brown. Brown initiated the journey, and he testified to their compatibility when prematurely deprived of Keats's company after some forty-five days, complaining, "It is a cruel disappointment. We have been as happy as possible together" (Letter 13). Keats profited immeasurably from having at his side a hearty, well-organized fellow who knew from experience how to stretch his pennies, chart out a route on "the Map" with chalk, calculate distances, hire guides, and monitor the writing and health of his younger friend.

Keats and Brown had known each other since the late summer of 1817, when they were introduced either by John Hamilton Reynolds or Charles Wentworth Dilke. Brown's first encounter with Keats made such a strong impression that he could recall it vividly years later: "It was on the Hampstead road that we were introduced to each other; the minutest circumstances attending our first meeting are strong in my memory. . . . Still, as in that interview of a minute I inwardly desired his acquaintanceship, if not his friendship, I will take this occasion of describing his personal appearance. He was small in stature, well proportioned, compact in form, and, though thin, rather muscular;—one of the many who prove that manliness is distinct from height and bulk" (Life of Keats, 43–44). Their friendship deepened on the walking tour, when they were constantly together sharing not only the experiences they regarded as important enough to write about but also the ordinary ones their readers could easily infer from their style of travel: probably sleeping in the same bed from time to time, using primitive toilet facilities, grooming and bathing without privacy, and figuring out expenses. By the end of their travels the two had established an affectionate fellowship that could be depended upon in adversity.

This was particularly fortunate for Keats the following winter, when Tom died. Brown, sensitive to his friend's aloneness, invited John to share his quarters. Brown's now famous description of the scene confirms the trust and love that had developed between the two men: "Early one morning I was awakened in my bed by a pressure on my hand. It was Keats, who came to tell me his brother was no more. I said nothing, and we both remained silent for awhile, my hand fast locked in his. At length, my thoughts returning from the dead to the living, I said—'Have nothing more to do with those lodgings,—and alone too. Had you not better live with me?' He paused, pressed my hand warmly, and replied,—'I think it would be better.' From that moment he was my inmate" (Life of Keats, 53). The friendship endured to the end of Keats's life and affected Brown long afterward. Brown cheered Keats, helped him with financial problems, and nursed him during some of his illness near the end of his life. After Keats died Brown continued to work on his behalf—advancing the poet's reputation, looking after the posthumous publication of his poems, sorting out financial disputes, and writing (though not publishing) a memoir. When Brown himself died at the age of fifty-five in New Zealand, where he had emigrated rather precipitously at the end of his life in order to give his grown son Carlino better prospects, the stone that was eventually placed over his grave read: "The Friend of Keats." And Brown's recent biographer, E. H. McCormick, begins the man's life with the assertion: "His feelings for Keats exceeded in depth and intensity those he bore for the only other human being who seems to have won his adult love—his son and namesake" (*Friend of Keats*, 1).

In 1818 both men lived in the suburb of London called Hampstead, Brown in his half of a two-family home he had built with his friend Charles Wentworth Dilke, and Keats in the apartment on Well Walk he shared with his two brothers. Eight and a half years Keats's senior, Brown had lived a life that was far more adventurous than Keats's. At eighteen Brown entered into an export business with his oldest brother, John, that took him to Russia, where he held down an office in the cosmopolitan city of St. Petersburg, while his brother remained in a London office. The business failed after five years, and Brown returned to England and dire financial problems. From then on he remained overly cautious about money. He drew an income again when he became the agent of another brother, James, who prospered as an East India Company resident in Sumatra, where he owned two nutmeg plantations and apparently engaged in independent trading. When James died, in 1815, he left Brown ten thousand pounds and a share of some property in Surrey.

In the interim, and probably far more to Brown's pleasure, a "Serio-Comic Opera, in Three Acts" that Brown had written "five years ago," according to its preface, was produced at Drury Lane (1814). "The Plot is founded on an event which occurred in Russia, during my residence there." The opera, *Narensky; or, The Road to Yaroslaf,* called for a robber's cave, song, and dance—a "Pas Deux, The National Country Dance to the original Russian Air." Brown's opera had some of the characteristics of the ballet of the period, and his overtly Russian setting reflected the trend to celebrate native Russian themes on the stage just as Pushkin wrote his ballads about country people. Choreographer Charles Didelot of the Russian Imperial Ballet produced divertissements based on Russian folk dances in London during 1812–1814. Brown's *Narensky* had a theatrical precedent, then, and its dancing, by "Mr. Oscar Byrne [a principal dancer at the King's Theatre] and Miss Smith, and Corps de Ballet," would have been in vogue. London was not dazzled, however. The reviewers took note of the principal singers, Mrs. Dickons, and John Braham, both well known on the London stage, but they had nothing to say about the overall production that would encourage Brown to write another opera soon. Braham, the tenor, had composed some of the music, and the critic for the *Champion* (January 15) attributed whatever success the play had to Braham's composition and performance. The production ran for only ten days. But Brown made three hundred pounds on his opera and was given free admission to all performances at the theatre.

Brown was the sixth of seven sons and thus accustomed to sharing, to accommodating, and, as the second-youngest, to caring and being cared for. Keats's closeness to Tom and George was something Brown understood. And the predominantly male household he grew up in contributed to his being quick on the rebound with harmless jibes and bawdy jokes. Brown's mother seems to be the source of the name Armitage. Her father, according to recent scholarship, was probably John Armitage, a manufacturer of starch. His father, a stockbroker, was Scottish, a fact that accounts for Brown's casual genealogical research when he and Keats were on Mull.

Brown is practically the only one among Keats's friends and relatives about whose health Keats did not seem to worry. His heartiness and strength always stand out in biographical portrayals of him. On the walking tour, however, Keats proved to be every bit his equal; in fact, Keats emerges as more interested in the sheer physical activity of the tour, more inclined to throw himself into a climb or an exploration. Brown gives out before Keats does; his blistered feet fail him in Inverary. Even when ill Keats exerts himself to the limit to climb Ben Nevis. Both men complain bitterly about the grim diet of oat cakes in Scotland; neither eschews the whiskey that was offered in the north as readily as a cup of tea in the south. Barring disease, to which Keats was susceptible, the two men were well matched.

Brown's interests were compatible with Keats's. From the travel writing alone it is clear that his taste in literature matched Keats's. Both men found Milton worth tackling on a rainy morning; Shakespeare came easily from their memories into

Bust of Charles Armitage Brown, by "SW."

position looking up to Keats's head, shown in profile, seems to betray Brown's recognition of the genius of his dear friend, who was, as Brown acknowledges later, in his memoir, "honoured as a superior being by me" (*Life of Keats*, 40). A long view of Keats's right arm, up to the closed hand on which the lower right cheek rests, directs the eye of the viewer to the head of dark curly hair, long brows, fixed gaze, perfectly proportioned nose, and full sensuous mouth (see the frontispiece to this book). The drawing provides documentation of Keats's robust intensity by someone who knew his subject from all angles and under almost all circumstances.

For a visual portrait of Brown there are but two images. Both require a special "reading" to see Keats's walking-tour companion as he was in 1818. One is a bust made in 1828 (see photo), while Brown was living in Florence, formerly thought to be by Andrew Wilson but now identified by the initials "SW" inscribed on the base. By then Brown had a receding hairline with thinning hair arranged to cover the baldness on the top of his head and long sideburns; he had a large nose, a small upper lip, and a dimpled chin, which was clean shaven. His full chest implies a physique of solid proportions belonging to a man of some height. The other image is a written one made by Keats in 1819 in the poem "Character of C.B.," and it, too, has to be interpreted. The poem is ironic, meaning the opposite of what it claims:

> He was to weet a melancholy carle,
>   Thin in the waist, with bushy head of hair,
> As hath the seeded thistle, when in parle
>   It holds the zephyr, ere it sendeth fair
> Its light balloons into the summer air;
>   Thereto his beard had not begun to bloom,
> No brush had touch'd his chin or razor sheer;
>   No care had touch'd his cheek with mortal doom,
> But new he was and bright as scarf from Persian loom.[3]

Brown lived his life methodically. One practice biographers never fail to note is that every summer he rented his half of the residence co-owned with Dilke. For the duration of the walking tour Brown leased his quarters to Mrs. Samuel Brawne, whose daughter Fanny, with the same name as Keats's young sister, soon figured so passionately in Keats's life.

Charles Brown seemed to be stepping into Keats's life just when his brother George was stepping out. In May 1819 Keats admitted, "My Brother George always stood between me and any dealings with the world" (*Letters*, 2, 113). Brown, ex-

their conversations. Brown could give Keats the plot of Scott's *Guy Mannering*. Keats recited his *Isabella* to Brown. Like Keats, Brown found pretentious people and fashionable travellers distasteful. Both men had associated with politically liberal friends like Leigh Hunt and his brother, who also lived in Hampstead. Both were skillful draftsmen and liked to sketch. (Some time after the tour Brown made a watercolour sketch of Lincluden College, the ruin they visited near Dumfries.) One of the most often reproduced images of Keats is the one Brown drew of him in 1819, most likely in the summer, when they were together on the Isle of Wight collaborating on their play *Otho the Great*. The perspective of one situated in a lower

perienced in business and confident he could always land on his feet, began to play that role during the summer of 1818. Ironically, Brown and George, in many ways similar in character and inclination, fell into a bitter dispute over Keats's finances after his death and ended up not only disliking each other but polarizing relationships among old friends in the Keats circle. The problem began when George, in need of money to get him over a financial crisis, returned to England for a brief visit in January 1820 to claim his share of Tom's inheritance. He accepted money that belonged to John as well, and Brown perceived this, as well as the fact George did not subsequently send money back to John, as clearly exploitative. Others close to John, aware that he was ill and having to borrow money himself, supported Brown's contention that George had harmed his brother. Indeed, according to Brown, Keats himself believed that George had not behaved well. After Keats's death Brown devoted much energy to documenting George's dereliction. The feud delayed the publication of any biography of Keats, because George retaliated against Brown by threatening an injuction against the publication of his brother's poetry. Brown's good friend Dilke sided with George, and their old friendship dissolved into permanent enmity.

But that summer Brown and George were equal and harmonious members of the party of travellers that left London in a coach for Liverpool. "It is a flaw / In happiness to see beyond our bourne," Keats wrote in "Dear Reynolds, as last night I lay in bed." Fortunately, Brown could not have that sight.

The Emigration of the George Keatses

John Keats left his brother and sister-in-law in Liverpool without being quite certain which ship they would sail on, when it would leave, and at what American port they would disembark. He addressed a letter to them at the Crown Inn on June 27, but they had gone by the time the letter arrived. In spite of all the distractions of new scenery in his own travels, he wished for hard facts about the outcome of George's arrangements, and on July 14 he wrote to Tom: "I want very much to know the name of the Ship George is gone in—also what port he will land in—I know nothing about it" (Letter 7). If Keats had been able to track down the particulars, he might have pieced together what appears to be a classic emigrant's tale.

Liverpool newspapers ran long narrow columns of one- to two-inch advertisements for places in ships sailing to all navigable points of the known world, especially America. George Keats had a gentleman's taste, whatever the constraints of birth or pocket. He responded to the promotion of a new American vessel, "the fine first-class American ship *Telegraph*." She was "a regular trader, coppered and copper-fastened," built in Boston, registered in Philadelphia the previous November 11, and owned by Wiggin & Whitney, merchants of Philadelphia. She had been in Liverpool since sometime before May, when the advertisements started appearing. If George and Georgiana looked at back issues of *Gore's Advertiser* during their stay at the Crown Inn (the destination of their coach from London), they apparently welcomed and believed the claims. The *Telegraph* was "remarkable for making quick passages, and...always delivered her cargoes in good order." The average sailing time to America was eight weeks; speed was a selling point. Comfort was also a priority, and "her accommodations for passengers are very superior—two cabins and twelve state rooms."

The *Telegraph* had been cleared for sailing on June 22, the same day the Keatses left London. She lay in the River Mersey, waiting for a wind, and continued to receive cargo and passengers. She had already taken on 300 tons of her 392-ton capacity. Most of the cargo was iron. Passengers were requested to be on board by Thursday, June 25. Liverpool's shipping and travel industries were booming, and the town, which had taken on the identity of a sophisticated resort as well as a port, was bustling with tourists and travellers at this time of year. Some came for the theatre, which now boasted among its "embellishments" a gaslight chandelier and new scenes painted by Mr. Westmacott. George had to absorb the town hurriedly, however, and attend to booking passage. He paid a bit more than average fare and secured one of the two cabins available on the *Telegraph*, endowing his passage with an air of gentility.

It would have taken a day at least to make all the final arrangements for boarding, since passage had not been booked in advance of arrival in Liverpool. The chronology probably ran something like this: they arrived at the Crown Inn in the late afternoon of June 23 (the run from London to Liverpool was generally thirty to thirty-two hours), settled into their room at the inn, and visited with John and Charles the rest of the evening, no doubt over a late meal. The farewells were said at night, so that the next morning John and Charles could set out and the emigrants could make some inquiries before deciding on a particular ship, negotiate price and accommodations, reorganize the baggage, do some shopping, and hire a horse-drawn cart to the dock. This could not have all been accomplished before 2:00 P.M. (the latest the *Telegraph* would accept goods and passengers) on June 24, so they spent another night at the Crown Inn and easily made it aboard early the next day. And so George and Georgiana made their way to their cabin on the *Telegraph*, carrying with them, according to the records in the National Archives and Records Administration (Washington, D.C.), "Beds Bedding & five packages."

At the very time John and Charles were beginning the first stretch of their walking tour, from Lancaster to Endmoor, George and Georgiana were settling in on board. There was no forecasting the wind. The ship lay in the River Mersey fifteen days from the time it cleared, waiting for enough wind to sail. For the Keatses there was an unexpected period of quiet in which to assess the rapid turn of events since their marriage in late May and to recognize the feelings of loss that had been hidden by anticipation until then. Georgiana, barely sixteen, was leaving her mother and brothers, Charles and Henry, who would be different people when and if she saw them again. (She did not return until 1828.) Her deceased father had been an adjutant of the Fifeshire Regiment of Fencible Infantry; though children of the military are sometimes forced to accept family separations at an early age, they are not necessarily inured to them. George, the twenty-one-year-old bridegroom, probably wondered about what kind of life, practically speaking, his generous and obviously gifted older brother John was going to carve out for himself.

Fresh in George's memory would have been a recent study in contrasts. On the way to Lancaster the coach, which had left the Swan with Two Necks Inn in London at 9:00 A.M., had stopped in Redbourne, near St. Albans. There John had met, by prior arrangement, his friend Henry Stephens, who had been a fellow student at Guy's Hospital. They had shared living quarters and spent much time together until they passed their exams in 1816. Now Stephens was established in a practice in Redbourne as a surgeon apothecary. George must have seen in Stephens that enviable expression of confidence and security one can always read in the faces of young professionals making their way with absolute trust in the equation of hard work with reward. This was the occasion when John had announced to Stephens his intention of being a poet rather than a physician, proclaiming his walking tour to be a rite of conversion. In his

daring brother, George must have found someone to admire and worry about all the way to America.

George also had Tom to think about. The extent to which he denied Tom's illness is easily surmised. But surely, in solitude now, awaiting the wind, he would have had to reconcile his own present joys with the likelihood that Tom would not live until that uncertain time when the brothers would reunite, on one soil or another. Fanny, on the other hand, was safe, if overly protected, with the Abbeys. John still thought of her as a child, but to George, whose wife was only a year older than his sister, Fanny must have seemed a young woman who should be able to reach maturity unscathed. And so his reflections would return full circle to John, the firstborn, hiking north with memories of the unmerciful reviews of his poetry and digging in his heels on the resolution to be a renowned literary artist.

As for the decision he made for himself, to marry and go to a promising new land, a twenty-one-year-old does not often entertain doubts at the peak of adventure, and besides, there was no turning back now. He had recently been reading the publications circulating in London that promoted land investments in frontier country like Illinois. Indiana, Ohio, and Kentucky might also have figured in his plans. In any case, he intended to parlay his inheritance into a fortune—a financial exploit that could never have been carried out in London with its poor economy.

The *Telegraph* finally sailed out of the Mersey and into the Atlantic on July 7. The journey to America took fifty-one days. By the time they arrived at Philadelphia, having made better time than most ships, just as the ad had promised, George and Georgiana must have gotten to know their fellow travellers—there were fifty-four in all—fairly well. Captain Coffin may have played the role of tutor in preparing passengers for their first contacts with America. He would have announced that the ship was to make its way through Delaware Bay up the Delaware River. Philadelphia, he might have warned, will seem very different from Liverpool: it is laid out quite regularly in a rectangle from the Delaware River to the Schuylkill River, with straight streets running perpendicular to each other. It will be easy to find your way, but you should avoid lingering in Philadelphia as there are many there who are anxious to take the money of innocent newcomers on false pretenses.

Some passengers took with them newspaper reprints of a work called "Travels in the Interior of America," by a Mr. Bradbury. The *Carlisle Patriot* for June 20 ran much of the text under the heading "Advice to Emigrants." The help was quite specific. For example: "For a very great portion of emigrants, the countries west of the Alleghenies, say Ohio, Indiana, Kentucky, Tennessee, or Illinois, offer by much the best prospects; and to go to those countries, Philadelphia or Baltimore are the best ports." For those emigrants taking Bradbury's advice, there were plenty of wagons leaving Philadelphia for Pittsburgh. The charge varied from five to seven dollars per hundred pounds, less if male passengers walked beside the wagons across the mountains. Once in Pittsburgh emigrants would meet numbers of Europeans and Americans who were arriving there every day, having learned that they must go west to find employment. If the traveller had to go down the Ohio River, he could share the expense of purchasing a seventy-five-dollar covered ark with other families. The flat-bottomed vessel was fifty feet long and fourteen feet wide, suited for clearing the falls at Louisville and narrow enough to pass between two rocks fifteen feet apart in the Indian chute. Bradbury helped them to foresee every contingency.

Cabin-class passengers discussed a work by Henry Bradshaw Fearon that had just come out in 1818 entitled *Sketches of America*. Its descriptive subtitle explained that it was "a narrative of a journey of five thousand miles through the eastern and western states of America; contained in eight reports addressed to the thirty-nine English families by whom the author was disputed [for *deputed*], in June 1817, to ascertain whether any, and what part of the United States would be suitable for their residence. With remarks on Mr. Birkbeck's 'Notes' and 'Letters.'" This was aimed at the kind of gentlemanly audience with which George preferred to identify.

The ceremony of immigration was for the Keatses what it would be for generations to follow, a kind of divestiture. Names misspelled. Information omitted. The American National Archives with the report and manifest for the *Telegraph* and files for each emigrant who landed in Philadelphia on August 26, 1818, poignantly depersonalize two vital young people. File 5416-K reads: "Family name: Keats. Given name: Mr. George. Accompanied by: Lady & Mrs. Georgianna. Age: not given. Sex: male. Occupation: not given. Nationality: not given. Destination: United States." And File 5417-K correspondingly registers: "Family name: Keats. Given name: Miss Georgianna. Accompanied by: Mr. George. Age: not given. Sex: female. Occupation: not given. Nationality: not given. Destination: United States."

Actually, George and Georgiana were headed for south-eastern Illinois, where there was a concentration of English settlers. George had borrowed from John Taylor, Keats's new publisher, a copy of Morris Birkbeck's *Letters from Illinois*, seven editions of which had been published in English in 1818. The letters described the advantages of settling in the Illinois territory. Birkbeck himself had explored the United States from Virginia to Illinois in 1817 (his *Notes on a Journey* was issued in eleven editions during 1817–1819) and had selected Illinois, in part because it was not a slave state and therefore true to the ideology of a free land.

A wealthy English farmer and the son of a Quaker preacher, Birkbeck was in his fifties when he began to develop settlements in Illinois, operating in partnership with another liberal Englishman, George Flowers, whose role in the spring of 1818 was to return to England and accompany a shipload of emigrants back to the settlement called Wanborough, after Birkbeck's English farm. By mid-June, when George attempted to make advance arrangements to acquire 640 acres in the settlement near the Boltenhouse Prairie where Birkbeck had his cabin, all the lots had been spoken for. George realized that "there will be no house to receive us," and he would have to find his own property and build his own cabin. He was not daunted but, in fact, enlivened by the prospect of such enterprising self-sufficiency, writing to Taylor, "I only feel an addition of pride to undertake and accomplish the whole task myself" (Keats, *Keats Circle*, 1, 29). His way of thinking was already quite American.

It took at least two months for George and Georgiana to reach Illinois taking the conventional route through the Alleghenies to Pittsburgh and then down the Ohio River to Shawneetown. By that time it was October, and an English settlement that was to become the village of Albion had been created on the virgin land near the Boltenhouse Prairie residence of George Flower. Albion probably provided the Keatses with a temporary base. They ultimately settled in Louisville, Kentucky, after a number of financial mishaps, including a disastrous investment in a steamboat enterprise that was one of the ill-conceived business schemes of John James Audubon in Henderson, Kentucky. The Keatses had eight children, two boys and six girls.[4] George had become a respected, influential member of Louisville society by the time he died of consumption in 1841, at the age of forty-four. Georgiana remarried (John Jeffrey, sixteen years her junior) in 1843 and died in 1879. But that part of their story belongs to a period well beyond John Keats's walking tour.

The farewells in Liverpool marked the beginning of a long

lapse in communication between John and George. John continued to write to America after he returned from his walk north, but the mail brought no news from the emigrants until May 1819.

The Westmorland Election

Political events intrude upon even the most rural rambling during the period of a general election. News of the Westmorland election in particular followed Keats and Brown for the better part of their walk north. Sensational accounts of slanderous and inflammatory speeches, as well as riots, were ventilated in public houses, post offices, and inns from Lancaster all the way to Gatehouse-of-Fleet and Creetown, where the pair settled down on July 4, the day the polls closed. And the significance of the outcome continued to stir reaction well past that point, as presses in Belfast, Ayr, Inverness, Glasgow, and of course Westmorland itself revealed in their editorials through August.

The contest in Westmorland exposed an irregular representation of two seats in Parliament.[5] An amazing cast of characters, both literary and political, rose to either justify or confront the election policy and the candidates. The prevailing conservative Tory party, whose supporters wore yellow ribbons and called themselves "Yellow Boys," was running two sons of the wealthy and influential earl of Lonsdale, William, Lord Lowther, and Colonel Henry Lowther, both of whom already represented the county of Westmorland in two seats of the House of Commons. The Lowther name carried a great deal of weight in Westmorland, associated as it was not only with conservative political views but with ownership of land and industry. The earl was Lord Lieutenant of the county; he controlled neighbouring Cumberland as well. The Lowthers had not been challenged in an election for more than a generation; unaccustomed to the fight, they were not sanguine. Yet support in deed as well as in spirit came from, among others, William Wordsworth, his sister Dorothy, and Thomas De Quincey, with Southey speaking out from Cumberland. The Westmorland Tory forces would seem to have been fortified with talent and prestige beyond vulnerability. But this was not the case.

Henry Brougham, of an old Westmorland and Cumberland family, accepted the solicitation of independents to be their candidate for the Whig party, whose colour was blue. Brougham aimed to unseat either one of the two Lowthers and thereby help to correct the flagrant abuse of family influence and political power that had produced a pocket borough. Both Brougham Castle (a ruin) and Brougham Hall ("the Windsor of the north") stood not far from Lowther Castle, solid emblems of the competition. Brougham had been born and educated in Edinburgh and was now an English barrister. Ambitious, passionate, and canny, he was a dazzling orator who could marshall perorations and exhortations to any end. His tall bony figure and dramatic style (for example, his sudden modulations from a loud to a soft voice) made him an imposing, even theatrical presence in the speakers' stands and at the windows of inns in the rural towns of the Lake District. To his detractors he was a dangerous and talented provocateur. In Brougham, the "Blue Boys" had for their candidate an educated, urbane Scot: a serious writer, who had published in the *Edinburgh Review* on topics that ran the gamut from literature to surgery. By 1818, the time of the Westmorland election, he had already gained a reputation for his opposition to the slave trade, and he would go on to be associated with those issues (such as education for the poor) that would lead to the important Reform Bill of 1832. And he would be remembered by literary historians for disconcerting Wordsworth.

For Keats, the name Brougham represented more than a liberal force in the Westmorland election. Brougham had been an ally to Leigh Hunt, the friend and mentor to whom Keats had dedicated his first book of poems. Hunt had nurtured Keats's early poetry and introduced him to some of the foremost artists and writers of the time. Keats had written two sonnets honouring Hunt, "On Receiving a Laurel Crown from Leigh Hunt" and "To Leigh Hunt, Esq.," the latter printed as the "Dedication" in *Poems* (1817). Brougham had defended Hunt in 1811 against the charge that he risked provoking a French military attack with his criticism of harsh military training practices in England (particularly that of flogging) in an article in his brother John's radical journal the *Examiner*. Later, when Hunt was fined and imprisoned for criticizing the prince regent (calling him an "Adonis in Loveliness . . . a corpulent gentleman of fifty"), Brougham visited him in prison.

Keats declared his own support of Hunt in his sonnet "Written on the Day That Mr. Leigh Hunt Left Prison" (February 2, 1815), though their friendship did not commence until later. Keats had already paid a penalty for that allegiance: Lockhart had implicated Keats in the three venomous attacks on Hunt that appeared in *Blackwood's*. Before he left on his walking tour with Brown, Keats had good reason to believe additional trouble from the Cockney School assailant was forthcoming. As a consequence, for the duration of his journey this summer one of the problems that Keats needed to leave behind from his recent past was stirred up by the frequent mention of the name Brougham.

A further layer of irritation developed because Wordsworth was involved in the Westmorland election. Keats and Brown crossed over into Westmorland on June 25, toward the climax of the campaigns, hoping that in the few days they would be in the area they might visit Wordsworth in his home in Rydal. The next day they dined at the White Lion Inn (now called the Royal Hotel) in Bowness, and afterward Keats wrote to Tom, in some amazement: "I enquired of the waiter for Wordsworth—he said he knew him, and that he had been here a few days ago, canvassing for the Lowthers. What think you of that—Wordsworth versus Brougham!! Sad—sad—sad— and yet the family [the Lowthers] has been his friend always. What can we say?" (Letter 1). In the repeated judgment "sad" lie hints of disillusionment that will grow. For the moment, however, Keats seemed to be making allowances for what he assumed to be personal loyalties, even indebtedness. Lord Lonsdale had helped Wordsworth buy a property, Broad How, in Patterdale in 1806, making him a freeholder, and had used his influence to help the poet obtain the position of Distributor of Stamps for the County of Westmorland in 1813. Keats no doubt was also aware that Wordsworth's father, John, had been a political agent for the old earl. Wordsworth had been in London with his wife and sister during the winter. Keats had spent time with him ("I have Seen Wordsworth frequently— Dined with him last Monday," he wrote to Taylor January 10, 1818 [*Letters*, 2, 202]); enough to form opinions of the character of the man that did not square with his belief in the genius of his poetry. On February 21 Keats wrote to his brothers: "I am sorry that Wordsworth has left a bad impression wherever he visited in Town—by his egotism, Vanity and bigotry—yet he is a great Poet if not a Philosopher" (1, 237). Now Keats might add "political conservative" to his complaints.

Whether Keats had an idea of the extent to which Wordsworth had set aside writing poetry in order to produce political addresses for the *Carlisle Patriot* and the *Kendal Chronicle*, write and distribute a broadside and a pamphlet ("Two Addresses"), and help establish the *Westmorland Gazette* in May, for the purpose of controlling the coverage of the Brougham-Lowther contest, we cannot be sure. But if he had chatted with others besides the waiter in Bowness, he might have learned that Brougham had been perceived by Wordsworth and other gentry as a demagogue and a rabble-rouser (there had been anti-Lowther riots in Kendal in February complete with stone throwing and mud slinging) and that Wordsworth had been exercised over the Brougham-Lowther contest since the previous autumn. And Keats had easily gleaned that Wordsworth was not living in the style hymned in the Lucy poems and "Michael." Simple people did not concern him now. "Lord Wordsworth, instead of being in retirement, has himself and his house full in the thick of fashionable visitors quite convenient to be pointed at all the summer long" (Letter 1). Affecting a lordship and courting the fashionable, Wordsworth appeared a poet of another colour to Keats.

Three local newspapers covered the contest. The *Carlisle Patriot*, for the county of Cumberland, represented principally the bias of the Tory "Yellow Boys." The *Kendal Chronicle* attempted to remain neutral at first, publishing some of Wordsworth's addresses to the freeholders (signed "A Friend to Truth") which advocated support of the Lowthers. Overall, however, the *Kendal Chronicle* was biased toward Brougham and the Whig "Blue Boys." A new paper was established to serve the interests of Wordsworth, the Lowthers, and the Tory "Yellow Boys." On May 23 the first number of the *Westmorland Gazette and Kendal Advertiser* appeared. By July 11 an impoverished Thomas De Quincey, who was living in Wordsworth's former house, Dove Cottage, took over as editor. The Tory party line was reflected in all that De Quincey published, and his indebtedness to Wordsworth, who had facilitated his receiving the editorship, was satisfied.

The small village of Ambleside was not the sort of place that could sweep its troubles under the carpet when the tourists came. A letter to the editor of the *Westmorland Gazette* dated June 18 captured the mood of the town Keats and Brown came upon. It was written by a "Yellow Boy."

> Sir—It is very generally acknowledged, that Ambleside and
> its neighbourhood afford to their visitors as delightful
> scenery and agreeable company as any part of Westmorland;
> but those who think them worthy of being honoured with
> their presence this season will find an additional
> entertainment for their leisure hours, when they are not
> viewing the beauties of the country, in laughing at the
> jacobinical and foolish cries of innumerable petty orators,
> whose constant business is to spout out their countrified

speeches concerning the politics of the nation. We have male and female grocers, weavers, colt-tamers, &c. &c. &c. exercising their strongest powers (though they are but weak) to become orators; endeavouring to speechify in every public as well as private place; degrading and bringing themselves below the level of the brute creation, by abusing their best friends and supporters. Wherever a respectable party of Gentlemen meet in support of the loyal cause, drums, fifes, shouts of "B——m forever," with the foulest of foul speeches ring in their ears till their separation. . . . Even the servants of such Gentlemen, at times amongst the number, if any one ventures to support the loyal cause, in the company of one of the above orators, such a torrent of abusive language is thrown upon him, that he is obliged to retire from the presence of one who, at other times, would be called a maniac.

If Mr B——m succeed (which is not to be feared) he may thank his petty orators, who have endeavoured, with all the eloquence they are possessed of (though that is very little), to turn the minds of the people against that family which, by its good endeavours, has supported this Country during their long and respectable representation of it in Parliament. I shall now conclude by observing that those famous petty orators would have been better employed behind their counters, in tanning colts, or using their looms, than by abusing their best friends, and endeavouring to displace him, whose power is (very probably) *too great for theirs*. The day of election will, I doubt not, prove the inefficacy of all their exertions, and expose the fulsome inutility of bringing charges without any means of proving them.——I am, Sir, yours,

A YELLOW BOY

Clearly no one in Ambleside was withholding a political opinion. Despite the fact that only freeholders could vote, all classes demanded a voice. This democratic spirit was something Brougham wished to engender and tap. His strategy had been to activate workers, women, children, Quakers—all non-Tory residents who deserved control over their destinies but did not have it—to express themselves and thereby influence the enfranchised voters. This is not to say, however, that he did not already have the votes of a significant number of freeholders who wanted to get out from under the Lowther domination. To his opposition he was definitely a force to be reckoned with.

In the wake of the election upheaval, Keats and Brown sought out the reputed beauties of Ambleside and its environs. The morning after they arrived, they arose early to see the Ambleside waterfall, which put them in an aesthetic frame of mind, and after breakfast they made their way to Rydal Mount to pay a call upon Wordsworth. But "he was not at home nor was any Member of his family—I was much disappointed. I wrote a note for him and stuck it up over what I knew must be Miss Wordsworth's Portrait and set forth again" (Letter 2), Keats wrote to George and Georgiana as matter-of-factly as possible. Wordsworth was not at home because he and his sister Dorothy had gone to Appleby, just north of Kendal, to be with the Lowthers just before the polls closed. Years later, when Brown began his biography of Keats, he remembered Keats's disappointment at finding Wordsworth absent: "The young poet looked thoughtful at this exposure of his elder" (*Life of Keats*, 49).

The polls opened in Appleby on June 30 and closed on July 4. By July 7, 1818, even the *Belfast News Letter* carried the results, broken down into a day-by-day account. Brougham had lost. Lord Lowther received 1,211 votes; Hon. Col. Lowther, 1,157; Brougham, 889. And on Thursday, July 16, the *Caledonian Mercury*, published in Edinburgh, carried an analysis of the election that would have upset Keats's sense of justice had he read it. The *Mercury* cited unfair tactics on the part of the conservative Lowther party. The land tax commissioners, all friends of the Lowther clan, had not met on April 30 as they should have, for the law required that landowners must pay taxes and have their names published in order to be eligible to vote. The commissioners stalled for almost a month, and then decided that the tax assessments couldn't take place until June 27, three days before the poll opened. They used as their ruse a supposed question of the legitimacy of some of the land titles of those who were willing to pay taxes to vote. By this "maneuver," reported the *Mercury*, "upwards of 200 freeholders, in Mr. Brougham's interest, were unable to vote, while only twenty of the Lowthers were prevented from the same cause." All in all, it had been a dirty fight, the *Mercury* informed its readers:

Lord L. retained every attorney in the county, except one, and his sons and friends commenced an active canvass.—They considered their castle attacked, and were resolved to spare neither labor nor money to carry their effort.

The Brougham party did not begin their canvass for nearly six weeks after the other. Almost the whole county immediately rose in favor of the independents, and there is no instance in the annals of electioneering of such entire unanimity prevailing. Even those in the Lowther lists, who dare not vote against their Lord and Master, were canvassing for Mr. Brougham. The decided opinion in the county was, that the cause would prevail against all influence of the Lowthers, and the bets were five to one in favor of Mr. Brougham.

The writer for the *Mercury* argues that had the land-tax trick not been played, Brougham would have had a majority of seventy votes. His estimate may not have been accurate: modern analyses reveal that Brougham would have lost anyway. But the *Mercury*'s exposure of the Lowther foul play has been found to be valid.

Brougham's fury on losing resulted in a fiery resolution: "They must meet me here at every election while I live.... A flame will break forth from my ashes which will utterly consume your Oppressors" (*Kendal Chronicle*, July 11, 1818). It is interesting to note, because it provides a commentary on the power of the Lowther stronghold in Westmorland, that Brougham lost again to the Lowthers in 1820 and in 1826.

Keats experienced the impact of the Westmorland election as an aftershock. He had travelled miles beyond the Lake District to Cairndow in Argyllshire. By mid-July he had mentioned neither the elections nor Wordsworth in his letters. The upheaval would seem to have been forgotten, until he was bitten by a gadfly after swimming in Loch Fyne across from the Cairndow Inn. Suddenly Keats unloaded his "dudgeon," as he called it—the anger and resentment that had been building up. His letter to Tom of July 17 (Letter 8), which begins with place-name puns, most having reference to the Lake District, contains a satiric song addressed to "All gentle folks who owe a grudge / To any living thing."

The poem begins with the commonplace, treated farcically, digresses to law, politics, and literature, apologizes "for deviating so," and returns to the commonplace. The deviation, stanzas four through eight, reflects on the Westmorland experience and its ramifications:

> Has any here a lawyer suit
>   Of 1743?
> Take lawyer's nose and put it [a gadfly] to't
>   And you the end will see.

> Is there a man in Parliament
>   Dumfounder'd in his speech?
> O let his neighbour make a rent
>   And put one in his breech.

> O Lowther, how much better thou
>   Hadst figur'd t' other day,
> When to the folks thou mad'st a bow
>   And hadst no more to say,

> If lucky gadfly had but ta'en
>   His seat upon thine a——e,
> And put thee to a little pain
>   To save thee from a worse.

> Better than Southey it had been,
>   Better than Mr. D——,
> Better than Wordsworth too, I ween,
>   Better than Mr. V——.

Lawyers are attacked, one of the Lowthers is ridiculed, and Wordsworth is juxtaposed with Southey, the Lake poet who also forsook liberalism for Toryism. The most serious indictment is of Wordsworth, whom Keats greatly admired as a poet and whom he would never have placed in the same category as Southey.

The gadfly is a monstrous creature in its family—even gothic in its menacing appearance. In a static pose, with its wings down and its six legs spread, it is more than an inch and a half long. Its bite is deep and painful. A good deal of anger underlies Keats's attack on Lowther, and the humour of the poem does not disguise the intensity of his dudgeon. Wordsworth is implicated in the Westmorland travesty, and if he is not to be the victim of the unromantic, vicious insect he is nonetheless the ultimate target of Keats's pique.

The Westmorland election had eclipsed in national interest other Parliamentary contests in the land that summer of 1818. Great Britain had its eye on the Lowther-Brougham struggle. No one can ever know how that mysterious rhythm of association and memory that all travellers experience as they move along, trying to reconcile where they have been with where they are now, worked for Keats—how the names of Hunt and Brougham and Lowther and Wordsworth tumbled around in his psyche with Cockney School attacks in *Blackwood's*, and the image of placing a note over Miss Wordsworth's portrait above the mantle sharpened and dissolved, until one small incident, being bitten by a gadfly, focused his vague discontent and released a poem. There was relief for Keats in unloading his dudgeon. The more complicated question remains of whether he was also ridding himself of the influence of a forty-eight-year-old giant, Wordsworth.

The Walking Tour as Travel Literature

Keats's letters and poems of the 1818 walking tour were intended to entertain, please, inform, and cheer his siblings (especially Tom) and a few friends. Keats had a keen sense of his audience and wished he could please them even more by knowing their emotional needs. "I wish I knew what humour you were in that I might accomodate myself to any one of your Amiabilities," he wrote to the George Keatses from his inn, the Nag's Head, in Wythburn on June 27 (Letter 2). In Maybole, on July 13, he wrote to his friend Reynolds: "I wish I knew always the humour my friends would be in at opening a letter of mine, to suit it to them nearly as possible," adding, "I could always find an egg shell for Melancholy—and as for Merriment a Witty humour will turn any thing to Account" (Letter 6). He expected his letters to be shared and circulated. The first letter of the journey, written to Tom, concludes: "Let any of my friends see my letters—they may not be interested in descriptions—descriptions are bad at all times—I did not intend to give you any; but how can I help it? I am anxious you should taste a little of our pleasure. . . . Content that probably three or four pair of eyes whose owners I am rather partial to will run over these lines I remain; and moreover that I am your affectionate brother John." So while Keats intended his writing to lift Tom's spirits and maintain his own closeness to Fanny, George, and Georgiana, he also thought about a wider readership for the letters. Until now they have never been published on their own, and if some of their impact comes from realizing that we are sharing in the disclosure of Keats's brotherly love, surely as much comes from recognizing that Keats wrote some extraordinary travel literature, in an era when this literature was changing as a genre.

Brown's journal of the tour complements Keats's letters beautifully, being more reportorial and more coherent as prose. Keats says he did not like to write description, and he had a certain disdain for the picturesque. There are times when he grows impatient of recounting his journey, as when he starts his letter to Reynolds by announcing that he would "not run over the Ground we have passed" because "that would be merely as bad as telling a dream" (Letter 6). Brown, on the other hand, was patient in recording details of a scene and seemed to have an eye trained to the picturesque. In fact he was so compulsive and methodical about writing in his journal that Keats, in a good-natured way, complained to Benjamin Bailey about his companion's nightly ritual: "Brown keeps on writing volumes of adventures to Dilke—when we get in of an evening and I have perhaps taken my rest on a couple of Chairs he affronts my indolence and Luxury by pulling out of his knapsack 1st his paper—2^{ndy} his pens and last his ink—Now I would not care if he would change about a little—I say now, why not Bailey take out his pens first sometimes—But I might as well tell a hen to hold up her head before she drinks instead of afterwards—" (Letter 9). It was not until 1840 that Brown published some of his journal in the *Plymouth and Devonport Weekly Journal*, October 1, 8, 15, and 22. The long delay resulted from the feud described above with Brown's good friend Charles Wentworth Dilke and others in the Keats circle concerning George Keats and money that was owed to John. In justifying its publication so many years later, Brown rationalized that the "beauty and sublimity of nature" simply did not change much over the years. "On this account, my pains-taking journal, written at the conclusion of each several stage, though full twenty years old, may serve as an itinerary for a traveller on a similar excursion, equally well as if I had just taken off my knapsack at the end of my northern walks. . . . Mine is literally a superficial view of nature; which has one recommendation at least—every body can understand it" (*Walks in the North*, Chapter 1). Brown obviously viewed his writing as travel literature in 1840, though today we value it primarily for its biographical portrait of Keats on the walking tour.

Keats's actual tour and the record he and Brown have left of it profit from being discussed as part of a tradition of travel writing that had been dramatized by noted Englishmen, adventurous Americans, a few venturesome women, and an impressive number of literati. From 1773, when Boswell and Johnson made their heroic visit to Scotland, riding ponies into remote, impoverished, wild islands of the Hebrides and sleeping on hay in shepherds' homes, the possibility of discovering unknown or mysterious people and places fascinated travellers and lured them to the North.

The travellers kept journals, drew sketches, and planned to enlighten the public on their return. Their works were published and read. They were even reviewed. As the body of literature built up, a genre of guide books developed in which the authors dealt with much more than topographical descriptions and anthropological analyses. Questions of taste, of Edmund Burke's distinctions between the beautiful and the sublime, of William Gilpin's concerns with the picturesque, and of politics appeared in the pages of these books. By the time Keats and Brown set out even the most commercial guide books prescribed experiences of the beautiful, the sublime, the picturesque, and the historical for travellers, encouraging anthropological questioning as well. Travel literature had become luxurious: it no longer had to deal primarily with concrete facts of mileage, lodging, food, weather, and expense. It could allow the journeyer-journalist to concentrate on perceiving and experiencing. And it began to make way for humour and anecdotes intended to enliven the text and entertain the reader. Not long after Keats's time, travel books like those of Thomas Frognall Dibdin (*A Bibliographical Antiquarian and Picturesque Tour in the Northern Counties of England and in Scotland*, 2 vols.) and William Beattie (*Scotland, Illustrated in a Series of Views taken Expressly for this Work*, 2 vols.), both published in 1838, featured handsome engravings and impressive cartography, not only for the sake of attracting readership but also to represent a new level of elegance in the guide book as a literary form.

Keats's journey was defined in part by what he had read and heard about the places he was visiting and in part by what his own creative imagination brought to the walk. The journey falls essentially into two major but unequal episodes for him: the visit to northern England, especially the Lake District (which by now had been identified as an extraordinary natural environment), and the visits to Scotland and briefly, Ireland, both clearly remote and, though British, foreign. The Lake District had already been eloquently particularized by Wordsworth in his poetry and in his prose *Guide to the Lakes*, written anonymously in 1810 as an introduction to a collection of drawings (of which Wordsworth did not think highly) by the Reverend Joseph Wilkinson and published separately in 1820. Keats would have known of the *Guide*, and its information would have been common to Keats's literary friends, who would also have known Thomas West's *Guide to the Lakes* (1778 and tenth ed. 1812) and William Gilpin's *Observations, Relative Chiefly to Picturesque Beauty, in Several Parts of England, Particularly the Mountains and Lakes of Cumberland and Westmoreland* (1786 and third ed. 1792), as well as the poet Thomas Gray's *Journal in the Lakes* (written 1769, published 1775).

Novelist Ann Radcliffe had written about her excursion to the Lake District, publishing it in 1795 with another, much longer travel piece as *A Journey Made in the Summer of 1794, through Holland and the Western Frontier of Germany, with a Return Down the Rhine: to Which Are Added Observations During a Tour to The Lakes of Lancashire, Westmoreland, and Cumberland.* In March, just a few months before he left on his trip with Brown, Keats wrote to Reynolds in an exuberant tone: "I am going among Scenery whence I intend to tip you the Damosel Radcliffe—I'll cavern you, and grotto you, and waterfall you, and wood you, and water you, and immense-rock you, and tremendous sound you, and solitude you" (*Letters*, 1, 245). Keats's remarks aptly preface his journal of the Lake District, in which, mercifully, he does not weight his prose with a Radcliffean appreciation of the sublime but instead takes a joyful, personal look at the required sights. There are passages of Radcliffe's *Observations*, however, that are far more engaging than the works of more strictly philosophical travel writers, and Keats could have found his own sense of the gothic validated in the images she captures. Her handling of the Druid Circle at Castlerigg is a case in point. Situated as it is in the vale of St. John, near Keswick, she sees that "such seclusion and sublimity were, indeed, well suited to the deep and wild mysteries of the Druids. Here, at moon-light, every Druid, summoned by that terrible horn, never awakened but upon high occasions, and descending from his mountain, or secret cave, might assemble without intrusion from one sacrilegious footstep, and celebrate a midnight festival by a savage sacrifice" (446). When Keats writes to Tom about his experience of the same place, he acknowledges "the gratification of seeing those aged stones, on a gentle rise in the midst of Mountains, which at that time darkened all round, except at the fresh opening of the vale of St. John" (Letter 3). Brown claims, "the spot is suited to render the human mind awestruck, and, possibly, with the ignorant, superstitious" (Chapter 3). Both men work at divesting the site of sensationalism so well that they call attention to it.

The Lake District was well established as a resort area, and the presence of a certain kind of tourist—the "London sharper," as Brown called him—must have given Keats pause to consider his own image as a traveller: he was a tourist too, there could be no denying that, but he was travelling as economically as possible, and he was, by recent declaration, a poet. Brown's portrait, in his journal, of the pretentious young man from London whom they met at Ambleside who had brought with him only his "fashionable boots," alluded to his uncle's carriage, found fault with the hotel in Bowness, and bragged about "the suppers he used to give at Oxford, interlarding this last account with sundry classic quotations, as evidence of his having been educated there" signals a change in the sensitivity of visitors to the placid Lakes setting.

Tourism had been growing since the time of Thomas West's original *Guide*. West recommended that his visitors position themselves at "stations," where they would view, with an orthodoxy he established for them, the landscape of Cumberland and Westmorland. He was interested in developing taste, and he had a method that was as disciplined as ballet barre work for dancers or scales for piano students. He mapped out a clear route from Lancaster to Kendal, which was followed, or at least nodded to, by travellers from Radcliffe to Keats and Brown. "The best season for visiting the lakes is from the beginning of June to the end of August," he advised, and that is when Keats and Brown travelled. His visitors should carry landscape mirrors, four inches in diameter, with them. The mirror is a "plano-convex glass, and should be the segment of a large circle; otherwise distant and small objects are not perceived in it; but if the glass be too flat, the perspective view of great and near objects is less pleasing, as they are represented too near." The traveller should stand with his back to the landscape; the glass "should be suspended by the upper part of the case, holding it a little to the right or left (as the position of the parts to be viewed require) and the face screened from the sun." The net gain of this odd way of distancing oneself from the landscape is that objects appear "in the soft colours of nature, and in the most regular perspective the eye can perceive, or science demonstrate" (*Guide*, 1789 ed., 12).

The painterly vision of West did not necessarily influence the touring habits of London sharpers, but it contributed to sensitizing visitors to the environment, and this was of profound concern to natives like Wordsworth, who realized that the trend toward tourism was irreversible and that it was therefore important to educate travellers and keep standards of respect for nature high. This was in some sense the first movement toward what we regard today as environmentalist politics. As a measure of how far the area had gone toward catering to visitors, Brown, writing of Keswick, tells us: "Nothing was wanting in the town, at least by attempts, to please a London taste. It was full of lures to pass away the time—a circulating library, a fossil museum, an exhibition of Mr. Green's drawings, and a camera obscura" (Chapter 3). The camera obscura—a box with a

pinhole or lens that admitted light to form an image on the opposite surface—gained new significance as an optical device at the beginning of the nineteenth century because Thomas Wedgwood, son of the famous pottery manufacturer, had experimented with a portable model in an attempt to fix images, anticipating photography. Along with the art show (most likely of the work of William Green of Ambleside, whose *Series of Sixty Small Prints* [1810] Wordsworth alludes to in his *Guide to the Lakes*), it placed Keswick on the map as a haven for the urbane traveller in the country for a holiday.

Keats begins to assume an independent character as he leaves the Lake District, his letters reflecting less of a desire to locate a world through Wordsworth's vision and more of an abandonment to being an empathic observer open to surprises in scenery and culture. He had much less preconception of the scenery that followed the lakes, falls, and mountains of Westmorland and Cumberland. Whatever travel information he may have gotten from a guide book prepared him only practically.

Brown refers to an "Itinerary" (Letter 13), and Nelson Bushnell conjectures (*Walk*, 285) that it may have been *The Traveller's Guide through Scotland* (2 vols., sixth ed., 1814).[6] Though the recommended routes (for example from Inverary to Oban) are not precisely the ones Keats and Brown followed, some of the language in which points of interest are described has a familiar ring. Bushnell notes the similarity of phrasing between Keats's description of Iona in Letter 10, for example. Keats says: "Columba in the Gaelic is Colm signifying Dove—Kill signifies church and I is as good as Island—so I-colm-kill means the Island of Saint Columba's Church." The *Traveller's Guide* says: "Iona, in Hebrew, signifies a *dove*, in allusion to St Columba, who landed here in 565. After his death the island retained his name, and was called Ycolmb-cill, or Columb's Cell, now Icolm Kill, or the island of Columba" (2, 208). And in giving the number of kings buried there Keats reports: "61 kings . . . 48 Scotch from Fergus 2nd to Macbeth 8 Irish 4 Norwegian and 1 french." The *Traveller's Guide* cites: "the remains of the 48 Scotish monarchs, from Fergus II to Macbeth. . . . 4 Irish monarchs. . . . 8 Norgwegian princes" (2, 208). But Bushnell is circumspect in advancing the parallel, stating of the description of the burial ground in Iona, "The phrases . . . are so like Keats's as to excite my wonder, yet so unlike as to leave it unsatisfied" (*Walk*, 295). And he refers to the "Itinerary" of Keats and Brown as the "mysterious Itinerary," an epithet I heartily endorse. Having examined the

Traveller's Guide, I find it does not support Keats's words consistently enough to rule out other possibilities, the most plausible of which, it seems to me, is that information on major sites was provided on the spot, orally, just as it is today, and it all sounded pretty much the same as what was in the guide books. Whatever Brown's "Itinerary," it is only one of many that guided the traveller through Scotland with generic diction and stock details.

For literary figures, the tour to Scotland held a compelling attraction. Johnson and Boswell had charted the archetypical exploration in their tour of August to November 1773. That Johnson was engaged on that trip in examining the authenticity of the Ossian poet and questioning the credibility of his purported translator, Macpherson, only added to the literary interest of their work. Burns, much closer to Keats aesthetically than Johnson was, had made a Highland tour during August and September 1787. Wordsworth, with his sister Dorothy and Coleridge, who remained a part of the threesome only until they arrived in the Highlands, travelled in an Irish car (a small, horse-drawn, open-air cart so close to the ground that one could get off and on while it was in motion) from Keswick through Scotland from August to September 1803, covering some of the same route Keats and Brown followed. As soon as they returned, Dorothy began to write about the trip, producing her journalistic *Recollections of a Tour Made in Scotland, A.D. 1803*. Wordsworth had already visited Scotland two years before this; he took another tour of Scotland with his wife and her sister in 1814, leaving Dorothy at home with the children this time. He made a final trip to Scotland in 1831.

A survey of the output of travel literature concerning Scotland from 1773, when Johnson made his trip, to 1819, when poet laureate Robert Southey published a measured yet attractive account of his tour of inspection with Scottish engineer Thomas Telford (*Journal of a Tour in Scotland in 1819*), reveals the burgeoning of a literary industry. Naturalist and antiquarian Thomas Pennant, who had already come out with his *Tour in Scotland* (1771), published from 1774 to 1776 a classic in travel literature, *A Tour in Scotland and Voyage to the Hebrides*. This was followed in 1793 by Robert Heron's *Observations Made in a Journey through the Western Counties of Scotland in the Autumn of 1793*. The bookseller's shelves then filled with: David Loch, *A Tour through Most of the Trading Towns and Villages of Scotland* (1778); John Lattice, *Letters on a Tour through Various Parts of Scotland in 1792* (1794); John Leyden, *Tour in the Highlands and Western Islands, 1800* (1803);

Sir John Stoddart, *Remarks on Local Scenery and Manners in Scotland* (1801); Alexander Campbell, *A Journey from Edinburgh through Parts of North Britain, Containing Remarks on Scotish Landscape and Observations on*, etc. (1802); Sarah Murray Aust, *A Companion and Useful Guide to the Beauties of Scotland*, etc. (1799, 1803, 1810); John Briston, *Anthroplanomenos: or A Pedestrian Tour through Part of the Highlands of Scotland* (1803); John Walker, *Essays on Natural History and Rural Economy* (1808); Washington Irving, *Tour in Scotland, 1817*; and John Gibson Lockhart, *Peter's Letters to his Kinfolk* (third ed. 1819). The list is far from exhaustive, and there were many other works growing out of travel experiences besides those whose titles specifically promised a tour. Benjamin Franklin, for example, toured Scotland twice, in 1759 and 1771; his correspondence contains the record of his trip. Sir Walter Scott produced a kind of travel literature with his poems and novels from 1802 on that celebrated the border country. Wordsworth's poems about Yarrow, Jedburgh, the site of Burns's grave, the waterfall at Cora Linn, Kilchurn Castle, an island ruin, and Loch Lomond all celebrate a physical place as directly as any travel narrative, albeit with more eloquent articulation. Whether with maps on a page or routes of the poetic imagination, literature about travel in Scotland ripened and propagated with each warm season.

Given the long-established postal routes, as well as General Wade's enduringly serviceable roads, constructed for the occupation of the highlands in the early part of the eighteenth century, the authors of guide books to Scotland tended to cover the same territory or routes, particularly for the Hebrides trips. Their descriptions of the stretch from Loch Lomond to Oban, for example, begin to read like repeated accidents of déjà vu: the inn at Arrochar being preferable to the one at Tarbet; the gloom and sublimity of Glen Croe; the various understandings and misunderstandings of "Rest and Be Thankful"; the comparison of Glen Kinglas to Glen Croe; the welcome arrival at the Cairndow Inn; the imposing sight of the duke of Argyll's castle at Inverary; the ruin of Kilchurn Castle on Loch Awe; the relative inadequacy, considering its critical position, of Oban. It was common among the travellers to note changes in the appearance of the inhabitants of the rural areas, villages, and towns. Some authors presumed to observe actual changes in the physiognomies of men and women as they put more and more miles between themselves and London. One author, for example, was certain he noted just the place where women's faces became more square. The use of Gaelic, the wearing of the plaid, the primitive nature of the living quarters of the Highlanders—all were remarked. It was noted with dismay that women in some parts of Scotland wore no shoes, or stomped in mud and slime while carrying their shoes and stockings in their hands till they got to town for a fair or celebration. The focuses were shared by the guide authors even though their intellectual and moral points of view might be quite disparate.

Of the several writing travellers whose ideas and works would have been public by the time Keats and Brown set out, two strike me as interesting to examine in conjunction with Keats because their works represent opposite extremes of the directions travel literature had taken, and because their polarities nicely encompass and gloss Keats's own travel writings.

The first is Sir John Stoddart, brother-in-law of Hazlitt (who was much admired by Keats), well educated at Oxford, a member of the College of Advocates, articulate and aggressive in advancing his views, and known in London in Keats's time because, after four years of being a leading writer with the *Times*, he had had a dispute with that publication and established his own newspaper, *The New Times*. In 1801 Stoddart published a remarkably detailed and reflective two-volume work based on his travels entitled *Remarks on Local Scenery and Manners of Scotland during the Years 1799 and 1800*. Stoddart wrote with the acumen that made him a successful journalist. He had read widely and knew his Edmund Burke as well as his native poets. Indeed, an important assumption underlying his work is that there is a moral gain to be found in travel, particularly if the traveller experiences nature *correctly*—that is, as Stoddart does and as he guides the reader to do.

The second figure is the author of another two-volume work (guide books always seemed to require more than one volume, thereby confounding portability), a woman named Sarah Murray Aust, who wrote under the name The Honourable Mrs. Murray of Kensington. (After the death in 1786 of her first husband, the Honourable William Murray, she married George Aust.) Mrs. Murray published in 1799 a lively, audience-oriented work called *A Companion and Useful Guide to the Beauties of Scotland, to the Lakes of Westmoreland, Cumberland, and Lancashire, and to the Curiosities in the District of Craven, in the West Riding of Yorkshire; to Which Is Added a More Particular Description of Scotland, Especially That Part of It Called the Hebrides*. In 1803 a second edition appeared and the title was enlarged to include the *Isles of Mull, Ulva, Staffa, I-Columbkill, Tirii, Coll, Eigg, Rum, Skye, Raza, and Scalpa*, and in 1810, a year before Sarah Murray Aust died at the age of sixty-seven, a third edition came out, whose sprawling title page now read: *To Which Is Now Added, An Account of the New Roads in Scotland, and of a Beautiful Cavern Lately Discovered in the Isle of Skye*. Mrs. Murray claimed she was not writing for fame or "bread," but only to offer a guide that would be useful to travellers. Nevertheless, the 1810 edition contained "puffs"—extracts of reviews acclaiming the 1803 edition. One reviewer's characterization of the author could attract readers even today: "Mrs. Murray appears to be possessed of such enthusiasm, that difficulties and dangers operate on her mind as inducements; and we frequently behold her exposing herself to situations from which the most hardy of the other sex would willingly retire. Impelled by a strong attachment to the beauties of Nature, she has visited scenes which were admirably calculated to gratify and reward her liberal curiosity" (2, xvi).[7] Despite her disclaimers, Mrs. Murray's guide was written to sell, and part of the work's appeal rests on the fact that she herself emerges as the plucky heroine of travel romance.

Stoddart addresses "a certain class of readers," the well-informed, educated man or woman who can follow his distinctions when he defines types of experiences of nature; who has seen the works of Reynolds, Salvator, Poussin, and Claude in the galleries, and who will understand his corrections of Samuel Johnson's and Thomas Pennant's commentaries on Scotland. He concludes his work with an essay on taste, working from a definition by Burke, "the greatest writer of modern days," toward his own position that the sublime and the beautiful in nature should be considered in the question of taste. Clearly, Stoddart was writing for a highly literate audience.

His work, therefore, gives us a sense of the issues with which the refined traveller engaged and of the place travel literature was assuming in the literary world. "Tours," he tells us in his preface, "are the mushroom produce of every summer, and Scotland has had her share." "Tours are read, as much as any other ephemeral productions; and some of them live," he notes, going on to cite the qualities (trivial occurrences, enumeration of milestones and public houses, accounts of accidents with the chaise, information on how the travellers dressed) that characterize the work of writers who will be forgotten and those ("either a communication of important physical facts, and discoveries, or an accurate tracing, and novel illustration of human feelings") that distinguish the writing of authors who aspire to permanence (*Remarks*, 1, viii). Stoddart counts himself in the latter category, of course, and not far into his preface we get a sense of the seriousness with which he approaches travel. The world he speaks of is the world Keats came to experience on his tour:

> This feeling [in response to nature] I had forcibly experienced on a visit long since to the delightful scenery of Westmoreland lakes—and I promised myself a still higher gratification from carrying my more ripened feelings to the noble landscapes of Scotland. I was not disappointed in my expectations of pleasure; but during my tour, I did not confine myself to the mere Observation of Nature. I opened my mind to all the diversity of impressions—from general character, and particular association—from ancient tradition, and recent celebrity—from customs and manners, dress and dialect, from appearance—from all that was appropriate to the scene, and all that was accidental to the traveller. Thus the general mass of feelings, recollectable and unrecollectable, was at once augmented and improved; and whilst I pursued the varieties of Nature and Chance, I strengthened the uniformities of sentiment and reflection. I persuaded myself, that if a just delineation were given of my feelings, together with the actual events, the local scenes, and the personal characters, which are essential to truth of description, it would create no unpleasing interest in the minds of a certain class of readers. (1, xi)

Stoddart's self-conscious relation to the external world and his scrupulous sorting-out of reactions before presenting them to the reader make serious reading for tour audiences.

Despite the cerebral character of his intentions, Stoddart's work has considerable vigour and occasional human warmth. At times he seems the prototypical Romantic hero, and he offers a virtual case study of the sublime experience. Standing on top of the north side of Ben Lomond, he feels "a degree of surprise arising almost to terror," and he tells us: "In such a situation, the most sublime sensations cannot be felt, unless you are alone. A single insulated being, carrying his view over these vast, inanimate masses, seems to feel himself attached to them, as it were, by a new kind of bond; his spirit dilates with magnitude, and rejoices in the beauty of the terrestrial objects" (1, 236). As if this were a Wordsworthian spot of time, he remembers a similar instance when he was on top of a mountain in Cumberland: "It was a bright, lovely day, and I stood contemplating with admiration a beautiful vale, with its glittering lake, rich woods, and numerous buildings. Gradually, a thick mist rolled, like a curtain, before it, and took away every

object from my view. I was left alone, on the mountain top, far above the clouds of the vale, the sun shining full upon my head; it seemed as if I had been suddenly transported into a new state of existence, cut off from every meaner association, and invisibly united with the surrounding purity and brightness" (1, 237). It was this kind of turning into oneself in order to arise to "a new state of existence" under conditions of "surprise arising almost to terror" that Stoddart offered, with himself as the model, to the Romantic traveller or the reader of the Romantic tour.

Stoddart in general likes first-hand experience, and he speaks of making friends with local people, for example, a shepherd of Glen Croe who showed him out-of-the-way places. William Gibb, the shepherd, entertained Stoddart in his cottage, and while his wife prepared refreshments, Gibb "conversed very intelligently on his own situation, and on the objects around him" (1, 247–248). What Gibb described, without giving them a label, were the controversial Highland "clearances" and their devastating effect on common people and on the landscape. With a keen political sense and a journalist's eye for news, Stoddart explains the shepherd's position for the reader and comments on the significance of the clearances:

> The system of farming, which now prevails over almost the whole of the Highlands, necessarily annihilates the population; and this part of the empire seems to be converted into a mere sheep-walk for the rest. I will not pretend to say, that this partial evil, in modern politics, is not compensated by the prevalence of manufactures, and other employments, in the more populous parts of the empire; but still it is an evil to the places where it prevails. The love of society is an appetite to the human mind; and we feel a sense of privation, when we behold whole regions depopulated. (1, 248)

It was rare indeed for a nineteenth-century tour book even to acknowledge the issue of the Highland clearances, much less to take a stand favouring the displaced shepherd. Staying close to the landscape and its people allows Stoddart the opportunity to be politically investigative.

He writes confrontationally and analytically, making a virtual science of his journey. After coming up out of Glen Croe, crossing Rest and Be Thankful, and entering Glen Kinglas, he notes, "Mr. Gilpin has unaccountably reversed the characters of Glen Croe, and this vale" (1, 251). Not only does he catch

Gilpin in an error, but he involves himself, at some length, in the still-current debate over the genuineness of the Ossian poems and the culpability of Macpherson (who claimed to have translated them), concluding his own provocative and linguistically sophisticated commentary with a sensible appraisal: "With all these defects, the poems of Ossian are highly valuable; they contain much that is beautiful, and much that is sublime; and it is proof at once of their worth and antiquity, that many passages in them have long been proverbial in the Highlands" (1, 279). He undertakes a defense of the construction of the Caledonian Canal, pointing out the importance of bringing industry to the Highlands. And he takes a jab—not his first—at Dr. Johnson, in a discussion of why Loch Ness does not freeze: whether, as Johnson and some others maintained, because of some sulphurous property, or whether, as Stoddart supposed, because of its depth. "We can scarcely forbear smiling, when we hear Dr. Johnson gravely arguing on the impossibility, that the depth of water should prevent its freezing; a subject on which his profound ignorance should at least have suggested to him the propriety of hesitation" (2, 94–95). For Stoddart the tour book provided a forum for all the ideas, aesthetic to political, that came to him as he travelled.

Such was not the case for Mrs. Murray. Her travel writing never strays much from her purpose, which is to guide people to places that ought to be seen, to advise them on how to fit out their chaises and on what the road conditions will be, to suggest clothing and necessities to be packed, and in general to give the best practical advice possible to travellers headed north, while at the same time entertaining them with occasional anecdotes about her own experiences. She claims to be breaking ground in travel literature. As she puts it in the address at the beginning of her book to the "Managers of the Literary Reviews": "I write because I think my Guide will be really useful to travellers, who may follow my steps through Scotland, and to the Lakes of Cumberland, Westmoreland, and Lancashire; by informing them of those objects which are worthy of notice, and at the same time acquainting them where, and by what means they can get at them in the safest and most comfortable manner. A plan, I believe, never attended to (in the way I have done) by any of my predecessors in Tour writing" (*Companion*, 1, vii). If Stoddart is even partially representative of her predecessors, she is certainly right.

Murray addressed the well-to-do, curious, and informed traveller. She was not interested in shaping morality through tests of the imagination or encounters with the sublime. Indeed, at times she confuses the beautiful with the sublime with refreshing carelessness: "When I went to Fort William it was a fine day, consequently the greater number of these torrents were quiet. It was the next day, on my return, when it rained hard, that I was so delighted with these beautiful dashers. Having two days of different weather between Fort Augustus and Fort William, I saw on one day that charming defile, sublime, bright, soft, and smiling; on the other, terrific, gloomy, and dripping" (1, 275). In general she meant to be practical, providing information, allaying worries, celebrating rewards, and giving encouragement. Mrs. Murray was one of the first to popularize travel to the North.

Her guide reads well even today—despite its lack of the high-mindedness Stoddart conceived necessary for immortality in travel literature—because she is not afraid to give plain details. Her advice on how to fit out a chaise and what to carry on the journey is a wonderfully graphic commentary on how the fashionable upper class travelled to see "The Beauties of Scotland":

Provide yourself with a strong roomy carriage, and have the springs well corded; have also a stop-pole and strong chain to the chaise. Take with you linch-pins, and four shackles, which hold up the braces of the body of the carriage; a turn-screw, fit for fastening the nuts belonging to the shackles; a hammer, and some straps.

For the inside of the carriage, get a light flat box, the corners must be taken off, next the doors, for the more conveniently getting in and out. This box should hang on the front of the chaise, instead of the pocket, and be as large as the whole front, and as deep as the size of the carriage will admit; the side next the travellers should fall down by hinges, at the height of their knees, to form a table on their laps; the part of the box below the hinges should be divided into holes for wine bottles, to stand upright in. The part above the bottles, to hold tea, sugar, bread, and meat; a tumbler glass, knife and fork, and salt-cellar, with two or three napkins: the box to have a very good lock. I would also advise to be taken, bed-linen, and half a dozen towels at least, a blanket, thin quilt, and two pillows; these articles will set a traveller quite at ease, with respect to accommodation; the blanket and quilt will be very seldom wanted; however, when they are, it is very pleasant to have such conveniences in one's power.

If a traveller would like to save a great deal of money, and render a servant more useful than on horseback, put a seat for him behind the carriage; and he being thus a part of the equipage, is always at hand for use, either in opening gates, or in case of accidents; besides, he never can be left behind at the inns where you stop, or elsewhere, which is for ever the case when a servant is on horseback: he is hardly ever with you, when you most want him; and often comes galloping after you, at the risk of his own neck, and to the great detriment of the poor post-horse. (1, 41–42)

Mrs. Murray, who travelled alone and claimed, "I think I have seen Scotland and its natural beauties more completely than any other individual" (1, 45), seemed wise about the anxieties of uninitiated travellers and catered to their worries by advising a kind of defensive approach to seeing the sights as comfortably as possible.

She does not, however, spare travellers the realities of Highland poverty in her guide, and she describes with remarkable precision the crude homes of the people of the moors:

The huts on this moor are very small and low, are soon erected and must very soon fall down. They consist of four stakes of birch, forked at the top, driven into the ground; on these they lay four other birch poles, and then form a gavel at each end by putting up more birch sticks, and crossing them sufficiently to support the clods with which they plaster this skeleton of a hut all over, except a small hole in the side for a window, a small door to creep in and out at, and a hole in the roof, stuck round with sticks, patched up with turf, for a vent, as they call a chimney. The covering of these huts is turf cut about five or six inches thick, and put on as soon as taken from the moor; therefore it seldom loses its vegetation, as I hardly saw any difference between huts and the moor; for what heath there was on either, was equally in bloom. In these huts they make a fire upon the ground, and the smoke issues in columns at every hole, so that if an inhabitant within be induced to take a peep at any travellers, they are seen in a cloud of smoke; notwithstanding which, the curshes (caps of Highland women) were as white as snow, and the faces of the children mostly fair and blooming. (1, 284–285)

Mrs. Murray's clarity and thoroughness in telling the reader about homes on this moor near Fort William and about so many other scenes that reflect human lives rival the reportorial skills of the best travel writers of her time.

Keats is a travel writer of a different order—different even from Brown, as well as from the more obviously contrasting authors of big travel works like those of Mrs. Murray and Stoddart. Keats's tour literature should be read with the understanding that he was a poet, travelling as close to the earth as possible, in the utterly simple sense that he was walking, not riding in a chaise. He and Brown aimed to travel as cheaply as possible, and they willingly took on physical discomfort (in Keats's case to the detriment of his health) in order to intensify their participation in the world they explored. Keats's vision was not coloured by title or wealth: he did not patronize, even when he enjoyed humour at the expense of the Scots.

Keats is not on the whole cerebral about nature, although he hopes to wrest from it a lesson for his soul. In fact, one of the pleasures of reading his letters is seeing how he virtually mocks the high Romantic aesthetic posture. We remember Stoddart on top of Ben Lomond assuming his Romantic pose, analyzing and fine-tuning his experience of the sublime, and we chuckle to find Keats almost parodying such self-absorption at the top of Ben Nevis. He stations himself on a fearful precipice, terrifying Brown, and composes a reflective sonnet, sublimating on the spot the kinds of Burkean energies that preoccupied Stoddart. And Keats's perceptual shortcut leads to a sonnet, contained in Letter 11, that deals primarily with human intelligence:

Read me a lesson, Muse, and speak it loud
    Upon the top of Nevis, blind in mist!
I look into the chasms, and a shroud
    Vaprous doth hide them; just so much I wist
Mankind do know of hell: I look o'erhead,
    And there is sullen mist; even so much
Mankind can tell of heaven: mist is spread
    Before the earth beneath me; even such,
Even so vague is man's sight of himself.
    Here are the craggy stones beneath my feet;
Thus much I know, that, a poor witless elf,
    I tread on them; that all my eye doth meet
Is mist and crag—not only on this height,
But in the world of thought and mental might.

The sonnet may not be one of Keats's finest pieces, but it is a considerable cut above the often self-indulgent reflections of the eyebrows-knit travellers observing nature. Keats can lose himself to nature and, welcoming imagination, produce poetry.

If Keats looks upon nature, that is, the physical world, with a serious eye, it is to establish an aesthetic for himself that will support his commitment to poetry. Seeing Lake Windermere for the first time charges him with the consciousness of how sensual perception can be transformed by way of imagination into a concrete image, or art. The two views he has had of the lake "refine one's sensual vision into a sort of north star which can never cease to be open lidded and stedfast over the wonders of the great Power" (Letter 1). Keats's modern readers usually leap from this metaphor to his "Bright Star" sonnet, satisfied only to note the germination of an idea. But what matters to Keats in the context of his journey and this setting is testing a creative process. Another rush of creative excitement came soon afterward, at the Ambleside waterfall. Considering what a modest natural phenomenon this is, even for the only moderately well travelled viewer, it seems almost naive of Keats to invest so much of himself in experiencing it. True, Ambleside was a traditional guide-book spot. Further, the spirit of Wordsworth, who figuratively owned this place, as well as so much of the rest of the Lake District, would certainly have beckoned the younger poet. But only the powerful urge to put himself on a valid course as a poet can explain the excess of his response and his declaration of the necessity to stockpile visual images for the future. "I shall learn poetry here and shall henceforth write more than ever," he proclaims (Letter 1). It is a plan that will work for him, given his distinctive capacity for empathic absorption of what he elects to take to himself from the external world and the intensity with which he actively discharges his imagination upon an object. He had written to his friend Benjamin Bailey on March 13, 1818: "As Tradesmen say every thing is worth what it will fetch, so probably every mental pursuit takes its reality and worth from the ardour of the pursuer—being in itself a nothing" (Letters, 1, 242). Now, at the beginning of his walking tour, he established himself as a mental tradesman, pursuing the new landscape with ardour.

The complex problem Keats works out for himself in this passage on the Ambleside waterfall is one of relation. What does the objective world present for the taking, and what does the subject (the poet) recognize as pregnant with sensory value in that world? The waterfall in particular, and other "such places," have energy beyond what he has anticipated. "What astonishes me more than any thing is the tone, the coloring, the slate, the stone, the moss, the rock-weed; or, if I may so say, the intellect, the countenance of such places. The space, the magnitude of mountains and waterfalls are well imagined before one sees them; but this countenance or intellectual tone must surpass every imagination and defy any remembrance" (Letter 1). "Intellectual tone," far from hinting at a transcendental agency, stands for the organic vigour the poet's mind may lay claim to in the world before him. So potent is this world that it does not require "a greeting of the spirit" to call it into existence, as would be the case for clouds or love, things which Keats called "semi real" in his letter to Bailey. A surfeit of perceptions cancels out any imagination or remembrance one might have had of the waterfall. And for the time being his own imagination, because it has been surpassed by the reality, is at rest. This would seem self-indulgent if it weren't for the ambition that is applied to the idea. He will (in the future) add to what has already been written "by the finest spirits," among whom is certainly Wordsworth, by converting the materials of the landscape into "etherial existence," or poems.

Along the way to losing himself to nature on the walking tour, however, Keats can be a bit of a clown, teetering atop a mountain or falling into a "squashy hole" at Lodore Falls with marvellous irreverence for the hallowed ground of the Lake District, and this makes for good entertainment for his readers, who would certainly have gotten the anti-sublime joke. Keats wanted to be humourous, especially for his brothers. Punning was his verbal sport ("I have been looking out my dear Georgy for a joke or a Pun for you," he wrote to his brother [Letter 2]), and he could strike hard, coming up, for example, with the parenthesis joke in Letter 5, the play on Fladgate's name in Letter 6, and the macho obscenities hidden behind place names at the beginning of Letter 8. For his male readers Keats seizes upon an anecdote of a fifty-year-old fat woman who tried to climb Ben Nevis and from that creates a burlesque poem, in which the old mountain, personified, orders his servants to get him stoked up so he can rape fat Mrs. Cameron, who faints in the nick of time.

A litany of praise for the Cairndow Inn had been registered by refined, even literary travellers before Keats visited. But not by Keats, who takes a swim in Loch Fyne opposite the inn, is bitten by a gadfly, and releases his anger at the Westmorland campaign in a satiric-comic poem. The inn's delights pale next to the discomforts of the flesh. In the same satiric frame of mind he tears into a drama and its bagpipe accompaniment performed in Inverary.

The comedian in Keats took a sweeter turn in his letter to Fanny (Letter 4), in his "naughty Boy" poem, the tale about himself travelling that stretches out in narrow lines like a highway north. He rounds out the letter with a delightful hoop image, describing his tiredness, followed by hyperbolic measures of his appetite for food. Also in a lighter tone are several mirrorings of himself and Brown as they appeared to the Scots and Irish. Brown's spectacles entertained onlookers and were a source of much curiosity; on Mull they frightened a child. The pair were taken for peddlers, excisemen, travelling jewellers and razor sellers, Frenchmen, criminals, soldiers, linen drapers, spies. Brown, too, enjoyed passing on to his correspondents Keats's image of him as Spenser's Red-Cross Knight, with his shadow bursting at the seams. They make themselves characters in their own autobiographies.

This is not to say that both Keats and Brown were not conventional in their travel pursuits and writing. They did, after all, follow the classic guide-book routes and both, Brown more than Keats, paid lip service to the appreciation of the sublime. When he first came on Ailsa Craig, Keats wrote: "Ailsa struck me very suddenly—really I was a little alarmed" (Letter 7). This was the appropriate response to a large but beautiful geological phenomenon, the kind of remark Stoddart might have made, as was Brown's proclamation about Ambleside: "Here are the beautiful and the sublime in unison" (Chapter 2). The tendency to generalize about cultures and to compare them, as Keats does with the Scots and Irish, is standard to travel literature. Even some of Keats's attitudes toward the Scots are conventional: that they are frugal, logical to a fault, and grave, and that their conversation is too cautious. As we have seen in Mrs. Murray's writing, anecdotes took a respectable place in the pages of travel books, and Keats relished those he turned out for his readers. Judgments about food and lodgings belonged as well to the canon of travel accounts, and Keats does not fail to mention practical details: the "dirty bacon dirtier eggs and dirtiest Potatoes with a slice of Salmon," a "nice carpeted Room with Sofa hair bottomed chairs and green-baized mehogany," far too many oatcakes and eggs, the smoke in the shepherd's hut. Brown reports that "many fleas were in the beds" at the Nag's Head in Wythburn.

But Keats approaches these things in a fresh way and with a prose style that is livelier than Stoddart's and more aggressive than Mrs. Murray's. His genuine concern for the harmful and far-reaching effects of the Scottish Presbyterian Church (and the Reformation generally) produce the journalistic editorializing common to travel writing, but, again, it reaches a different, psychological level in Keats, who is concerned about the damage done to healthy sensuality in human beings and to preexisting religious institutions with their own innocent integrity.

The literariness of Keats's letters most clearly sets them apart as travel pieces. He both quotes and makes poetry, and in doing so takes his writing well out of the realm of topographical reporting. At a juncture when a lesser mind might be complaining about discomfort or disappointments, Keats quotes from Shakespeare, Wordsworth, Burns, and Milton, and lines are not so much summoned as surrendered to a place. The only literary sources Keats and Brown specifically mention taking with them for leisure reading are volumes of Milton and Dante.

The effect on Keats of being in Burns country comes through in his language and poetry. Veneration for the Scottish poet might have been satisfied by a visit to his home, the grave and mausoleum in St. Michael's Churchyard, and Tam o' Shanter's haunts. But Keats pushes beyond the cliché of attempting a kind of seance with a famous figure through contact with his grounds. With a poet's ear for the melody in words (and therefore for dialect), and with an easy command of Burns's metrics, Keats wrote three ballads. One, "Old Meg she was a gipsey," paints a rich though fairly static picture of Meg Merriles in her setting on the moors; the second, "Ah! ken ye what I met the day," adopts the Scottish dialect and experiments with the ballad meter of the fourteener, by cutting off the final stress of every second line so that the poem rushes through its horseback wedding procession with a slightly irregular canter of thirteen syllables; and the third, "All gentle folks who owe a grudge," develops its satire through tightly structured, regular ballad stanzas. The endings of the first two poems look forward to "La Belle Dame sans Merci": an extended image or narrative performance that has been in sharp focus is suddenly dissolved, leaving the reader with a sense of loss or sadness or isolation or unresolved disturbance.

The portraiture in Keats's letters is virtually Chaucerian. Probably the most haunting of the characters to turn up is the Duchess of Dunghill. Physically repulsive, she is the consummate impoverished old person who strikes simultaneously the conscience and the vanity of the beholder. Barely human, she is offensive to the eye. Keats was close enough to her, however, to observe even the thinness of her lids: "On our return from Belfast we met a Sadan—the Duchess of

Dunghill—It is no laughing matter tho—Imagine the worst dog kennel you ever saw placed upon two poles from a mouldy fencing—In such a wretched thing sat a squalid old Woman squat like an ape half starved from a scarcity of Buiscuit in its passage from Madagascar to the cape—with a pipe in her mouth and looking out with a round-eyed skinny lidded, inanity—with a sort of horizontal idiotic movement of her head—squat and lean she sat and puff'd out the smoke while two ragged tattered Girls carried her along—" (Letter 5). The Duchess of Dunghill remains a dark reality and a difficult one as well. Keats follows the description of her with the remark, "What a thing would be a history of her Life and sensations," but he promptly drops the complex idea of exploring her, and goes on to another thought. She remains locked in his memory as an unresolved experience. In a letter written to Reynolds a few days later (Letter 6), Keats brings her up again. He can never forget her, he says, adding, "I wish I may be able to give you an idea of her," but he makes no attempt to do so. Her coarse image is left to roam the imagination of the reader without compensatory pathos.

Most of Keats's characters are quick studies, fit for a crowded letter that had to be a "single," and drawn by means of dialect and dialogue rather than physical characteristics. The driver of the coach in Dumfries whose greeting is "How is it wi yoursel," Richard Radshaw the "notorious tippler" (celebrated in Brown's account as well), the barefoot girls, the two whiskey-drinking men in the house of entertainment somewhere between Donaghadee and Belfast, the "mahogany faced old Jackass" who drank and told anecdotes, both to excess, in Burns's cottage, the "Traveller" who boasted of having seen Edmund Kean in a performance of Shakespeare and proceeded to get his characters and plays mixed up, the "old grandmother" with shoes but no stockings, and her "Guid Man" in Ford, where mostly Gaelic was spoken, the shepherd and his family in the hut on Mull whose faces cannot be seen because of smoke, the silent young woman who threw on a wrap and guided Keats and Brown in the rain for a mile to get them on their path when they'd lost their way, the guide who snored and sang Gaelic songs on Mull, the "old Schoolmaster" on Iona—short (even compared to Keats), whiskey drinking, "ignorant" but "reckoned very clever," and indeed full of facts—the guide wearing "the Tartan and Cap" who served whiskey as he led the climb up Ben Nevis, and of course the characters of his poems—Meg, the wedding party, Mrs. Cameron, and the naughty boy: all people the tale of the 1818 walking tour.

Keats had written to Tom: "I shall endeavour that you may follow our steps in this walk—it would be uninteresting in a Book of Travels—it can not be interesting but by my having gone through it" (Letter 7). Today's reader will marvel at how wisely Keats invested himself in his Book of Travels.

[1] Letters from the Travel Literature are cited by number.

[2] Brown developed his biography, or memoir, of Keats as a lecture in 1836, while living in Plymouth. It was given on December 29, 1836, to the Plymouth Institution. In 1841, just before he emigrated to New Zealand, Brown entrusted his memoir of Keats and all the copies of Keats's unpublished poems in his possession to Richard Monckton Milnes, whose 1848 *Life, Letters, and Literary Remains, of John Keats*, 2 vols., became the first major biography of Keats.

[3] All quotations of the poetry of Keats are from *The Poems of John Keats*, ed. Jack Stillinger.

[4] The child who was the poet's namesake, John Keats, became a civil engineer in Missouri. The *Southern Literary Messenger* for August 1941 provides a list of George Keats's living descendants up to that time. For a fuller discussion of George and Georgiana in Kentucky, see *Keats Circle*, 1, xcvi–cviii.

[5] For a fuller discussion of the Westmorland election of 1818 see: Mary Moorman, *Wordsworth: The Later Years*, 344–363; John Edwin Wells, "Wordsworth and De Quincey in Westmorland Politics, 1818," *PMLA*, 1940, 63, 1080–1128; and Wallace W. Douglas, "Wordsworth in Politics: The Westmorland Election of 1818," *Modern Language Notes*, November 1948, 43, no. 7, 437–449.

[6] Bushnell describes it as "a light, compact little book, over five hundred pages, two volumes in one, such as could very easily be slipped into a knapsack" (*Walk*, 285). However, the 6th edition I examined was distinctly two volumes. Again Bushnell is impressed with the idea that this work "carries the traveler even as far as John o' Groats" (285), but I noticed there nothing called John o' Groats on the map. Bushnell's copy was lent to him by an Inverness librarian; the copy I examined was in the library of the Yale Center for British Art.

[7] All references to Murray's *Companion* are to the third (1810) edition.

THE ITINERARY

Nelson Bushnell developed this itinerary from the evidence of Keats's walking tour letters and Brown's journal. Since its publication in 1936 (as "Keats's Schedule," in *A Walk after John Keats*, 301–302) it has served as the principal reference for Keats scholars. The question marks call attention to conjecture in the absence of indisputable evidence. Bushnell's own journey after Keats, recounted in his book, lends validity to his outline of the walking tour.

Wednesday, June 24, 1818: Liverpool to Lancaster, by coach.

Thursday, June 25: through Bolton-le-Sands and Burton-in-Kendal, to Endmoor.

Friday, June 26: through Kendal and Bowness, to Ambleside.

Saturday, June 27: through Rydal and Grasmere, to Wythburn.

Sunday, June 28: to Keswick; with side trips around Derwentwater and to the Druid Circle.

Monday, June 29: up Skiddaw, and to Ireby.

Tuesday, June 30: through Wigton, to Carlisle.

Wednesday, July 1: through Gretna Green to Dumfries by coach.

Thursday, July 2: side trip to Lincluden; and to Dalbeattie.

Friday, July 3: through Auchencairn and Dalbeattie, to Kirkcudbright.

Saturday, July 4: through Gatehouse-of-Fleet, to Creetown?

Sunday, July 5: through Newton Stewart, to Glenluce.

Monday, July 6: through Stranraer, to Portpatrick; and by boat to Donaghadee.

Tuesday, July 7: to Belfast.

Wednesday, July 8: to Donaghadee, and by boat to Portpatrick.

Thursday, July 9: through Stranraer and Cairn Ryan, to Ballantrae.

Friday, July 10: to Girvan.

Saturday, July 11: through Kirkoswald and Maybole, to Ayr.

Sunday, July 12: to Kilmarnock?

Monday, July 13: through Kingswells, to Glasgow.

Tuesday, July 14: to Dumbarton?

Wednesday, July 15: to Tarbet?

Thursday, July 16: at Tarbet?

Friday, July 17: through Cairndow, to Inverary.

Saturday, July 18: to Cladich.

Sunday, July 19: through Port-in-Sherrich, to Ford.

Monday, July 20: to Kilmelfort.

Tuesday, July 21: to Oban.

Wednesday, July 22: by ferry, through Kerrera, to Lochdonhead?—and into Mull (Glen More?).

Thursday, July 23: to Bunessan?

Friday, July 24: by boat, to Iona, Staffa, and through Loch Na Keal; to Salen?

Saturday, July 25: by ferry, through Kerrera, to Oban?

Sunday, July 26: at Oban.

Monday, July 27:
Tuesday, July 28: } at Oban?
Wednesday, July 29:

Thursday, July 30: to Portnacroish?

Friday, July 31: to Ballachulish?

Saturday, August 1: to Fort William?

Sunday, August 2: up Ben Nevis.

Monday, August 3: to Letterfinlay.

Tuesday, August 4: to Fort Augustus?

Wednesday, August 5: to Foyers?

Thursday, August 6: to Inverness.

Friday, August 7:
Saturday, August 8, 1818: } at Inverness, and by coach through Beauly to Cromarty.

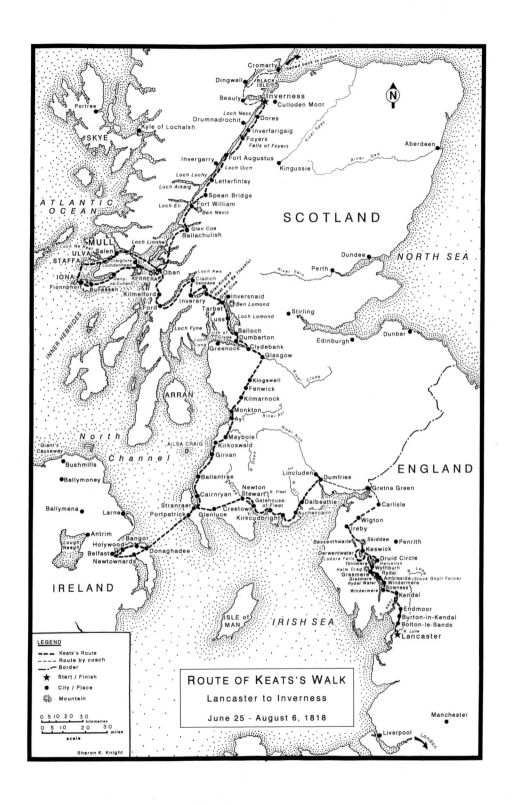

ROUTE OF KEATS'S WALK
Lancaster to Inverness
June 25 - August 6, 1818

LEGEND
— — — Keats's Route
– – – – Route by coach
–··–··– Border
★ Start / Finish
● City / Place
✳ Mountain

0 5 10 20 30
kilometres
0 5 10 20 30
miles
scale

Sharon K. Knight

A PHOTOGRAPHIC RETRACING OF THE WALKING TOUR

PROLOGUE

In April, Keats had written that his walking tour was expected "to make a sort of Prologue to the Life I intend to pursue," of writing and study. He looked forward to "an accumulation of stupendous recollolections." But at the beginning of his tour he would have been looking back as well, with a mood of melancholy over his recent farewell to George and Georgiana at the Crown Inn in Liverpool and at thoughts of Tom, left behind in Hampstead, and his youngest sibling, Fanny, sequestered with her guardian, Richard Abbey, invading his excitement. He wrote to them all, but especially to Tom, who "with an exquisite love of life" was in fact dying. Keats tried to bolster Tom's spirits, to include him on the journey by proxy. He kept a journal in letters for Tom. And he wrote poems, which he included in the letters.

Brief passages from Keats's letters and from the letters and journal of his walking companion, Charles Brown, are quoted in the captions to the photographs. The full texts of these letters and the journal are given in the section following the photographs.

1. Lancaster. The market square and town hall, built in 1781 (now a museum).

On Thursday, June 25, 1818, John Keats and Charles Brown began their walking tour in Lancaster. They were wearing oilskin capes, and they carried knapsacks crammed with toiletries, changes of clothing, writing paper, pens, ink, a translation of Dante's *Divine Comedy* in three small volumes, and a compact text of Milton. They had maps and an itinerary.

2. Lancaster. Entrance to the Carpenter's Arms, an old inn on what was in 1818 the highway to the north, Bridge Lane.

Lancaster was a dynamic city: active port, political center, and heart of the weaving industry. Keats and Brown arrived to find themselves in the midst of a national election, the town crowded with voters. "'The aspiring blood of Lancaster' deprived us of all comfort," Brown wrote in his journal. "There we had to wait two hours for our promised dinner; and were then told—'Not a bed in the house, gentlemen!' Fortunately a private house received us—better than a public one on such roaring occasions."

3. Lancaster. Penny's Almshouses, built in 1720 to offer shelter to
"12 poor old men of the town."

> The weariness, the fever, and the fret
>   Here, where men sit and hear each other groan;
> Where palsy shakes a few, sad, last gray hairs,
>   Where youth grows pale, and spectre-thin, and dies;
>   Where but to think is to be full of sorrow.

("Ode to a Nightingale," ll. 23–27)

4. Bolton-le-Sands. The parish church that Keats and Brown saw as they entered town.

Brown: "Four miles brought us into Bolton to breakfast, when the rain came down heavily again."

The two had arisen at four in the morning, but it was raining so heavily that they read Milton's *Samson Agonistes* for three hours and then set out into a Scotch mist. They had agreed on a regimen. Each morning they would arise at four or five, walk several miles before breakfast, and after a meal (and occasionally some letter writing) press on.

5. Burton-in-Kendal. The King's Arms.

Dinner time found them competing with crowds for food and lodging. The Green Dragon turned them away, but the King's Arms could provide a meal—and an agitated landlady, who exclaimed: "Ah! gentlemen, the soldiers are upon us! The Lowthers had brought 'em here to be in readiness.... Dear me! dear me!—at this election time to have soldiers upon us, when we ought to be making a bit of money.... You can't sleep here, gentlemen; but I can give you a dinner."

6. Kendal. The castle.
   Keats: "We have passed the two castles, Lancaster and Kendal."

7. Kendal. The River Kent.
   Keats: "We set out from Endmoor this morning, breakfasted at Kendal with a soldier who had been in all the wars for the last seventeen years."

8. Windermere. The first glimpse of the lake.

    Keats: "June 26—I merely put *pro forma*, for there is no such thing as time and space, which by the way came forcibly upon me seeing for the first hour the Lake and Mountains of Winander—I cannot describe them—they surpass my expectation."

9. Lake Windermere.

Keats: "The two views we have had of it are of the most noble tenderness—they can never fade away—they make one forget the divisions of life; age, youth, poverty and riches; and refine one's sensual vision into a sort of north star which can never cease to be open lidded and stedfast over the wonders of the great Power."

10. Bowness, Lake Windermere. The White Lion in Keats's time; the Royal Hotel today.

Here Keats and Brown dined on fish they had fetched themselves, and Keats began his search for Wordsworth: "We have walked to Bowness to dinner. . . . I took an oar to one of the islands to take up some trout for dinner, which they keep in porous boxes. I enquired of the waiter for Wordsworth—he said he knew him, and that he had been here a few days ago, canvassing for the Lowthers. What think you of that—Wordsworth versus Brougham!!"

Brown carped at the ambience: "We thought the many luxuries, together with the cold, civil, professional formality attending them, but ill accorded with the view from the window; nay, the curtains, furnished by some gay upholsterer, about that very window, might almost be construed into something like an affront."

11. Ambleside. The Salutation Inn.

They spent the night of June 26 at the Salutation Inn.

Brown: "In the evening he repeated to me his beautiful and pathetic poem of 'Isabella,' which he had just written, before he left Teignmouth" (*Life of Keats*, 49).

12. Ambleside. Stock Ghyll Force, or the Ambleside waterfall, as Keats called it.

Keats: "The waterfall itself, which I came suddenly upon, gave me a pleasant twinge. First we stood a little below the head about half way down the first fall, buried deep in trees, and saw it streaming down two more descents to the depth of near fifty feet—"

"...then we went on a jut of rock nearly level with the second fall-head, where the first fall was above us, and the third below our feet still—at the same time we saw that the water was divided by a sort of cataract island on whose other side burst out a glorious stream —then the thunder and the freshness."

"... We afterwards moved away a space, and saw nearly the whole more mild, streaming silverly through the trees."

"What astonishes me more than any thing is the tone, the coloring, the slate, the stone, the moss, the rock-weed."

13. Near Ambleside.

14. Rydal. Rydal Mount, the home of Wordsworth.
    Keats: "We ate a Monstrous Breakfast on our return...and after it proceeded to Wordsworths. He was not at home nor was any Member of his family—I was much disappointed."

15. Rydal Mount. Interior. The dining room with mantelpiece.
    Keats: "I wrote a note & left it on the Mantlepiece."
    The entrance to Wordsworth's home was through an alcove in the dining room. The portrait of Burns now over the mantelpiece was given to Wordsworth by Burns's sons.

16. Grasmere. Dove Cottage.

Wordsworth lived here in the leaner years of his life (1799–1808). Keats would have passed it as he left Rydal Mount. Its charm and the realization that Wordsworth wrote some of his best poetry while living here must have compensated somewhat for the disillusionment of finding Wordsworth away from Rydal Mount campaigning for the Tory candidates.

De Quincey resided here at the time Keats and Brown passed it.

17. Helm Crag.
On top of the mountain range seen from Grasmere one sees the configuration of an old woman bent forward.
Keats: "I have seen Kirkstone, Loughrigg and Silver How—and discovered without a hint 'that ancient woman seated on Helm Craig.'"

18. Wythburn, just within Cumberland. The site of the Nag's Head.

At one time there was an inn called the Nag's Head right on the water's edge. Here Keats wrote the first poem of the walking tour—an acrostic for his new sister-in-law, Georgiana.

Brown called Wythburn "a pretty place," but had a problem with the Nag's Head: "During the night there had fallen much rain; many fleas were in the beds."

19. Keswick. The Royal Oak Hotel.

Keats and Brown were in Keswick on Sunday, June 28, and most likely stayed at the Royal Oak Hotel, called the Oak Inn then and frequented by the fashionable.

Brown: "At the inn here, near mid-day, came a yawning dandy from his bed-room, and sat at his breakfast reading a bouncing novel!"

20. Derwentwater. View from the west side.

Keats: "The Approach to derwent water is rich and magnificent beyond any means of conception—the Mountains all round sublime and graceful and rich in colour—Woods and wooded Islands here and there—at the same time in the distance among Mountains of another aspect we see Basenthwaite."

21. Derwentwater. Lodore Falls, near the southern end.

    Keats: "We took a complete circuit of the Lake going about ten miles, & seeing on our way the Fall of Low-dore. I had an easy climb among the streams, about the fragments of Rocks & should have got I think to the summit, but unfortunately I was damped by slipping one leg into a squashy hole."

"...There is no great body of water, but the accompaniment is delightful; for it ooses out from a clef in perpendicular Rocks, all fledged with Ash & other beautiful trees. It is a strange thing how they got there."

22. Castlerigg. The Druid Circle.
    Brown: "In the evening we visited the Druidical remains. . . . Surrounded by a majestic panorama, the spot is suited to render the human mind awestruck, and, possibly, with the ignorant, superstitious."

23. Millbeck.

    The next morning the pair arose at four to climb Skiddaw. On their way they probably passed Millbeck and perhaps began their climb from a footpath beyond the little village.

24. Skiddaw.
   Keats: "It promised all along to be fair,"

". . . & we had fagged & tugged nearly to the top, when at halfpast six there came a mist upon us & shut out the view; we did not however lose anything by it."

25. Ireby.

In this old, quiet town, which Brown described as "a dull, beggarly looking place," Keats seems to have come into his own as a travel writer. Wordsworth country was behind him, and the expectations raised by guide books no longer held him. His responses to Ireby are fresh and entirely his own. For the first time he seems to have felt close to the natives and desired to identify with them. The children appealed to him, and he experienced a sense of patriotism.

26. Ireby. Fountain and bench.
   Perhaps they rested here before searching out an inn for the night.

27. Ireby. The Sun Inn.
   Brown: "Our inn was remarkably clean and neat, and the old host and hostess were very civil and preposessing."

The Sun Inn. Dining room.

Here Keats and Brown became aware that in an upstairs hall a travelling dancing master was giving a class to the children of local farmers.

Brown: "But, heyday! what were those obstreperous doings over head?"

The Sun Inn. Entrance to the dancing hall.

Keats: "We were greatly amused by a country dancing school, holden at the Sun, it was indeed 'no new cotillion fresh from France.' No they kickit & jumpit with mettle extraordinary, & whiskit, & fleckit, & toe'd it, & go'd it, & twirld it, & wheel'd it, & stampt it, & sweated it, tattooing the floor like mad."

28. Ireby. Men on a bench.
    Keats: "This is what I like better than scenery. I fear our continued moving from place to place, will prevent our becoming learned in village affairs; we are mere creatures of Rivers, Lakes, & mountains."

29. Wigton.
    Keats: "Our yesterday's journey was from Ireby to Wigton,"

30. Carlisle Castle.
". . . & from Wigton to Carlisle. . . . The Castle is very Ancient, & of
Brick."

SCOTLAND

31. Dumfries. St. Michael's Churchyard.

Keats: "We shall ride 38 miles to Dumfries, where we shall linger a while."

Fudging on their walking commitments, the pair took a coach to Dumfries. Brown justified this concession by claiming, "there was nothing interesting in the country between Carlisle and Dumfries, and . . . consequently, it would be toil without remuneration" to walk. Robert Burns was on Keats's mind, and they arrived early enough to visit St. Michael's Churchyard before dinner.

Keats: "Burns' tomb is in the Churchyard corner."

32. St. Michael's Churchyard. The Burns Mausoleum.

Keats: found the tomb "not very much to my taste, though on a scale, large enough to show they wanted to honour him." But after dinner he wrote "On Visiting the Tomb of Burns" for Tom.

The town, the churchyard, and the setting
    sun,
  The clouds, the trees, the rounded hills
    all seem,
  Though beautiful, cold—strange—as in
    a dream
I dreamed long ago.

Brown: "Such memorials to great men in the intellectual world, especially over their graves, should not be neglected. They may excite emulation; they must inspire reverence and gratitude, two feelings of which man is susceptible to the improvement of his nature."

33. North of Dumfries. Lincluden College, a ruined abbey.

It was only a one-mile walk (two, according to Brown) to these ruins the next morning to see Lincluden, founded as a Benedictine Convent in 1146.

Brown: "Praise for great beauty may be honestly bestowed on the Chapel."

"...It was once admirable for much fine workmanship about the cornices and capitals, but it is now nearly effaced; the stone being rather soft, and the climate rather hard."

"... There are several vaults beneath, very like the dungeons we read
of, for the heretical, the refractory, or the frail."

34. Between Dalbeattie and Auchencairn. Meg Merrilies country.

Brown: "There was a little spot, close to our pathway, where, without a shadow of doubt, old Meg Merrilies had often boiled her kettle, and, haply, cooked a chicken. It was among fragments of rock, and brambles, and broom" (*Life of Keats*, 1, 439).

35. Dundrennan Abbey.

Brown: "The road to Kirkcudbright is ten miles; but we chose to add a couple more to them, in order to pass through Dundrennan, and see the Abbey. It is the ruin of a stately building, and must have bordered on the magnificent in its original state. Trees were not only growing about, but on the walls. There was, especially, a flourishing ash, that did not appear to derive any nourishment from earth; the root spreading itself down the wall, curving its branches between the stones, some forty feet from the ground, and feeding, as far as we could judge, on the mortar alone. Probably the mortar was in a nutritious state of decay."

36. Approaching Kirkcudbright.

Brown: "With the town not far before us, we were enchanted with
the view; the winding bay—the wood-covered hills—the blue mountains beyond them . . . all formed a scene that even Keats confessed to
be equal and similar to the best parts of his favourite Devon. As we
nearer approached the town, through the valley, every thing was in a
most luxuriant state; the trees, the corn, the verdure, and even the
hedges—nothing could surpass them."

37. Kirkcudbright.
    Keats to Fanny: "We have walked through a beautiful Country to Kirkud-bright—at which place I will write you a song about myself—"

> There was a naughty boy
>   A naughty boy was he
> He would not stop at home
>   He could not quiet be—

38. Kirkcudbright.

> This knapsack
> Tight at 's back
> He rivetted close
> And follow'd his nose
> To the north
> To the north
> And followed his nose
> To the north—

"My dear Fanny I am ashamed of writing you such stuff, nor would I if it were not for being tired after my days walking, and ready to tumble into bed so fatigued that when I am asleep you might sew my nose to my great toe and trundle me round the town like a Hoop without waking me."

39. Gatehouse-of-Fleet. The Murray Arms.

   Brown: "To arrive at Gate House costs four miles to the top of a hill, and four more to the bottom."

   On July 4 Keats and Brown may have breakfasted at the Murray Arms, a coaching inn on the Dumfries-to-Stranraer stage route. The inn was added on to the original gatehouse (now a coffee house) and could boast that Burns had written his "Scots, Wha Hae" there. Scott set some of *Guy Mannering* in the town.

40. Cardoness Castle.

   Standing high on a bluff that Keats and Brown passed as they left Gatehouse-of-Fleet.

41. The seaside road to Creetown.

Brown: "Taking the sea-side road to Cree Town, four miles longer than the usual road, we became acquainted with a custom which I wish were more general in all countries. We soon met, returning to Gate House, men, women and children, of all ages and descriptions. It looked like an emigration, and we inquired the reason; when 'The salt water' was the reply; and truly the greater proportion of population had taken the opportunity of high tide to wash and be clean, where a jutting rock on the coast separated the sexes; and, moreover, they told us it was their daily custom."

42. Creetown. The Barholm Arms.
Here the pair undoubtedly spent the night of July 4. Mr. and Mrs. King, the present proprietors, were able to locate deeds that showed the inn had been sold in 1808 and that the deed for that year indicated two previous sales.
Keats: "Our Landlady . . . said very few Southrens passed these ways—The children jabber away as in a foreign Language."

43. Newton Stewart. The Galloway Arms.
Keats: "We are lodged and entertained in great varieties—we dined yesterday on dirty bacon dirtier eggs and dirtiest Potatoes with a slice of Salmon."

44. Glenluce. The Auld King's Arms Hotel.
   Keats: "We breakfast this morning in a nice carpeted Room with Sofa hair bottomed chairs and green-baized mehogany."
   The original King's Arms of Glenluce, this inn served as a post for coaches on the London-Portpatrick service—the Irish Mail.

45. Glenluce. The King's Arms Hotel.
   This smaller hotel was a private house in Keats's time.

46. Glenluce Abbey. Founded 1192.
    Keats: "Yesterday Morning we set out from Glenluce going some distance round to see some Ruins—they were scarcely worth the while."

47. Portpatrick. The harbour.

Keats: "We went on towards Stranrawier in a burning sun and had gone about six Miles when the Mail overtook us—we got up—were at Portpatrick in a jiffy."

Portpatrick had been the principal port for sailings to northern Ireland since the mid-sevententh century.

48. Portpatrick. A view from Dunskey Castle.

49. Dunskey Castle.
 The ruined castle stands on a coastal bluff at Portpatrick, and Keats and Brown would have seen it as they sailed across the rough sea to Ireland, twenty-one miles away.

IRELAND

50. Donaghadee.

Now a quiet fishing village, Donaghadee was Portpatrick's counterpart in Ireland. Larne replaced Donaghadee as the principal port, just as Stranraer did Portpatrick, when steamers took over the work of sailing vessels in the mid-nineteenth century.

Keats: "It is not so far to the Giant's Cause way as we supposed—we thought it 70 and hear it is only 48 Miles—so we shall leave one of our knapsacks here at Donoghadee, take our immediate wants and be back in a week."

51. Belfast. Checkpoint on Ann Street.
    What would have been Keats's surprise if his other knapsack had
been searched as he went from zone to zone in central Belfast.

52. Belfast. The Linen Hall Library, above the Gramophone Shop.
   Called the Belfast Library in Keats's day and established by the Belfast Society for Promoting Knowledge. Its first librarian, Thomas Russell, was a radical.

53. Belfast. Kelly's.
   A possible retreat in Belfast.

54. Donaghadee.

Keats: "I will tell you that it is as dear living in Ireland as at the Hummums—thrice the expence of Scotland—it would have cost us £15 before our return—Moreover we found those 48 Miles to be Irish ones which reach to 70 English—So having walked to Belfast one day and back to Donoghadee the next we left Ireland with a fair breeze."

SCOTLAND

55. The road to Ballantrae. Milestone.
　Keats: "Yesterday we came 27 Miles from Stranraer—entered Ayrshire a little beyond Cairn, and had our path through a delightful Country. I shall endeavour that you may follow our steps in this walk—it would be uninteresting in a Book of Travels —it can not be interesting but by my having gone through it."

56. To Ballantrae.
　Keats: "Our Road lay half way up the sides of a green mountainous shore, full of Clefts of verdure and eternally varying— sometimes up sometimes down."

"...After two or three Miles of this we turned suddenly into a magnificent glen finely wooded in Parts—"

"...with a Mountain Stream winding down the Midst—"

"...the sides of the Hills covered with sheep—"

57. Ailsa Craig.
"... At the end we had a gradual ascent and got among the tops of the
Mountains whence in a little time I descried in the Sea Ailsa Rock
940 feet hight—it was 15 Miles distant and seemed close upon us....
Ailsa struck me very suddenly—really I was a little alarmed."

58. Ballantrae. The old bridge.
    Keats wrote a "gallowy song" in Ballantrae, inspired by a wedding party he saw as he came into town.

<blockquote>
As I stood where a rocky brig
    A torrent crosses,
I spied upon a misty rig
    A troup o' horses—
</blockquote>

59. Ballantrae. The King's Arms.

Brown: "At nearly the close of our day's journey the rain fell in earnest, and we hastened down to Ballantrae, near the sea-shore, taking up our quarters in that little town, at a dirty inn—the first of that description we had entered in Scotland. We had been warned not to go to the Post-chaise-inn, as things might not be quite comfortable there, because the landlord was a little in trouble. A little in trouble!— he had been just taken up for being concerned in robbing the Paisley bank!"

60. Coastal route to Girvan.
   On the way to Girvan they passed rugged formations with smugglers' caves.

61. Girvan. The King's Arms.
They checked into the King's Arms. The Exciseman Lounge hints at the inn's character when Keats visited.
   Keats: "We are in comfortable Quarters."

62. Ailsa Craig. At dusk, seen from the shore behind the King's Arms. In the evening Keats wrote the sonnet "To Ailsa Rock."

Hearken, thou craggy ocean pyramid,
   Give answer by thy voice, the sea fowls' screams!
   When were thy shoulders mantled in huge streams?
When from the sun was thy broad forehead hid?

63. On the way to Maybole. Crossraguel Abbey.
  Keats: "Maybole—Since breakfast . . . we have examined in the way two Ruins, one of them very fine called Crossragual Abbey."

64. On the way to Maybole. Baltersan Castle.
  The second of the two ruins, Baltersan Castle, is very near Crossraguel.

65. Crossraguel Abbey. Winding stair.
    Keats: "There is a winding Staircase to the top of a little Watch Tower."

66. Ayr. The Brig o' Doon.
Keats: "The bonny Doon is the sweetest river I ever saw overhung with fine trees as far as we could see—"

"...we stood some time on the Brig across it, over which Tam o'Shanter fled—we took a pinch of snuff on the key stone—"

67. Alloway. Kirk Alloway.
"...Then we proceeded to 'auld Kirk Alloway.'"

68. Alloway. Robert Burns Cottage.

Keats: "We proceeded to the Cottage he was born in—there was a board to that effect by the door Side—...We drank some Toddy to Burns's Memory with an old Man who knew Burns—damn him—and damn his Anecdotes."

Keats wrote "This mortal body of a thousand days" in Burns's cottage: "I wrote a sonnet for the mere sake of writing some lines under the roof."

69. Burns Cottage. Window.

Yet can I ope thy window-sash to find
The meadow thou has tramped o'er and o'er,—
("This mortal body of a thousand days")

70. Ayr. The bridges.
 Keats: "Next we walked into Ayr Town and before we went to Tea, saw the new Brig and the Auld Brig and Wallace tower."

71. On the road to Glasgow. Fenwick. Fenwick Church.

72. Near Glasgow. Kingswell.
    James I of England (James VI of Scotland) made this inn famous by stopping there. Now a private residence.

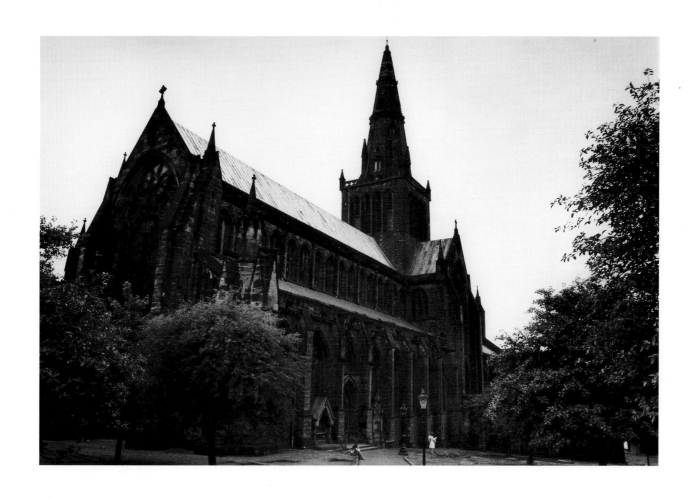

73. Glasgow. Glasgow Cathedral.
    Keats: "We shall see the Cathedral this morning—they have devil-led it into a 'High Kirk!'"

74. Clydebank today.
Keats: "The Banks of the Clyde are extremely beautiful."

75. Loch Lomond. Balloch, at the lower end of the lake.
   Keats: "Steam Boats on Loch Lomond and Barouches on its sides
take a little from the Pleasure of such romantic chaps as Brown and I."

76. Loch Lomond. On the west side, above Luss.

   With Ben Lomond in sight as they made their way along the loch,
Keats probably remembered his Prologue to Life: "I will clamber
through the Clouds and exist. . . . I intend to straddle ben Lomond—
with my Soul!"

77. Loch Lomond. The north end viewed from Tarbet.
   At Tarbet Keats was moved by this view of the loch to sketch it for Tom.

78. Keats's letter to Tom with a sketch of Loch Lomond.
   "The north End of Loch Lomond grand in excess—the entrance at the lower end to the narrow part from a little distance is precious good—the Evening was beautiful nothing could surpass our fortune in the weather—yet was I worldly enough to wish for a fleet of chivalry Barges with Trumpets and Banners just to die away before me into that blue place among the mountains—I must give you an outline as well as I can—."

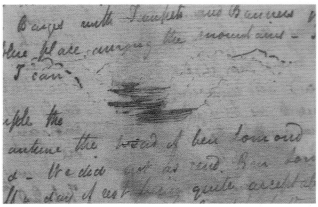

79. Glen Croe.

    Brown: "At the top of the glen my Itinerary mentioned a place called 'Rest and be thankful' nine miles off; now we had set out without breakfast, intending to take our meal there,"

80. Rest and Be Thankful.

"...when, horror and starvation! 'Rest and be thankful' was not an Inn, but a stone seat!"

This stone is at the top of the pass and looks down on a winding road in Glen Croe, built, like so many of the paths Keats trod, by General Wade.

81. Glen Kinglas.
   Another glen before breakfast.

82. The Cairndow Inn.
   Breakfast at last. Keats: "We were up at 4 this morning and have walked to breakfast 15 Miles through two tremendous Glens—at the end of the first there is a place called rest and be thankful which we took for an Inn—it was nothing but a Stone and so we were cheated into 5 more Miles to Breakfast—"

83. Loch Fyne. Just opposite the Cairndow Inn.

    Keats: "I have just been bathing in Loch fine a saltwater Lake opposite the Window—quite pat and fresh but for the cursed Gad flies—damn 'em they have been at me ever since I left the Swan and two necks."

    The gadfly becomes the subject of a ribald poem for Tom:

> Has any here an old grey mare
>   With three legs all her store?
> O put it to her buttocks bare
>   And straight she'll run on four.

The verses grow bawdier.

84. Inverary. Inverary Castle.

Keats: "Last Evening we came round the End of Loch Fine to Inverary—the Duke of Argyle's Castle is very modern magnificent and more so from the place it is in—the woods seem old enough to remember two or three changes in the Crags about them."

85. Inverary. Popular entertainment.

Keats, who had been a pugnacious child, an initiator of schoolyard fights, would have enjoyed this modern entertainment advertised in Inverary. When Keats and Brown entered Inverary, there was a dramatic performance in town, at the barn. "On entering Inverary we saw a Play Bill—Brown was knock'd up from new shoes—so I went to the Barn alone where I saw the Stranger accompanied by a Bag pipe." Keats described the performance of *The Stranger* unfavourably. But a mock-serious sonnet grew out of that night's entertainment.

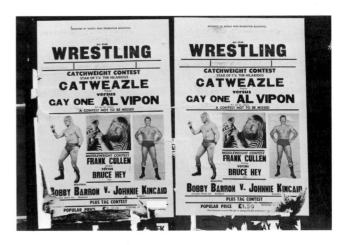

86. Cladich. Twins in front of their home.

After pausing in Inverary for part of the day in deference to Brown's pained feet, the two pressed on to Cladich, at the northeast end of Loch Awe. They rested there for the night.

There appear to be only three houses in modern Cladich and a charming church.

87. Loch Awe. Innischonnel Castle.
 Keats: "We walked 20 Miles by the side of Loch Awe—every ten steps creating a new and beautiful picture—sometimes through little wood—there are two islands on the Lake each with a beautiful ruin—one of them rich in ivy."

88. Loch Awe. Innish Errich.
The second of the two islands Keats noticed was Innish Errich.

89. The road to Ford.

As he wound along Loch Awe toward Ford, Keats would have found a silent partner in Brown, whose feet were so blistered he was "scarcely able to walk." He had time to reflect on women: "When I was a Schoolboy I thought a fair Woman a pure Goddess, my mind was a soft nest in which some one of them slept though she knew it not—I have no right to expect more than their reality. I thought them etherial above Men—I find them perhaps equal."

90. Ford. Private residence, at one time an inn.
    The evening of July 19, Keats and Brown dined on a supper of eggs and oat cake. "The Inn or public is by far the best house in the immediate neighbourhood—It has a white front with tolerable windows."

91. Ford. Interior of former inn.
    Keats: "Opposite the Window there are hills in a Mist—a few Ash trees."

92. Kilmelford. Post office and general store.
    Keats wrote letters in Kilmelford: "We are detained this morning by the rain."

93. Oban.
   Keats and Brown arrived in Oban after a fifteen-mile walk in a soaking rain. They looked into the cost of the tour to Staffa and Iona, found it impossibly expensive, and decided to proceed instead to Fort William. But after a good night's sleep in Oban, they negotiated a better deal with the man they'd talked to the day before, and headed across the water to see the "Curiosities."

94. Kerrera.
    Keats: "We set out, crossed two ferries, one to the isle of Kerrara of little distance, the other from Kerrara to Mull 9 Miles across—we did it in forty minutes with a fine Breeze."

95. Mull. Duart Castle.
    Their first sight of Mull would have been Duart Castle.

96. Mull. Grasspoint.
   The mouth of the loch at the north end of Mull where ferries from Kerrera still land.

97. Grasspoint. The Drover's Inn.
   Two hundred and fifty years old, this was in the nineteenth century the site of some riotous gatherings of whiskey-drinking cattle drovers awaiting transportation for themselves and their cattle to the mainland.

98. Mull. Drover's Road, also called Pilgrim's Road.

Pilgrims to Iona who landed at Grasspoint began their journey on this road, the oldest in Mull. As Keats travelled this path with Brown and their guide, a poem began to take shape in his mind, which he recorded later in the day.

There is a joy in footing slow across a silent
  plain,
. . . .
There is a joy in every spot made known by
  times of old,
New to the feet, although the tale a hundred
  times be told.

99. Mull. The journey across Glen More.

Keats: "The road through the Island, or rather the track is the most dreary you can think of—between dreary Mountains—over bog and rock and river with our Breeches tucked up and our Stockings in hand."

100. Mull. A wild place.

Brown: "There's a wild place! Thirty seven miles of jumping and flinging over great stones along no path at all, up the steep and down the steep, and wading thro' rivulets up to the knees, and crossing a bog, a mile long, up to the ancles."

101. Mull. A bog.

Months later Keats wrote of his "bad sore throat which came of bog trotting in the Island of Mull."

102. Glen More. Ruined shepherd's hut.

Keats spent his first night on Mull in a shepherd's hut, sleeping, most likely, in damp clothes and developing the sore throat from which he was never fully to recover: "We have come over heath and rock and river and bog to what in England would be called a horrid place—yet it belongs to a Shepherd pretty well off perhaps—The family speak not a word but gaelic and we have not yet seen their faces for the smoke which after visiting every cranny, (not excepting my eyes very much incommoded for writing), finds its way out at the door." Under these most uncomfortable circumstances Keats finished the letter to his friend Bailey in which he confessed his problems with women.

103. Glen More. Doorway to a ruined shepherd's hut.

Keats: "About eight o Clock we arrived at a shepherd's Hut into which we could scarcely get for the Smoke through a door lower than my shoulders."

104. Glen More. Derry-na-cullen.

The most important clue to his route across Mull is the heading "Dun an cullen" on Keats's letter to Tom from where he and Brown had breakfast on July 23. "This morning we came about six Miles to Breakfast by rather a better path and we are now in by comparison a Mansion." Translated from the Gaelic, *Derry-na-Cullen*, as the place is correctly called, means "house under the waterfall." It was known throughout Glen More as the Mansion, and judging by the chunks of slate at the site of the ruin today, it was elegant compared to any shepherd's hut in the area. The waterfall in the mountains just behind the Mansion flowed into the nearby Coladoir River.

105. Mull. Farm building in the Rossal area near Derry-na-Cullen.

106. Rossal area. Lambing pen on a farm.

107. The Ross of Mull. Reedy marsh.
   Heading toward Fionnphort they walked through Bunessan and the
Ross of Mull.

108. Fionnphort. A point of departure from Mull.
    From the pier at Fionnphort one catches a little boat to Iona, which
appears in the distance.

109. Iona, or Icolmkill, as Keats called it, Hebrides. The Nunnery.

Their first sight on this small sacred island across from Mull to which Christian pilgrims had come for centuries was the Nunnery, built before 1200.

Keats: "The Beginning of these things was in the sixth Century under the superstition of a would-be Bishop-saint who landed from Ireland and chose the spot from its Beauty—for at that time the now treeless place was covered with magnificent Woods. Columba in the Gaelic is Colm signifying Dove—Kill signifies church and I is as good as Island—so I-colm-kill means the Island of Saint Columba's Church —Now this Saint Columba became the Dominic of the barbarian Christians of the north and was famed also far south—but more especially was reverenced by the Scots the Picts the Norwegians the Irish. In a course of years perhaps the Iland was considered the most holy ground of the north."

The women of Iona and the surrounding islands were buried in the Nunnery, in a tradition of segregation that lasted until about 1780.

Keats: "When I am among Women I have evil thoughts, malice spleen—I cannot speak or be silent—I am full of Suspicions and therefore listen to no thing—. . . . I must absolutely get over this."

110. Iona. Reilig Oran, or St. Oran's Churchyard.

Said to be the most hallowed ground in Iona, St. Oran's Churchyard was exclusively a burial place for men. At the time Keats visited, the ground was solidly covered with tombstones: "We were shown a spot in the Churchyard where they say 61 kings are buried 48 Scotch from Fergus 2nd to Macbeth 8 Irish 4 Norwegian and 1 french—they lie in rows compact."

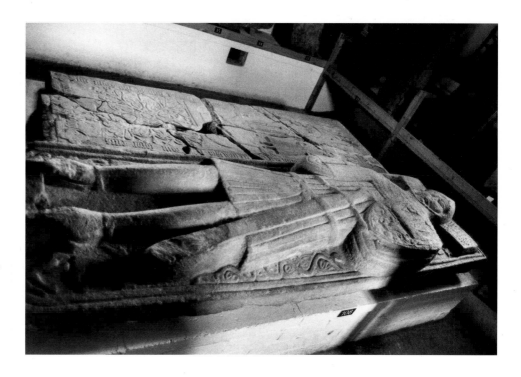

111. Iona Abbey. Tombstone with effigy.

Keats: "Then we were shown other matters of later date but still very ancient—many tombs of Highland Chieftains—their effigies in complete armour face upwards—black and moss covered—Abbots and Bishops of the island always of one of the chief Clans."

Such tombs today are sheltered within the Iona Abbey, to which they have been moved. Most monuments and stones of this sort were thrown into the sea during the Reformation.

114. Iona. The Street of the Dead.

Johnson and Boswell in 1773, Campbell in 1795, Sir Walter Scott in 1810, Keats and Brown in 1818, and Wordsworth in 1835 walked along this ancient stone path, once the route over which the royal dead were carried to burial. It was for a long time the only road to the Abbey on Iona.

113. Iona. St. John's Cross.

Keats: "There have been 300 crosses in the Island but the Presbyterains destroyed all but two, one of which is a very fine one and completely covered with a shaggy coarse Moss."

112. Iona. St. Oran's Chapel, Iona's oldest standing building.

Keats: "There were plenty Macleans and Macdonnels, among these latter the famous Macdonel Lord of the Isles."

The single stone marking the tomb of three MacDonalds, who were Lords of the Isles in succession, was in St. Oran's Chapel, which at the time Keats visited was roofless.

115. Iona Abbey. The cloisters.
    Keats: "Who would expect to find the ruins of a fine Cathedral Church, of Cloisters, Colleges, Monasteries and Nunneries in so remote an Island?"

116. Sailing to Staffa, Hebrides.

Keats: "We took a boat at a bargain to take us to Staffa and land us at the head of Loch Nakgal whence we should only have to walk half the distance to Oban again and on a better road—All this is well pass'd and done with this singular piece of Luck that there was an intermission in the bad Weather just as we saw Staffa at which it is impossible to land but in a tolerable Calm Sea."

117. Approach to Staffa.
    Keats: "As we approached in the boat there was such a fine swell of the sea that the pillars appeared rising immediately out of the crystal."

118. Staffa. Surface.

    Keats: "One may compare the surface of the Island to a roof—this roof is supported by grand pillars of basalt standing together as thick as honey combs."

119. Staffa. Fingal's Cave.

    Keats: "The finest thing is Fingal's Cave—it is entirely a hollowing out of Basalt Pillars. Suppose now the Giants who rebelled against Jove had taken a whole Mass of black Columns and bound them together like bunches of matches—and then with immense Axes had made a cavern in the body of these columns—"

"...so that we walk along the sides of the cave on the pillars which are left as if for convenient Stairs."

120. Mull and Loch Na Keal, near Kellan. Skyscape.
Keats and Brown probably disembarked at or near Kellan.

121. Salen, Mull. Salen Hotel.
  Keats and Brown very likely found a resting spot in Salen for the last night of their Hebrides tour, July 24.

122. Salen. The pier.
  Boats to Oban departed from Salen.

123. Mull. Sunset.
A last sight perhaps.

124. Oban. Harbour.

125. Oban. Oban Hotel.
  Keats: "I have a slight sore throat and think it best to stay a day or two at Oban."

126. Oban. Street with flowing water.
  Brown: "For some time he had been annoyed by a slight inflammation in the throat, occasioned by rainy days, fatigue, privation, and, I am afraid, in one instance, by damp sheets. It was prudently resolved, with the assistance of medical advice, that if, when we reached Inverness, he should not be much better, he should part from me, and proceed from the port of Cromarty to London by sea" (*Life of Keats*, 52).

127. Leaving Oban.

Scanty the hour and few the steps beyond
the bourn of care,
Beyond the sweet and bitter world—beyond
it unaware;
Scanty the hour and few the steps, because a
longer stay
Would bar return and make a man forget his
mortal way.
("There is a joy in footing slow across a
silent plain")

128. Ballachulish. Ferry crossing.
On July 31, on their way north to climb Ben Nevis, they paused in Ballachulish Ferry, named for the ferry crossing, with two jetties, whose function has now been supplanted by a modern bridge.

129. Ben Nevis. Ascent.

Keats injudiciously undertook this strenuous climb soon after the fatiguing Hebrides episode. His energy level was low, his sore throat getting worse. Yet his lengthy account to Tom reflects exhilaration, curiosity, adventurousness, and a range of attitudes from the puckish to the philosophic: "We set out about five in the morning with a Guide in the Tartan and Cap and soon arrived at the foot of the first ascent which we immediately began upon—"

". . . after much fag and tug and a rest and a glass of whiskey apiece we gained the top of the first rise and saw then a tremendous chap above us which our guide said was still far from the top—"

"... we began upon the next ascent more formidable by far than the last and kept mounting with short intervals of rest.... There came on a Mist,"

"... so that from that part to the verry top we walked in a Mist."

"...Before we had got half way up we passed large patches of snow and near the top there is a chasm some hundred feet deep completely glutted with it—Talking of chasms they are the finest wonder of the whole—they appear great rents in the very heart of the mountain though they are not, being at the side of it, but other huge crags arising round it give it the appearance to Nevis of a shattered heart or Core in itself—."

"...On one part of the top there is a handsome pile of stones done pointedly by some soldiers of artillery, I climed onto them and so got a little higher than old Ben himself."

The ascent accomplished, Keats became a kind of stunt-man poet and terrified Brown as he sat on a fearful precipice to compose a reflective sonnet, "Read me a lesson, Muse, and speak it loud."

130. Letterfinlay. Letterfinlay Inn, now a private residence.
    On August 4, when Keats and Brown stopped at Letterfinlay Inn,
the Ben Nevis climb was still a fresh experience, and he crammed the
letter he was writing to Tom with excited details and yet another Ben
Nevis poem, this one a bawdy comic dialogue between a fat fifty-year-
old woman named Mrs. Cameron and old Ben Nevis personified.

131. Letterfinlay. Pipers.
  Keats: "There are not many Kilts in Argylshire—At Fort William they say a Man is not admitted into Society without one—the Ladies there have a horror at the indecency of Breeches."

132. Laggan. Laggan Lochs.
  Opening into Loch Lochy, at the southwest end of the Caledonian Canal, the Laggen Lochs were the engineering masterpiece of Thomas Telford, which was under construction when Keats and Brown passed. They would have heard the steam engines and dredging machines and seen men with wheelbarrows.

133. Loch Ness. A view from its southern tip, above Fort Augustus.

At Fort Augustus more work of the wizard of the Caledonian Canal was in progress, and much as Keats and Brown might have liked to bypass the industry there, they must have realized that Telford and his engineering plan would be part of the picture they would have of Loch Ness.

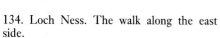

134. Loch Ness. The walk along the east side.

By June enough work had been completed on the canal to allow ships to come into Loch Ness from the Moray Firth, and Keats and Brown might have seen some making their way to Fort Augustus.

135. Loch Ness. Foyers. The Falls of Foyers.

Brown: "I must mention my having seen the grandest fall of water in Europe—called the Falls of Foyers."

136. Loch Ness. Continuing the twenty-two miles along its east side.

As Keats and Brown walked along General Wade's military road, the principal route to Inverness on the east side of the lake, they would have turned their heads to Loch Ness, on their left many times, and perhaps debated the popular notion that the water, which was understood to be 129 fathoms deep, never freezes.

And in the depths of his own consciousness, Keats may have been realizing that he would not be able to complete his walking tour.

137. Inverness. The vaulted tower of the fourteenth-century High Parish Church.
Keats: "My Sore throat is not quite well and I intend stopping here a few days."

138. Inverness. At night.

Keats made an important decision here. Brown had insisted that Keats see a doctor about his sore throat, and the doctor had advised him to return to London. Brown: "Mr Keats . . . is too unwell for fatigue and privation. I am waiting here to see him off in the Smack for London. He caught a violent cold in the Island of Mull, which far from leaving him, has become worse, and the Physician here thinks him too thin and fevered to proceed on our journey. It is a cruel disappointment."

They booked passage and took a coach to the port of Cromarty, travelling by way of Beauly and Dingwall.

139. Beauly Priory.

140. Beauly Priory. Skull and crossbones tombstone.

141. Beauly Priory. Skull and crossbones tombstone.

Keats and Brown together wrote a poem on these images at Beauly. It distracted Keats and sealed their friendship before they went their separate ways—Brown on to John o' Groats, and Keats, home. The poem, "On Some Skulls in Beauley Abbey, near Inverness" (reprinted below), was not published until 1822.

142. Dingwall. The bar at Canon Bridge Inn.
  The camaraderie, the chance encounters at inns and pubs, the
"whusky," and the letter writing of the walking tour to the north all
ended forty-five days after they began.

143. Cromarty. House dating from 1813.

144. Cromarty. The harbour.
"For at the cable's length / Man feels the gentle anchor pull and gladdens in its strength." ("There is a joy in footing slow across a silent plain")

145. Cromarty Firth. The narrows through which Keats sailed on his smack *The George*, on his way to London on August 8, 1818.

Keats: "I have got wet through day after day, eaten oat cake, & drank whiskey, walked up to my knees in Bog, got a sore throat, gone to see Icolmkill & Staffa, met with wholesome food, just here & there as it happened; went up Ben Nevis, & N.B. came down again."

EPILOGUE

Keats was back in London and home at Well Walk, in Hampstead, by August 18. In his knapsack were pebbles from Iona for his sister, Fanny. He found Tom critically ill, his "lingering state" having grown much worse. With little regard for his own health, Keats attended his brother until Tom's death on December 1, shortly after his nineteenth birthday.

During that period the most serious of the famous Cockney School attacks on Keats appeared.

During that period he met Fanny Brawne.

And during that period he began to write *Hyperion*, the major product of the walking tour.

By the time Tom died, Keats had been physically and emotionally tried, but he was on the threshold of his highest creative period as a poet and of his love affair with Fanny Brawne.

It was his good friend from the walking tour, Charles Brown, who would see him through the transition.

THE TRAVEL LITERATURE

I have based my text for Keats's letters primarily on the Hyder Rollins edition, *The Letters of John Keats, 1814–1821*, though I have consulted the Hampstead Keats, edited by H. Buxton Forman and revised by his son, Maurice Buxton Forman (*The Poetical Works and Other Writings of John Keats*), as well as the Richard Monckton Milnes (Lord Houghton) edition (*Life, Letters, and Literary Remains, of John Keats*). My own changes in the text are conservative, infrequent, and I hope not troublesome to purists among my readers, for the adjustments have to do with minor punctuation matters, paragraphing, and spacing. Dates in brackets are Rollins's. Letters 13 and 14, from Brown to Dilke, Sr., and to Snook, are from *The Letters of Charles Armitage Brown*, edited by Jack Stillinger.

All the poems in Keats's letters, as well as the two poems not included in the letters—"This mortal body of a thousand days" and "On Some Skulls in Beauley Abbey, near Inverness"—are from Jack Stillinger's edition of *The Poems of John Keats*. Charles Brown's journal of his walk with Keats comes from the edition of Keats's letters by Hyder Rollins, who in turn takes his text from the *Plymouth and Devonport Weekly Journal*, 1840.

Keats's extant letters from the walking tour are works of graphic art in themselves. They were written in brown ink on a single sheet of what Keats described as "coarse" paper, the average dimensions of which were 13 by 16½ inches. The sheet, referred to as a *single* by the postal service, was folded in the center, widthwise, to create three pages, each 13 by 8¼ inches, on which to write, with a blank fourth side. Halving the paper again created a fourth page of 6½ by 8¼ inches and a page for the address. The final two folds for mailing resulted in a tidy document of about 6¾ by 3½ inches. The letters in the Houghton Library at Harvard (2, 5, 9, 10, and 11) vary in size by only a fraction of an inch, suggesting that the cuts of paper were a standard size.

The letters went by mail coaches, which had been in operation since 1784, along routes that were not always safely paved, though the service was remarkably efficient and swift. In 1797 there were forty-two mail coach routes in operation, and by Keats's time there were more; a letter posted in London for Edinburgh would reach its destination in forty-three hours, with the coach's six horses travelling an average of seven to eight miles an hour. It was in Keats's interest to keep letters down to one sheet, because postal charges were by the sheet and by the mile, and rates were at an all-time high. (They

remained so for twenty-five years after the Battle of Waterloo, since they had become a source of revenue to pay for the Continental war.) The cost of a single travelling less than eighty miles was two pence, and rates rose proportionately, with an extra two pence charged for letters carried on the branch posts. The mileage was stamped on the letter when it was posted. Prepayment was optional, and from the letters we have of Keats's walking tour, it is unclear whether he prepaid or intended his recipients to pay. As economy on this tour was of prime concern, I think it likely he wished his correspondents to pay.

The letters are distinct artifacts. The photograph of Letter 8, which I was able to take by permission of the Keats Museum in Hampstead, reveals the sketch made of Loch Lomond from Tarbet, and in it we see his sense of space on the page. But the gamut of Keats's graphic modes is nicely demonstrated in the Houghton Library letters. The earliest, Letter 2 to George and Georgiana, is written in a relaxed hand; the text is clear, with an open, spatially liberal expansion on the page. The acrostic to Georgiana is accorded its own space, while the second poem, "Sweet, sweet is the greeting of eyes," occurs on "page" 3, again clearly displayed, though a fragment of paper is missing from the manuscript. In the letter he writes to Tom, from July 3 to 9 (Letter 5), Keats uses broken lines, created with dashes, to mark off an area of the first, largest "page" for his Meg Merrilies poem.

A much more complicated visual experience awaits the viewer of the letter to Bailey (Letter 9), written between July 18 and 22. The poem "There is a joy in footing slow across a silent plain" is written on top of and perpendicular to the text of the first page, carrying over to and across the second page and part of the third. The effect is an amazing grid of manuscript. An important peculiarity of this letter is that much of the text in which Keats reveals his most intimate concerns about women is exposed and readable.

The letter to Bailey is surpassed in difficulty of decipherment by Letter 11, to Tom, written on August 3 in Letterfinlay after the climb up Ben Nevis. This letter is crammed full of news and description of the climb and two poems that grew out of the experience: the serious sonnet "Read me a lesson, Muse, and speak it loud," and the comic dialogue "Upon my life, Sir Nevis, I am piqu'd." Both poems are crossed over the prose to Tom in tight grids, spanning both horizontal and vertical directions, with the Ben Nevis poem starting on the third page, in both directions, and continuing onto the fourth page, where the reader finds a note from Keats to "turn to the beginning." "Ben Nevis" is completed across the first page. One can imagine the first editors of Keats beholding this letter with a wild surmise.

The original manuscript for Letter 1 has been lost. It was printed, apparently not in its entirety, in June 1836 in the *Western Messenger*, published by James Freeman Clarke, in Louisville, Kentucky. George Keats, who lived in Louisville then, had loaned the letter to Clarke.

[1] Winander, Winandermere, and Windermere are the same place, the last of these being the name that has carried over to modern times. Wordsworth's Boy of Winander (*Prelude*: book 5) may have come to Keats's mind here.

[2] Lake Windermere. See photo of the White Lion Inn, now called the Royal Hotel, where Keats and Brown dined. "Bowne's" is Bowness, which Keats later (in Letter 2) spells Bownes.

[3] See Introduction: The Westmorland Elections; Letter 8 and notes.

[4] Keats's sonnet "Bright star, would I were stedfast as thou art" echoes this imagery.

Letter 1

TO TOM KEATS

[25–27 June 1818]

Here beginneth my journal, this Thursday, the 25th day of June, Anno Domini 1818. This morning we arose at 4, and set off in a Scotch mist; put up once under a tree, and in fine, have walked wet and dry to this place, called in the vulgar tongue Endmoor, 17 miles; we have not been incommoded by our knapsacks; they serve capitally, and we shall go on very well.

June 26—I merely put *pro forma*, for there is no such thing as time and space, which by the way came forcibly upon me on seeing for the first hour the Lake and Mountains of Winander[1]—I cannot describe them—they surpass my expectation—beautiful water—shores and islands green to the marge—mountains all round up to the clouds. We set out from Endmoor this morning, breakfasted at Kendal with a soldier who had been in all the wars for the last seventeen years—then we have walked to Bowne's to dinner—said Bowne's situated on the Lake where we have just dined,[2] and I am writing at this present. I took an oar to one of the islands to take up some trout for dinner, which they keep in porous boxes. I enquired of the waiter for Wordsworth—he said he knew him, and that he had been here a few days ago, canvassing for the Lowthers. What think you of that— Wordsworth versus Brougham!![3] Sad—sad—sad—and yet the family has been his friend always. What can we say? We are now about seven miles from Rydale, and expect to see him to-morrow. You shall hear all about our visit.

There are many disfigurements to this Lake—not in the way of land or water. No; the two views we have had of it are of the most noble tenderness—they can never fade away—they make one forget the divisions of life; age, youth, poverty and riches; and refine one's sensual vision into a sort of north star which can never cease to be open lidded and stedfast[4] over the wonders of the great Power. The disfigurement I mean is the miasma of London. I do suppose it contaminated with bucks and soldiers, and women of fashion—and hat-band ignorance. The border inhabitants are quite out of keeping with the romance about them, from a continual intercourse with London rank and fashion. But why should I grumble? They let me have a prime glass of soda water—O they are as good as their neighbors. But Lord Wordsworth, instead of being in retirement, has himself and his house full in the thick of fashionable visitors quite convenient to be pointed at all the summer long. When we had gone about half this morning, we began to get among the hills and to see the mountains grow up before us—the other half brought us to Wynandermere, 14 miles to dinner. The weather is capital for the views, but it is now rather misty, and we are in doubt whether to walk to Ambleside to tea—it is five miles along the borders of the Lake. Loughrigg will swell up before us all the way—I have an amazing partiality for mountains in the clouds. There is nothing in Devon like this, and Brown says there is nothing in Wales to be compared to it. I must tell you, that in going through Cheshire and Lancashire, I saw the Welsh mountains at a distance. We have passed the two castles, Lancaster and Kendal. 27th—We walked here to Ambleside[5] yesterday along the border of Winandermere all beautiful with wooded shores and Islands—our road was a winding lane, wooded on each side, and green overhead, full of Foxgloves—every now and then a glimpse of the Lake, and all the while Kirkstone and other large hills nestled together in a sort of grey black mist. Ambleside is at the northern extremity of the Lake. We arose this morning at six, because we call it a day of rest, having to call on Wordsworth who lives only two miles hence—before breakfast we went to see the Ambleside water fall. The morning beautiful—the walk easy among the hills. We, I may say, fortunately, missed the direct path, and after wandering a little, found it out by the noise—for, mark you, it is buried in trees, in the bottom of the valley—the stream itself is interesting throughout with "mazy error over pendant shades."[6] Milton meant a smooth river—this is buffetting all the way on a rocky bed ever various—but the waterfall itself, which I came suddenly upon, gave me a pleasant twinge. First we stood a little below the head about half way down the first fall, buried deep in trees, and saw it streaming down two more descents to the depth of near fifty feet—then we went on a jut of rock nearly level with the second fall-head, where the first fall was above us, and the third below our feet still—at the same time we saw that the water was divided by a sort of cataract island on whose other side burst out a glorious stream—then the thunder and the freshness. At the same time the different falls have as different characters; the first darting down the slate-rock like an arrow; the second spreading out like a fan—the third dashed into a mist—and the one on the other side of the rock a sort of mixture of all these. We afterwards moved away a space, and saw nearly the whole more mild, streaming silverly through the trees. What astonishes me more than any thing is the tone, the coloring, the

[5] See photo of the Salutation Inn, where they stayed on the night of June 26.

[6] Keats quotes Milton, *Paradise Lost*, 4, 239, though Milton describes a "River large" running through Eden, rising, falling, and dividing, much like the Ambleside waterfall. Keats and Brown had been reading Milton (Brown mentions *Samson Agonistes*) while waiting for the rain to stop before embarking on their first day's walk.

slate, the stone, the moss, the rock-weed; or, if I may so say, the intellect, the countenance of such places. The space, the magnitude of mountains and waterfalls are well imagined before one sees them; but this countenance or intellectual tone must surpass every imagination and defy any remembrance. I shall learn poetry here and shall henceforth write more than ever, for the abstract endeavor of being able to add a mite to that mass of beauty which is harvested from these grand materials, by the finest spirits, and put into etherial existence for the relish of one's fellows. I cannot think with Hazlitt that these scenes make man appear little.[7] I never forgot my stature so completely—I live in the eye; and my imagination, surpassed, is at rest—We shall see another waterfall near Rydal to which we shall proceed after having put these letters in the post office. I long to be at Carlisle, as I expect there a letter from George and one from you. Let any of my friends see my letters—they may not be interested in descriptions—descriptions are bad at all times—I did not intend to give you any; but how can I help it? I am anxious you should taste a little of our pleasure; it may not be an unpleasant thing, as you have not the fatigue. I am well in health. Direct henceforth to Port Patrick till the 12th July. Content that probably three or four pair of eyes whose owners I am rather partial to will run over these lines I remain; and moreover that I am your affectionate brother John.

[7] In his essay "Mr. Wordsworth's New Poem, *The Excursion*," Hazlitt, characterizing the people who live in the mountainous area described by Wordsworth, claims: "Their egotism becomes more concentrated, as they are more insulated, and their purposes more inveterate, as they have less competition to struggle with. The weight of matter which surrounds them, crushes the finer sympathies. Their minds become hard and cold, like the rocks which they cultivate. The immensity of their mountains makes the human form appear insignificant. . . . Their physiognomy expresses the materialism of their character, which has only one principle—rigid self-will" (*Works*, 19, 23–24).

Letter 2

TO GEORGE AND GEORGIANA KEATS

[27, 28 June 1818]

Foot of Helvellyn June 27

My dear George,
We have passed from Lancaster to Burton from Burton to Enmoor,[1] from Enmoor to Kendal from Kendal to Bownes on turning down to which place there burst upon us the most beautiful and rich view of Winandermere and the surrounding Mountains—we dined at Bownes on Trout which I took an oar to fetch from some Box preserves close on one of the little green Islands. After dinner we walked to Ambleside down a beautiful shady Lane along the Borders of the Lake with ample opportunity for Glimpses all the way—We slept at Ambleside not above two Miles from Rydal the Residence of Wordsworth. We arose not very early on account of having marked this day for a day of rest—Before breakfast we visited the first waterfall I ever saw and certainly small as it is it surpassed my expectation, in what I have mentioned in my letter to Tom, in its tone and intellect its light shade slaty Rock, Moss and Rock weed—but you will see finer ones I will not describe by comparison a teapot spout—We ate a Monstrous Breakfast on our return (which by the way I do every morning) and after it proceeded to Wordsworths. He was not at home nor was any Member of his family—I was much disappointed. I wrote a note for him and stuck it up over what I knew must be Miss Wordsworth's Portrait[2] and set forth again & we visited two Waterfalls in the neighbourhood, and then went along by Rydal Water and Grasmere through its beautiful Vale—then through a defile in the Mountains into Cumberland and So to the foot of Helvellyn whose summit is out of sight four Miles off rise above rise—I have seen Kirkstone, Loughrigg and Silver How—and discovered without a hint "that ancient woman seated on Helm Craig."[3] This is the summary of what I have written to Tom and dispatched from Ambleside—I have had a great confidence in your being well able to support the fatigue of your Journey since I have felt how much new Objects contribute to keep off a sense of Ennui and fatigue 14 Miles here is not so much as the 4 from Hampstead to London. You will have an enexhaustible astonishment; with that and such a Companion you will be cheered on from day to day—I hope you will not have sail'd before this Letter reaches you[4]—yet I do not know for I will have my Series to Tom coppied and sent to you by the

The holograph manuscript for Letter 2 is in the Houghton Library at Harvard. The letter was addressed to Mr George Keats at the Crown Inn in Liverpool, but George and Georgiana had already boarded their ship by the time the letter arrived on July 1. See Introduction.

[1] Endmoor.

[2] Most likely a portrait of Wordsworth's sister Dorothy rather than his daughter Dora. The note has been lost. A portrait of Burns now hangs over the mantel.

[3] In Wordsworth's "To Joanna" (from his series "Poems on the Naming of Places"), the poet describes how the mountains echo with the young maid Joanna's laughter. One peak resembles an old woman with her head bent over: "The Rock, like something starting from a sleep, / Took up the Lady's voice, and laughed again; / That ancient Woman seated on Helm-Crag / Was ready with her cavern" (ll. 54–57). Keats spells "crag" with an "i," as the Scots do, though this may be accidental.
[4] George had not sailed, but he and Georgiana had boarded and the ship was waiting in the Mersey for clearance to sail.

[5] Robert Burns's "Epistle to a Young Friend" is filled with advice to a young person going off to "try the world." The first stanza concerns the kind of poem to send the friend:

> I lang hae thought, my youthfu' friend,
>   A something to have sent you,
> Tho' it should serve nae ither end
>   Than just a kind memento:
> But how the subject-theme may gang,
>   Let time and chance determine:
> Perhaps it may turn out a sang;
>   Perhaps, turn out a sermon. (ll. 1–8)

[6] Read vertically, the initial letters of the lines spell GEORGIANA AUGUSTA KEATS.

[7] From the Greek, literally, "man-eating." Keats probably had in mind the violent giants who were also cannibals, called Laestrygonians, whom Ulysses (Odysseus) encountered in his wanderings in Homer's *Odyssey*. See also *Othello* 1.3.128–68, the speech in which Othello explains how he wooed Desdemona with tales of his adventures among dangerous and exotic people. The stanza is puzzling, but seems to contain a compliment to Georgiana, who has inspired it. Keats, of course, never meant the poem to be taken seriously as literature, as he himself writes when he sends it again over a year later in September 1819 (because the first letter never reached Georgiana): "I wrote it in a great hurry which you will see. Indeed I would not copy it if I thought it would ever be seen by any but yourselves" (*Letters*, 2, 195).

[8] They slept at the Nag's Head, an inn in Wythburn situated beside what is now Thirlmere. Brown claims "many fleas were in the beds" (Chapter 2). It is interesting to note that in 1865 *Black's Guide to the Lakes* lists the Nag's Head as a desirable place to stay. The 1901 Baedeker lists the Nag's Head in Wythburn, describing Wythburn as a "hamlet with a quaint little church, where all the coaches stop" (416). In 1931 Nelson Bushnell paused to look at "the old Nag's Head Inn" and found it had been "demoted a few years ago into a private house" (*Walk*, 52). When I visited in 1979 I was told by a native of the area that she and her siblings had been born at the Nag's Head, which had been closed as an inn in 1929. The Nag's Head no longer exists; all that remains of Wythburn today is a church with a graveyard.

first Packet you have from England. God send you both as good Health as I have now. Ha! my dear Sister George, I wish I knew what humour you were in that I might accomodate myself to any one of your Amiabilities—Shall it be a Sonnet or a Pun or an Acrostic, a Riddle or a Ballad—"perhaps it may turn out a Sang, and perhaps turn out a Sermon"[5] I'll write you on my word the first and most likely the last I ever shall do, because it has strucke me—what shall it be about?

> Give me your patience, sister, while I frame
> Exact in capitals your golden name:[6]
> Or sue the fair Apollo and he will
> Rouse from his heavy slumber and instill
> Great love in me for thee and Poesy.
> Imagine not that greatest mastery
> And kingdom over all the realms of verse
> Nears more to heaven in aught than when we nurse
> And surety give to love and brotherhood.
>
> Anthropophagi[7] in Othello's mood,
> Ulysses stormed, and his enchanted belt
> Glow with the muse, but they are never felt
> Unbosom'd so and so eternal made,
> Such tender incense in their laurel shade,
> To all the regent sisters of the Nine,
> As this poor offering to you, sister mine.
>
> Kind sister! aye, this third name says you are;
> Enchanted has it been the Lord knows where.
> And may it taste to you like good old wine,
> Take you to real happiness and give
> Sons, daughters, and a home like honied hive.

June 28th I have slept[8] and walked eight miles to Breakfast at Keswick on derwent water—We could not mount Helvellyn for the mist so gave it up with hopes of Skiddaw which we shall try tomorrow if it be fine—to day we shall walk round Derwent water, and in our Way see the Falls of Low-dore—The Approach to derwent water is rich and magnificent beyond any means of conception—the Mountains all round sublime and graceful and rich in colour—Woods and wooded Islands here and there—at the same time in the distance among Mountains of another aspect we see Basenthwaite—I shall drop like a Hawk on the Post Office at Carlisle to ask for some Letters from you and Tom—

Sweet, sweet is the greeting of eyes,
And sweet is the voice in its greeting,
When adieux have grown old and goodbyes
Fade away where old time is retreating.

Warm the nerve of a welcoming hand,
And earnest a kiss on the brow,
When we meet over sea and o'er land
Where furrows are new to the plough.[9]

This is all I did in the morning—please answer my Letters as possibly then[10] We will before many Years are over have written many folio volumes which as a Matter of self-defence to one whom you understand intends to be immortal in the best points and let all his Sins and peccadillos die away—I mean to say that the Booksellers will rather decline printing ten folio volumes of Correspondence printed as close as the Apostles creed in a Watch paper[11]—I have been looking out my dear Georgy for a joke or a Pun for you—there is none but the Names of romantic Misses on the Inn window Panes. You will of course have given me directions brother George where to direct on the other side of the Water. I have not had time to write to Henry[12]—for I have a journal to keep for Tom nearly enough to employ all my leisure—I am a day behind hand with him—I scarcely know how I shall manage Fanny and two or three others I have promised—We expect to be in Scotland in at most three days so you must if this should catch you before you set sail give me a line to Port-Patrick—

God bless you my dear Brother and Sister.

John—

[9] These lines caused Amy Lowell, the first scholar to publish them, a considerable pang of conscience. Her problem was that "while the scheme of this book makes it imperative that I sedulously put in whatever verse I discover which is certainly by Keats and has not heretofore been published, regardless of its merits, this poem is so singularly poor that poetically nothing would have been lost had it remained in oblivion" (*John Keats*, 2, 29). It seems to me Lowell over-reacted, since the poem does not pretend to be anything but a simple expression of loss with the concomitant desire for reconciliation.

[10] Keats's words are barely decipherable, owing to a tear in the paper. I have represented Rollins's best estimate of what Keats was saying.

[11] The outer case of a watch might have had in it, as a lining, a small disc of paper on which a design was painted or a rhyme inscribed.

[12] Henry Wylie, Georgiana's brother.

Letter 3 is based on a copy of the original manuscript transcribed by John Jeffrey.

Letter 3

TO TOM KEATS

[29 June, 1, 2 July 1818]

Keswick—June 29th 1818

My dear Tom

I cannot make my Journal as distinct & actual as I could wish, from having been engaged in writing to George. & therefore I must tell you without circumstance that we proceeded from Ambleside to Rydal,[1] saw the Waterfalls there, & called on Wordsworth, who was not at home, nor was any one of his family. I wrote a note & left it on the Mantlepiece.[2] Thence on we came to the foot of Helvellyn, where we slept,[3] but could not ascend it for the mist. I must mention that from Rydal we passed Thirlswater,[4] & a fine pass in the Mountains from Helvellyn we came to Keswick on Derwent Water.[5] The approach to Derwent Water surpassed Winandermere—it is richly wooded & shut in with rich-toned Mountains. From Helvellyn to Keswick was eight miles to Breakfast, After which we took a complete circuit of the Lake going about ten miles, & seeing on our way the Fall of Low-dore. I had an easy climb among the streams, about the fragments of Rocks & should have got I think to the summit, but unfortunately I was damped by slipping one leg into a squashy hole. There is no great body of water, but the accompaniment is delightful; for it ooses out from a cleft in perpendicular Rocks, all fledged with Ash & other beautiful trees.[6] It is a strange thing how they got there. At the south end of the Lake, the Mountains of Burrowdale, are perhaps as fine as any thing we have seen—On our return from this circuit, we ordered dinner, & set forth about a mile & a half on the Penrith road, to see the Druid temple.[7]

[1] A small village near the east end of Rydal Water. Keats was eager to reach Rydal Mount, the home of Wordsworth. They had arrived at Rydal on June 27.

[2] See Letter 2, n.3.

[3] At the Nag's Head. See Letter 2.

[4] In 1879 Thirlmere was flooded to make a reservoir, and the lake and surrounding country became the property of the Manchester Corporation. The few cottages that made up the little town were inundated as the water level was gradually raised.

[5] In his *Guide to the Lakes* Wordsworth commented that "A squirrel (so I have heard the old people of Wytheburn say) might have gone from their chapel to Keswick without alighting on the ground" (43). According to Bushnell, Keats and Brown were in Keswick on Sunday, June 28, and most likely stayed at what was then called the Oak Inn, now the popular Royal Oak Hotel. Southey was living in Keswick (at Greta Hall, now a school) at the time, writing his *History of Brazil*. His absence in Keats's letters here is perhaps noteworthy.

[6] Brown remarks that the fall "disappointed us," though he describes the movement of the water even more specifically than Keats. Observing rocks and trees at Lodore Falls was obligatory for travellers, and the assessment of the falls as not large enough to inspire awe was standard. As early a traveller as Thomas Gray noted in 1769 that "the quantity of water was not great," but described the leaping and flowing of the water among the rocks in terms similar to those of Keats and Brown (*Journal in the Lakes*, 255–56). A century after Gray's visit, *Black's Guide* (1865) describes "the celebrated cascade" with close observation: "The beautiful wooded glen down which the torrent is precipitated is guarded on both sides by crags, the one on the left being called Gowder Crag, and that on the right Shepherd's Crag" (113). In 1901 Baedeker advised, "The falls . . . are romantically framed with tall wooded crags; but as there is usually more rock than water, Southey's jingling verses are responsible for a good deal of disappointment" (426). (Southey's nursery rhyme, "The Cataract of Lodore" [1820], emphasized the sound of water.) Significantly, Keats dutifully admires the picturesque setting but undermines the aesthetic experience by describing his fall into a "squashy hole."

[7] Also known as a Druid circle. The Castlerigg stone circle attracted a growing number of tourists. Wordsworth describes it in his 1810 *Guide to the Lakes* acknowledging that "though it is not to be compared with Stonehenge, [I have] not seen any other remains of those dark ages, which can pretend to rival it in singularity and dignity of appearance" (53). His remarks are followed by verse about the circle. Keats's *Hyperion* alludes to the spot:

like a dismal cirque
Of Druid stones, upon a forlorn moor,

We had a fag up hill, rather too near dinner time, which was rendered void, by the gratification of seeing those aged stones, on a gentle rise in the midst of Mountains, which at that time darkened all round, except at the fresh opening of the vale of St. John. We went to bed rather fatigued, but not so much so as to hinder us getting up this morning, to mount Skiddaw.[8] It promised all along to be fair, & we had fagged & tugged nearly to the top, when at halfpast six there came a mist upon us & shut out the view; we did not however lose anything by it, we were high enough without mist, to see the coast of Scotland; the Irish sea; the hills beyond Lancaster; & nearly all the large ones of Cumberland & Westmoreland, particularly Helvellyn & Scawfell. It grew colder & colder as we ascended, & we were glad at about three parts of the way to taste a little rum which the Guide brought with him, mixed, mind ye with mountain water, I took two glasses going & one returning—It is about six miles from where I am writing to the top, so we have walked ten miles before Breakfast today. We went up with two others, very good sort of fellows. All felt on arising into the cold air, that same elevation,[9] which a cold bath gives one—I felt as if I were going to a Tournament. Wordsworth's house is situated just on the rise of the foot of mount Rydall, his parlor window looks directly down Winandermere; I do not think I told you how fine the vale of Grassmere is, & how I discovered "the ancient woman seated on Helm Crag."[10]—We shall proceed immediately to Carlisle, intending to enter Scotland on the 1st of July via—[11]

July 1st—We are this morning at Carlisle—After Skiddaw, we walked to Ireby the oldest market town in Cumberland—where we were greatly amused by a country dancing school, holden at the Sun, it was indeed "no new cotillion fresh from France."[12] No they kickit & jumpit with mettle extraordinary, & whiskit, & fleckit, & toe'd it, & go'd it, & twirld it, & wheel'd it, & stampt it, & sweated it, tattooing the floor like mad. The difference between our country dances & these scotch figures, is about the same as leisurely stirring a cup o' Tea & beating up a batter pudding. I was extremely gratified to think, that if I had pleasures they knew nothing of, they had also some into which I could not possibly enter. I hope I shall not return without having got the Highland fling, there was as fine a row of boys & girls as you ever saw, some beautiful faces, & one exquisite mouth. I never felt so near the glory of Patriotism, the glory of making by any means a country happier. This is what I like better than scenery. I fear our continued moving from place to place, will prevent our becoming learned in

When the chill rain begins at shut of eve,
In dull November, and their chancel vault,
The heaven itself, is blinded throughout night. (2, 34–38)

[8] The mountain north of Derwentwater. In his detailed account of the climb Brown indicates that they arose at 4:00 A.M.; this was their daily habit (Chapter 3). Wordsworth advises: "It is not likely that a mountain will be ascended without disappointment, if a wide range of prospect be the object, unless either the summit be reached before sunrise, or the visitant remain there until the time of sunset, and afterwards" (*Guide to the Lakes*, 97).
[9] Keats no doubt intends a double meaning for this word, often used by Wordsworth and others to describe experiences of the sublime, as, for example, in Wordsworth's: "Now, every one knows that from amenity and beauty the transition to sublimity is easy and favourable, but the reverse is not so; for, after the faculties have been elevated, they are indisposed to humbler excitement" (*Guide to the Lakes*, 97). Keats's reduction of his experience to the practical and athletic here is characteristic of his rejection of the sublime posture and his desire to be virile and obliquely off color (as in the beginning of Letter 5) in writing to Tom.
[10] See Letter 2, n.3.
[11] See the Itinerary.

[12] Keats simulates Burns's "Nae cotillion brent new frae France" ("Tam o' Shanter," l. 116).

[13] See photo of Carlisle Castle. It is in fact of local red sandstone.

[14] Letter 2 is the only one that remains.

village affairs; we are mere creatures of Rivers, Lakes, & mountains. Our yesterday's journey was from Ireby to Wigton, & from Wigton to Carlisle—The Cathedral does not appear very fine. The Castle is very Ancient, & of Brick.[13] The City is very various, old whitewashed narrow streets; broad red brick ones more modern—I will tell you anon, whether the inside of the Cathedral is worth looking at. It is built of a sandy red stone or Brick. We have now walked 114 miles & are merely a little tired in the thighs & a little blistered. We shall ride 38 miles to Dumfries, where we shall linger a while, about Nithsdale & Galloway, I have written two letters[14] to Liverpool. I found a letter from sister George, very delightful indeed. I shall preserve it in the bottom of my knapsack for you.

[2 July]

On Visiting the Tomb of Burns

The town, the churchyard, and the setting sun,
The clouds, the trees, the rounded hills all seem,
Though beautiful, cold—strange—as in a dream
I dreamed long ago. Now new begun,
The short-lived, paly summer is but won
    From winter's ague, for one hour's gleam;
    Though saphire warm, their stars do never beam;
All is cold beauty; pain is never done
For who has mind to relish, Minos-wise,
    The real of beauty, free from that dead hue
        Sickly imagination and sick pride
Cast wan upon it! Burns! with honour due
    I have oft honoured thee. Great shadow, hide
Thy face—I sin against thy native skies.

You will see by this sonnet that I am at Dumfries, we have dined in Scotland. Burns' tomb is in the Churchyard corner, not very much to my taste, though on a scale, large enough to show they wanted to honour him—Mrs Burns lives in this place, most likely we shall see her tomorrow—This Sonnet I have written in a strange mood, half asleep. I know not how it is, the Clouds, the sky, the Houses, all seem anti-Grecian & anti-Charlemagnish—I will endeavor to get rid of my prejudices, & tell you fairly about the Scotch[15]—

In Devonshire they say "Well where be yee going." Here it is, "How is it wi yoursel"—A man on the Coach said the horses took a Hellish heap o' drivin—the same fellow pointed out Burns' tomb with a deal of

[15] Keats's expression "the Scotch" would offend a present-day Scot; this may have been true for the Scots of 1818 as well.

life, "There de ye see it, amang the trees; white, wi a roond tap." The first well dressed Scotchman we had any conversation with, to our surprise confessed himself a Deist. The careful manner of his delivering his opinions, not before he had received several encouraging hints from us, was very amusing—Yesterday was an immense Horse fair at Dumfries, so that we met numbers of men & women on the road, the women nearly all barefoot, with their shoes & clean stockings in hand, ready to put on & look smart in the Towns. There are plenty of wretched Cottages, where smoke has no outlet but by the door—We have now begun upon whiskey, called here *whuskey* very smart stuff it is—Mixed like our liquors with sugar & water 'tis called toddy, very pretty drink, & much praised by Burns.

Letter 4 should be read in close correlation to Brown's account, which fleshes out much of what Keats alludes to. The holograph manuscript for this letter is in the Pierpont Morgan Library. It is addressed to Miss F. M. Keats, Rich[d] Abbey's Esq[re], Walthamstow, Middlesex—; it was posted in Newton Stewart on the 5th and delivered at 10 o'Clock FN[n] (before noon) on July 8.

[1] Keats spells the word *Kirkcudbright* incorrectly throughout. The town's name is pronounced Kir-kou´-bree.

[2] According to Amy Lowell, Keats and his party stopped for dinner in Redbourne on the way to Liverpool. There Keats visited with a friend from medical school, Henry Stephens, who had a practice in Redbourne (*John Keats*, 2, 13). Richard Monckton Milnes interpreted this encounter as having particular significance: "On the road he stopped to see a former fellow-student of Guy's, who was settled as a surgeon in a country town, and whom he informed that he had definitely abandoned that profession and intended to devote himself to poetry" (*Life, Letters*, 1, 152).

[3] Brown gives the name as Radshaw; see Chapter 1.

[4] Meg Merrilies is a figure in Sir Walter

Letter 4

TO FANNY KEATS

[2, 3, 5 July 1818]

Dumfries July 2nd

My dear Fanny,

I intended to have written to you from Kirkudbright[1] the town I shall be in tomorrow—but I will write now because my knapsack has worn my coat in the Seams, my coat has gone to the Taylors and I have but one Coat to my back in these parts. I must tell you how I went to Liverpool with George and our new Sister and the Gentleman my fellow traveller through the Summer and Autumn—We had a tolerable journey to Liverpool[2]—which I left the next morning before George was up for Lancaster—Then we set off from Lancaster on foot with our knapsacks on, and have walked a Little zig zag through the mountains and Lakes of Cumberland and Westmoreland—We came from Carlisle yesterday to this place—We are employed in going up Mountains, looking at Strange towns prying into old ruins and eating very hearty breakfasts. Here we are full in the Midst of broad Scotch 'How is it a' wi yoursel'—the Girls are walking about bare footed and in the worst cottages the Smoke finds its way out of the door—I shall come home full of news for you and for fear I should choak you by too great a dose at once I must make you used to it by a letter or two—We have been taken for travelling Jewellers, Razor sellers and Spectacle venders because friend Brown wears a pair—The first place we stopped at with our knapsacks contained one Richard Bradshaw a notorious tippler[3]—He stood in the shape of a 𝄞 and ballanced himself as well as he could saying with his nose right in M[r] Browns face 'Do—yo u sell Spect—ta—cles?' M[r] Abbey says we are Don Quixotes—tell him we are more generally taken for Pedlars—All I hope is that we may not be taken for excisemen in this whiskey country—We are generally up about 5 walking before breakfast and we complete our 20 Miles before dinner—Yesterday we visited Burns's Tomb and this morning the fine Ruins of Lincluden—I had done thus far when my coat came back fortified at all points—so as we lose no time we set forth again through Galloway—all very pleasant and pretty and with no fatigue when one is used to it—We are in the midst of Meg Merrilies' country of whom I suppose—you have heard[4]—

Old Meg she was a gipsey,
    And liv'd upon the moors;
Her bed it was the brown heath turf,
    And her house was out of doors.

Her apples were swart blackberries,
    Her currants pods o' broom,
Her wine was dew o' the wild white rose,
    Her book a churchyard tomb.

Her brothers were the craggy hills,
    Her sisters larchen trees—
Alone with her great family
    She liv'd as she did please.

No breakfast had she many a morn,
    No dinner many a noon,
And 'stead of supper she would stare
    Full hard against the moon.

But every morn of woodbine fresh
    She made her garlanding,
And every night the dark glen yew
    She wove and she would sing.

And with her fingers old and brown
    She plaited mats o' rushes,
And gave them to the cottagers
    She met among the bushes.

Old Meg was brave as Margaret Queen
    And tall as Amazon:
An old red blanket cloak she wore;
    A chip hat had she on.
God rest her aged bones somewhere—
    She died full long agone!

If you like these sort of Ballads I will now and then scribble one for you—if I send any to Tom I'll tell him to send them to you—I have so many interruptions that I cannot manage to fill a Letter in one day— since I scribbled the Song we have walked through a beautiful Country to Kirkudbright—at which place I will write you a song about myself—

        There was a naughty boy
        A naughty boy was he

Scott's novel *Guy Mannering*. Scott's character was so popular that a race horse was named after her. The *Air Advertiser* (July 9, 1818) announces that at the August 2 Bogside Races the six-year-old thoroughbred Meg Merrilies will be sold ("For Meg Merrilies' performance see the Racing Calendar for 1815"). Bushnell represents local Galwegians as believing a Gypsy named Flora Marshall was the original of Meg Merrilies, but reminds us that "Scott himself identified Meg with one Jean Gordon" (*Walk*, 100).

He would not stop at home
He could not quiet be—
    He took
    In his knapsack
    A book
    Full of vowels
    And a shirt
    With some towels—
    A slight cap
    For night cap—
    A hair brush
    Comb ditto
    New stockings
    For old ones
    Would split O!
    This knapsack
    Tight at 's back
    He rivetted close
    And follow'd his nose
    To the north
    To the north
    And follow'd his nose
    To the north—

There was a naughty boy
    And a naughty boy was he
For nothing would he do
    But scribble poetry—
        He took
        An inkstand
        In his hand
        And a pen
        Big as ten
        In the other
        And away
        In a pother
        He ran
        To the mountains
        And fountains
        And ghostes
        And postes
        And witches

And ditches
And wrote
In his coat
When the weather
Was cool
Fear of gout
And without
When the weather
Was warm—
Och the charm
When we choose
To follow one's nose
To the north
To the north
To follow one's nose to the north!

There was a naughty boy
    And a naughty boy was he
He kept little fishes
    In washing tubs three
        In spite
        Of the might
        Of the maid
        Nor afraid
        Of his granny-good—
        He often would
        Hurly burly
        Get up early
        And go
        By hook or crook
        To the brook
        And bring home
        Miller's thumb
        Tittlebat
        Not over fat
        Minnows small
        As the stall
        Of a glove
        Not above
        The size
        Of a nice

Little baby's
Little finger—
O he made
'Twas his trade
Of fish a pretty kettle
A kettle—a kettle
Of fish a pretty kettle
A kettle!

There was a naughty boy
  And a naughty boy was he
He ran away to Scotland
  The people for to see—
    There he found
    That the ground
    Was as hard
    That a yard
    Was as long,
    That a song
    Was as merry,
    That a cherry
    Was as red—
    That lead
    Was as weighty
    That fourscore
    Was as eighty
    That a door
    Was as wooden
    As in England—
    So he stood in
    His shoes
    And he wonder'd
    He wonder'd
    He stood in his
    Shoes and he wonder'd—

My dear Fanny I am ashamed of writing you such stuff, nor would I
if it were not for being tired after my days walking,[5] and ready to
tumble into bed so fatigued that when I am asleep you might sew my
nose to my great toe and trundle me round the town like a Hoop
without waking me—Then I get so hungry—a Ham goes but a very
little way and fowls are like Larks to me—A Batch of Bread I make no

[5] Bushnell believes they walked twenty-one miles that day, from Kirkcudbright to Creetown, spending the night in Creetown.

166

more ado with than a sheet of parliament; and I can eat a Bull's head as easily as I used to do Bull's eyes—I take a whole string of Pork Sausages down as easily as a Pen'orth of Lady's fingers[6]—Oh dear I must soon be contented with an acre or two of oaten cake a hogshead of Milk and a Cloaths basket of Eggs morning noon and night when I get among the Highlanders—Before we see them we shall pass into Ireland and have a chat with the Paddies, and look at the Giant's Cause-way which you must have heard of—I have not time to tell you particularly for I have to send a Journal to Tom of whom you shall hear all particulars or from me when I return—Since I began this we have walked sixty miles to Newton Stewart at which place I put in this Letter[7]—tonight we sleep at Glenluce—tomorrow at Portpatrick and the next day we shall cross in the passage boat to Ireland—I hope Miss Abbey[8] has quite recovered—Present my Respects to her and to M[r] and M[rs] Abbey—God bless you—

Your affectionate Brother John—

Do write me a Letter directed to *Inverness*. Scotland—

[6] Dorothy Hewlett explains: " 'Parliament' was a thin flat cake made of sticky gingerbread; 'Lady's fingers' large white peppermints pink ringed" (*Life of Keats*, 206). Bull's eyes are candies with soft centers.

[7] The letter appears to have arrived three days after it was posted in Newton Stewart (see headnote to this letter). Not all of the post marks (those that come after the time of delivery) are legible.

[8] Richard Abbey and his wife had an adopted daughter about whom little is known. Fanny Keats, who was now fifteen and would remain in the guardianship of the Abbeys until she came of age in 1824, grew up with her; John here acknowledges her with dutiful formality.

The holograph manuscript for Letter 5 is in the Houghton Library at Harvard. Addressed to Mr Thos. Keats at Well Walk, Hampstead, Middlesex, it was identified as a single and postmarked 13 July 1818, at 10:00; "D" (either for "Day" or "Delivered") 13 July 1818, at 10 o'Clock, with ½ pence due. Curiously, it is endorsed by Tom "Received 13 July." Thus the postmarks seem to refer to the point of arrival rather than the point of posting in Scotland.

[1] Charles Wentworth Dilke (1789–1864) was, with his wife, Maria, a friend to Keats and his brothers, entertaining them at their home called Wentworth Place (now Keats House) in Hampstead. Dilke and Brown had been school friends, and they built Wentworth Place together. Dilke was a publisher, an editor (of *Old English Plays*, for example), a literary scholar, and an early archivist for Keats's letters and works. The Dilkes had one son, Charles, who was about eight in 1818. Keats apparently sent Dilke a letter containing the Meg Merrilies poem, but the letter has been lost.

[2] Keats was writing this letter concurrently with Letter 4 to Fanny.

[3] Keats skips Saturday, July 4, in both the letter to Fanny and this one to Tom. It would seem that the walk through Gatehouse-of-Fleet to Creetown was not conducive to writing.

[4] Wigtown (not Wigton, the Cumberland town Keats passed through on June 30) is six miles south of Newton Stewart. Most likely he means that he has travelled six miles into the county of Wigtownshire and has used the county town, Wigtown, as a point of reference. He did not go to that town. See Bushnell (*Walk*, 238) for other possible explanations.

[5] At Newton Stewart, but it is not known where. I myself had a fine high tea at 6:00 P.M. at an honest place at the foot of the bridge called simply "Restaurant." The River Cree runs through the town.

[6] They were enjoying their morning meal in Glenluce, where they had spent the night of July 5, no doubt at the King's Arms—but which one? There are two establishments bearing that name, Auld King's Arms (the larger of the two), and the perfect little King's Arms in the middle of town. In 1978 I talked to the owner of the small inn, but when he

Letter 5

TO TOM KEATS

[3, 5, 7, 9 July 1818]

Auchencairn July 3rd

My dear Tom,

I have not been able to keep up my journal completely on account of other letters to George and one which I am writing to Fanny from which I have turned to loose no time whilst Brown is coppying a song about Meg Merrilies which I have just written for her—We are now in Meg Merrilies county and have this morning passed through some parts exactly suited to her—Kirkudbright County is very beautiful, very wild with craggy hills somewhat in the Westmoreland fashion—we have come down from Dumfries to the sea coast part of it—The song I mention you would have from Dilke:[1] but perhaps you would like it here—"Old Meg she was a gipsey / And liv'd upon the moors" [Keats copies the poem from Letter 4]. Now I will return to Fanny[2]—it rains. I may have time to go on here presently.

July 5—You see I have missed a day from Fanny's Letter.[3] Yesterday was passed in Kirkudbright—the Country is very rich—very fine—and with a little of Devon—I am now writing at Newton Stuart six Miles into Wigton[4]—Our Landlady of yesterday said very few Southrens passed these ways—The children jabber away as in a foreign Language—The barefooted Girls look very much in keeping—I mean with the Scenery about them—Brown praises their cleanliness and appearance of comfort—the neatness of their cottages &c. It may be—they are very squat among trees and fern and heaths and broom, on levels slopes and heights—They are very pleasant because they are very primitive—but I wish they were as snug as those up the Devonshire vallies—We are lodged and entertained in great varieties—we dined yesterday[5] on dirty bacon dirtier eggs and dirtiest Potatoes with a slice of Salmon—we breakfast this morning[6] in a nice carpeted Room with Sofa hair bottomed chairs and green-baized mehogany—A spring by the road side is always welcome—we drink water for dinner diluted with a Gill of wiskey.

[*To Ireland*]

revealed that his wife had just died a month previously I thought it tasteless to press him into conversation. The next year when I went

back I checked into the larger hotel, where I found the furnishings had not been upgraded much since Keats's "hair bottomed chairs and

July 7th Yesterday Morning we set out from Glenluce going some distance round to see some Ruins[7]—they were scarcely worth the while—we went on towards Stranrawier in a burning sun and had gone about six Miles when the Mail overtook us—we got up—were at Portpatrick[8] in a jiffy, and I am writing now in little Ireland[9]—The dialect on the neighbouring shores of Scotland and Ireland is much the same—yet I can perceive a great difference in the nations from the Chambermaid at this nate Inn[10] kept by M[r] Kelly—She is fair, kind and ready to laugh, because she is out of the horrible dominion of the Scotch kirk—A Scotch Girl stands in terrible awe of the Elders—poor little Susannas[11]—They will scarcely laugh—they are greatly to be pitied and the kirk is greatly to be damn'd. These kirkmen have done Scotland good (Query?) they have made Men, Women, Old Men Young Men old Women, young women boys, girls and infants all careful—so that they are formed into regular Phalanges of savers and gainers—such a thrifty army cannot fail to enrich their Country and give it a greater appearance of comfort than that of their poor Irish neighbours—These kirkmen have done Scotland harm—they have banished puns and laughing and kissing (except in cases where the very danger and crime must make it very fine and gustful. I shall make a full stop at kissing for after that there should be a better paren*t*-thesis:[12]

green-baized mehogany." I ventured back to the smaller King's Arms and spoke to Mr. Mellar, the proprietor, who said of the history of his inn that coaches stopped there on the way to or from Portpatrick, and that correspondence from that period contained references to "going up the hill" or "going down the hill," because the coaching inn was on a small rise in town. This was all very well and good, but I was staying in the large inn, whose proprietors maintained that this was certainly the original one and therefore the one where Keats and Brown breakfasted in 1818.

It would be some weeks before I could resolve the problem. When I returned to the United States I wrote to Stanley Pilling, FAS Scot at the District Museum in Stranraer, who promptly offered this arbitration:

"In reply to your letter about the inn in Glenluce where Keats stayed on his visit to Northern Ireland, it would seem that this was the one now known as the 'Auld King's Arms.' The name was usually given

to an inn which was a staging post for mail coaches, the innkeeper being the Postmaster for that stage and entitled to show the Royal Arms so that anyone would know that letters could be handed in there and passengers picked up. The London-Portpatrick service (The Irish Mail) had such a post in Glenluce during the time in which it was running, from 1789 or 90 to 1861, when it ceased on the advent of the railway.

"Presumably, because of the loss of this trade, the inn closed shortly afterwards and was used for a period for the letting of rooms to elderly single ladies. Some of these supported themselves by handicrafts, etc. and, perhaps because of this, or of the noise they made when they got together, the place became known as the 'Beehive.' The place now known as the 'King's Arms' lower down the Main Street, which had been a private house, took the name on becoming a hotel, at some date prior to 1890. About 1950, it was decided to re-

open the old inn as a hotel and the proprietor wished to use the original name, but the owner of the other establishment was unwilling to change, and so the name became the 'Auld King's Arms.'"

[7] Keats and Brown did not need to digress far from their path to visit the Abbey of Glenluce, "founded in 1192," according to a current Department of the Environment leaflet, "by Rolland, Lord of Galloway and Constable of Scotland." Though Keats found them "Scarcely worth the while," Robert the Bruce had visited them in 1329 as had James IV much later, while on a pilgrimage to Whithorn. Keats might at least have been intrigued if he had known that some of the detached buildings had not yet been excavated.

[8] Today ferries to Ireland leave from Stranraer (which Keats spelled Stranrawier), not Portpatrick. But in 1818 Portpatrick was a major port as well as a postal packet terminus. Portpatrick (still called Port Patrick in some modern literature) had figured as the most important port of departure for packets since the days of Queen Elizabeth. It was the shortest crossing (twenty-one miles to Donaghadee) in the north. The port is named for Saint Patrick, who is said to have bounded over to Scotland from Ireland in a single leap and landed here.

[9] Donaghadee, where the packet docked in Ireland. Like Portpatrick, this is a quiet port with traces of its past in the wall about the harbour. The ferries from Stranraer now dock above Belfast in Larne.

[10] Keats engages in a play on words here: *nation* from *nate Inn*; probably *nates* (meaning *buttocks*) intended as well.

[11] In the Old Testament story of Susanna and the Elders (Book of Daniel), churchmen of power and authority behave lasciviously and hypocritically toward the unsuspecting sensuous bather, Susanna.

[12] More word play, with *parent* standing for the consequences of not stopping after gustful kissing as well as for the punctuation mark. Interestingly, Keats's concern for the repression of feelings and spontaneity imposed by the kirkmen ("These kirkmen have done Scotland harm") was not shared by Brown, who four years later published an article entitled "The State of Religion in the

"Highlands" (*New Monthly Magazine*, 1822, 4, 329–333). In it, Brown represents the Protestants and Papists as coexisting harmoniously and the clergy in general as having no great flaws except "their want of a suitable education."

13 Had the adventurers gotten to their destination, they would have found, on the coast north of Belfast, a promontory of enormous basalt columns, like the ones they were to see in the Hebrides on Staffa. The Giant's Causeway was one of those sights the travellers of Keats's time and before understood they *must* see. Even today it is often referred to as the "eighth wonder of the world." Most of the columns are hexagonal, though some are three-, five-, seven-, and eight-sided, having been so formed by the slow cooling of lava. One traveller who visited the Giant's Causeway some twelve or thirteen years before Keats was an Englishman named Richard Phillips, who was seeing the sights with "three very intelligent companions." His account of the experience of viewing the Giant's Causeway was probably standard: "Very early, on a dismal morning, Saturday, August 18th, the rain pouring in torrents, we set out with a guide to view the Giant's Causeway. The first place to which we were conducted was a cave, at the mouth of which the sea broke tremendously. It is a sublime cathedral, built by the God of nature himself, and where the elements worship him. We next visited the Three Causeways, one of which is a plain surface of hexagonal stones, more nicely shaped and adapted to each other than the feeble hand of art could effect; and over this we walked as on the level of the sea. . . . But Pleskin, the last causeway, is the most striking, being that of which drawings are generally taken, and of which there is a model in the museum of Trinity College, Dublin" (*Journal of a Tour in Ireland &tc &tc*, 22).

14 The Battle of the Boyne took place in northern Ireland on the River Boyne, near Drogheda, on July 1, 1690. It involved William III (William of Orange) and King James II, who was defeated and fled to France, ending the Jacobite efforts and leaving Ireland to the Orangemen. July 12 is the day Orangemen celebrate the Battle of the Boyne.

15 The line is from the tenth stanza of "Robin Hood and the Bishop of Hereford":

and go on to remind you of the fate of Burns. Poor unfortunate fellow—his disposition was southern—how sad it is when a luxurious imagination is obliged in self defence to deaden its delicacy in vulgarity, and riot in things attainable that it may not have leisure to go mad after things which are not. No Man in such matters will be content with the experience of others—It is true that out of suffrance there is no greatness, no dignity; that in the most abstracted Pleasure there is no lasting happiness: yet who would not like to discover over again that Cleopatra was a Gipsey, Helen a Rogue and Ruth a deep one? I have not sufficient reasoning faculty to settle the doctrine of thrift—as it is consistent with the dignity of human Society—with the happiness of Cottagers—All I can do is by plump contrasts—Were the fingers made to squeeze a guinea or a white hand? Were the Lips made to hold a pen or a kiss? And yet in Cities Man is shut out from his fellows if he is poor, the Cottager must be dirty and very wretched if she be not thrifty—The present state of society demands this and this convinces me that the world is very young and in a verry ignorant state—We live in a barbarous age. I would sooner be a wild deer than a Girl under the dominion of the kirk, and I would sooner be a wild hog than be the occasion of a Poor Creature's pennance before those execrable elders—It is not so far to the Giant's Cause way[13] as we supposed—we thought it 70 and hear it is only 48 Miles—so we shall leave one of our knapsacks here at Donoghadee, take our immediate wants and be back in a week—when we shall proceed to the County of Ayr. In the Packet Yesterday we heard some Ballads from two old Men—one was a romance which seemed very poor—then there was the Battle of the Boyne[14]—then Robin Huid as they call him—'Before the king you shall go, go, go, before the king you shall go.'[15]

[Return to Scotland]

There were no Letters for me at Port Patrick so I am behind hand with you I dare say in news from George. Direct to Glasgow till the 17th of this month. 9th We stopped very little in Ireland and that you may not have leisure to marvel at our speedy return to Portpatrick I will tell you that it is as dear living in Ireland as at the Hummums[16]—

"Therefore make haste, and come along with me, / For before the king you shall go." See Helen Child Sargent and George Lyman Kittredge, eds., *English and Scottish Popular Ballads* (Boston: Houghton Mifflin, 1932), no. 144.

16 A fashionable hotel in Keats's time, the Hummums stood in the Piazza, Covent Garden. Rollins identifies it as "C. and G. Harrison's 'new' hotel at 13 Great Russell Street, Covent Garden" (Keats, *Letters*, 1, 320). Keats and Brown may have checked into

thrice the expence of Scotland—it would have cost us £15 before our return—Moreover we found those 48 Miles to be Irish ones which reach to 70 English[17]—So having walked to Belfast one day and back to Donoghadee the next we left Ireland with a fair breeze—We slept last night at Port Patrick where I was gratified by a letter from you. On our walk in Ireland we had too much opportunity to see the worse than nakedness, the rags, the dirt and misery of the poor common Irish—A Scotch cottage, though in that some times the Smoke has no exit but at the door, is a pallace to an Irish one—We could observe that impetiosity in Man Boy and Woman—We had the pleasure of finding our way through a Peat-Bog—three miles long at least—dreary, black, dank, flat and spongy: here and there were poor dirty creatures and a few strong men cutting or carting peat. We heard on passing into Belfast through a most wretched suburb that most disgusting of all noises worse than the Bag pipe, the laugh of a Monkey, the chatter of women *solus* the scream of a Macaw—I mean the sound of the Shuttle[18]—What a tremendous difficulty is the improvement of the condition of such people[19]—I cannot conceive how a mind "with child" of Philanthropy could grasp at possibility—with me it is absolute despair. At a miserable house of entertainment half way between Donaghadee and Belfast were two Men Sitting at Whiskey one a Laborer and the other I took to be a drunken Weaver—The Laborer took me for a Frenchman and the other hinted at Bounty Money saying he was ready to take it—On calling for the Letters at Port Patrick the man snapp'd out 'what Regiment'?

On our return from Belfast we met a Sadan[20]—the Duchess of Dunghill—It is no laughing matter tho—Imagine the worst dog kennel you ever saw placed upon two poles from a mouldy fencing—In such a wretched thing sat a squalid old Woman squat like an ape half starved from a scarcity of Buiscuit in its passage from Madagascar to the cape,—with a pipe in her mouth and looking out with a round-eyed skinny lidded, inanity—with a sort of horizontal idiotic movement of her head—squat and lean she sat and puff'd out the smoke while two ragged tattered Girls carried her along—What a thing would be a history of her Life and sensations. I shall endeavour when I know more and have thought a little more, to give you my ideas of the difference between the Scotch and Irish—The two Irishmen I mentioned were

the Donegall Arms or the White Cross on High Street in Belfast and found they were paying the prices of wealthy merchants.

[17] In Keats's time, and apparently even now, the definition of a mile in Great Britain is inconsistent. According to the *Oxford English* *Dictionary* (1978), "The legal mile in the British Empire and the U.S. is now 1,760 yards. The Irish mile of 2,240 yards is still in rustic use." Although Keats does not raise the point in his letters, the Scottish mile also differed from the English mile. The *OED* indicates: "The obsolete Scottish mile was longer than the English, and probably varied according to time and place; one of the values given for it is 1,976 yards."

[18] There were several large cotton factories in Belfast, some of which were driven by steam engines. Keats uses "Shuttle" here as a metaphor for the industry itself, which was everywhere visible and apparently audible.

[19] The misery Keats was so struck by was the consequence of poor wages and some exploitation of the many rural Irish who had flocked to the city to find work in the factories. According to Jonathan Bardon, Belfast had nearly a 47 percent increase in population between 1801 (when it was 19,000) and 1811 (when it was 27,832: *Belfast*). There had been an economic depression after the Battle of Waterloo, and manufacturers had reduced wages, but in 1818 the economy rose briefly. In fact, just before Keats and Brown visited in June, a weavers' strike had effected some improvement of the wages. But workers' living conditions were wretched. In addition to industrially induced cheerlessness, Belfast suffered from a dreadful typhus epidemic; some 7,000 weavers are said to have died of the fever in a period of three years. The *Belfast News Letter* for the weeks surrounding Keats's visit published continuous reports from the Belfast Fever Hospital of the number of afflicted. For the week ending June 27 the paper reported that since May 1, 1818, 284 patients had been admitted; 215 had been dismissed cured; and 11 had died. Keats's medical training would have made him acutely aware of the danger of typhus and contributed to his impression of a tainted, hopeless population. Though he does not mention typhus in his correspondence, it is interesting to speculate whether fear of contagion figured in the decision to return to Scotland without seeing the Giant's Causeway.

[20] Sedan.

[21] William Haslam was one of Keats's dearest friends, whose affection and loyalty were reciprocated both in boyhood, when they were schoolfellows, and in adulthood, when Haslam, a solicitor, was in a position to lend Keats money and to offer help and kindness.

[22] Benjamin Bentley was the village postman in Hampstead and the landlord of the Keats brothers in their residence on Well Walk. John here asks Tom to greet Mrs. Bentley as well since she had been looking in on Tom. The house no longer stands, but it was located next to what is now called the Wells Hotel (then the Green Man).

There is a sad irony in the fact that Tom, who was dying, lived on a street called Well Walk (after the springs discovered in the eighteenth century that were considered to have medicinal value) near a heath called the Vale of Health (because of its supposed tonic effect on those who breathed its air). The irony is compounded when Keats returns to Well Walk with his sore throat.

speaking of their treatment in England when the Weaver said—'Ah you were a civil Man but I was a drinker.' Remember me to all—I intend writing to Haslam[21]—but dont tell him for fear I should delay—We left a notice at Portpatrick that our Letters should be thence forwarded to Glasgow—Our quick return from Ireland will occasion our passing Glasgow sooner than we thought—so till further notice you must direct to Inverness

Your most affectionate Brother John—

Remember me to the Bentleys[22]

Letter 6

TO JOHN HAMILTON REYNOLDS

[11, 13 July 1818]

Maybole July 11

My dear Reynolds,

I'll not run over the Ground we have passed; that would be merely as bad as telling a dream—unless perhaps I do it in the manner of the Laputan printing press[1]—that is I put down Mountains, Rivers, Lakes, dells, glens, Rocks, and Clouds, with beautiful enchanting, gothic picturesque fine, delightful, enchanting, Grand, sublime—a few Blisters &c—and now you have our journey thus far: where I begin a letter to you because I am approaching Burns's Cottage very fast—We have made continual enquiries from the time we saw his Tomb at Dumfries[2]—his name of course is known all about—his great reputation among the plodding people is "that he wrote a good many sensible things"—One of the pleasantest means of annulling self is approaching such a shrine as the Cottage of Burns—we need not think of his misery—that is all gone—bad luck to it—I shall look upon it hereafter with unmixed pleasure as I do upon my Stratford on Avon

[1] In Jonathan Swift's *Gulliver's Travels*, part 3, chapter 5 ("A Voyage to Laputa, Balnibarbi, Luggnagg, Glubbdubdrib, and Japan"), a twenty-foot-square wooden frame, filled with words and manipulated by iron handles tended by students, was placed in the center of a room. At the professor's command the students turned the handles and the words were scrambled and juxtaposed anew.

[2] Burns died July 21, 1796, and was buried in a modest grave in St. Michael's Churchyard, Dumfries; there was no money for an elaborate tombstone. His funeral was most dramatic, with his pregnant widow going into labour during the ceremony. Mrs. Burns eventually provided a simple tombstone with the poet's name and age on it. In 1813 a subscription was opened to raise money for a mausoleum. Burns's remains were removed to this conspicuous monument on June 5, 1815. The original tombstone was buried under the new monument. The daughter of Mrs. Dunlop, Burns' friend and patroness, is buried in the original grave.

Wordsworth, his sister Dorothy, and Coleridge visited the original grave on their 1803 tour through Scotland, and Dorothy Wordsworth in her "journal entry" for Thursday, August 18, recorded: "We looked at the grave with melancholy and painful recollections" (*Recollections*, 6). Dorothy indicates that the grave was "at a corner of the churchyard" (5), which suggests that Keats viewed both the original grave site and the mausoleum. From Dorothy's journal we know as well that "the churchyard is full of gravestones and expensive monuments in all sorts of fantastic shapes" (6); this too would have been part of Keats's visual experience. If Keats approached Burns's grave in a genuine spirit of homage, he must also have done so with a sense of following the pattern and sensibilities of major poets of his time.

Letter 6 is based on a transcript made by a clerk; it is from the Woodhouse letter-book.

John Hamilton Reynolds, poet, theatre critic, and attorney, falls in the rich category of dear friend to John Keats. Reynolds came to know Keats through Leigh Hunt in 1816 and was acquainted as well with Brown, Dilke, and others in the Keats circle, most significantly perhaps with Benjamin Bailey, with whom Reynolds co-published "Poems by Two Friends" in 1816. A prepossesing character, Reynolds seems to have been sought after and respected by intellectual and literary figures in London. Byron looked favourably upon *Safie* (1814), the book-length poem Reynolds dedicated to him, and considered him a promising young poet. When Keats's first book of poems came out in 1817, Reynolds reviewed the work favourably in the *Champion*. In the spring of 1818 Keats wrote "Dear Reynolds, as last night I lay in bed," a substantial and complex verse epistle containing the germs of his most brilliant works to come in 1819. Keats and Reynolds enriched each other's thoughts about poetry, and Reynolds is said to have inspired the poems "Robin Hood" and *Isabella*. At the time of the walking tour Keats was acquainted with Reynolds's parents ("To Mrs. Reynolds's Cat" was written for his mother) and siblings and enjoyed the family. He admired but later disliked Reynolds's sisters. An excellent study of the friendship between Keats and Reynolds is found in Leonidas Jones's *Life of John Hamilton Reynolds*.

[3] Keats had visited Shakespeare's birthplace with his friend Benjamin Bailey (see Letter 9) on October 2, 1817.

[4] Burns's lyric "It was upon a Lammas night" has a recurring line: "Amang the rigs o' barley." Burns was particularly pleased with his final stanza, which concludes:

> But a' the pleasures e'er I saw,
>   Tho' three times doubl'd fairly—
> That happy night was worth them a',
>   Amang the rigs o' barley,
>   Corn rigs, an' barley rigs,
>   An' corn rigs are bonnie:
> I'll ne'er forget that happy night,
>   Amang the rigs wi' Annie. (ll. 33–40)

(This and all subsequent quotations from Burns are from *The Poetical Works of Burns*, ed. Raymond Bentman.)

[5] Burns's "The Banks o' Doon" begins: "Ye banks and braes o' bonnie Doone, / How can ye chant, ye little birds." The setting readily triggers Keats's association with Burns's verse tale "Tam o' Shanter" and Tam's flight away from the haunted Kirk Alloway over the bridge across the river Doon. See also Letter 7. Kirk Alloway, roofless for well over half a century before Keats saw it, was only two yards to the north of the Auld Brig of Doon.

[6] Burns's poem "The Brigs of Ayr" personifies the old bridge and the new one (erected 1785–1788), giving them a dialogue in which they speak competitively about their strength and endurance.

[7] Reynolds worked in the law office of Francis Fladgate with Fladgate's son Frank, who is referred to here. Reynolds was learning the law with Frank in an apprenticeship arrangement made by Reynolds's friend James Rice, who paid the senior Fladgate £110 to take Reynolds on, with the idea that when Rice took over his father's legal practice Reynolds would become his partner. Keats's unflattering punning on Fladgate's name suggests Fladgate was longwinded and that Reynolds had given Keats the ammunition for such a joke. "Floodgate" was first used as a pun by Keats in a bawdy passage of a letter to his brothers (January 5, 1818, from Teignmouth) in which he recounted a crude chamberpot incident. Rice was present on the occasion. "On proceeding to the Pot in the Cupboard it soon became full on which the

day with Bailey[3]—I shall fill this sheet for you in the Bardies Country, going no further than this till I get into the Town of Ayr which will be a 9 miles' walk to Tea—

[13 July] We were talking on different and indifferent things, when on a sudden we turned a corner upon the immediate County of Ayr—the Sight was as rich as possible—I had no Conception that the native place of Burns was so beautiful—the Idea I had was more desolate, his rigs of Barley[4] seemed always to me but a few strips of Green on a cold hill—O prejudice! it was rich as Devon—I endeavour'd to drink in the Prospect, that I might spin it out to you as the silkworm makes silk from Mulbery leaves—I cannot recollect it—Besides all the Beauty, there were the Mountains of Arran Isle, black and huge over the Sea—We came down upon every thing suddenly—there were in our way, the 'bonny Doon,' with the Brig that Tam O' Shanter cross'd—Kirk Alloway,[5] Burns's Cottage and then the Brigs of Ayr[6]—First we stood upon the Bridge across the Doon; surrounded by every Phantasy of Green in tree, Meadow, and Hill,—the Stream of the Doon, as a Farmer told us, is covered with trees from head to foot—you know those beautiful heaths so fresh against the weather of a summers evening—there was one stretching along behind the trees.

I wish I knew always the humour my friends would be in at opening a letter of mine, to suit it to them nearly as possible. I could always find an egg shell for Melancholy—and as for Merriment a Witty humour will turn any thing to Account—my head is sometimes in such a whirl in considering the million likings and antipathies of our Moments—that I can get into no settled strain in my Letters—My Wig! Burns and sentimentality coming across you and frank Flood-gate[7] in the office—O scenery that thou shouldst be crush'd between two Puns—As for them I venture the rascalliest in the Scotch Region—I hope Brown does not put them punctually in his journal—If he does I must sit on the cuttystool[8] all next winter. We went to Kirk Alloway "a Prophet is no Prophet in his own Country"[9]—We went to the Cottage and took some Whiskey—I wrote a sonnet for the mere sake of writing some lines under the roof—they are so bad I cannot transcribe them—The

Court door was opened Frank Floodgate bawls out, Hoolloo! here's an opposition pot" (*Letters*, 1, 200–201).

[8] A low stool formerly used in the Scottish church to expose offenders during the service while the minister rebuked them.

[9] A biblical idea occurring in three New Testament Gospels: Mark 6: 4; John 4: 44; and Luke 4: 24, which reads, "No prophet is accepted in his own country."

Man at the Cottage[10] was a great Bore with his Anecdotes—I hate the rascal—his Life consists in fuz, fuzzy, fuzziest—He drinks glasses five for the Quarter and twelve for the hour,—he is a mahogany faced old Jackass who knew Burns—He ought to be kicked for having spoken to him. He calls himself "a curious old Bitch"[11]—but he is a flat old Dog—I should like to employ Caliph Vatheck[12] to kick him—O the flummery of a birth place! Cant! Cant! Cant! It is enough to give a spirit the guts-ache—Many a true word they say is spoken in jest—this may be because his gab hindered my sublimity.—The flat dog made me write a flat sonnet—My dear Reynolds—I cannot write about scenery and visitings—Fancy is indeed less than a present palpable reality, but it is greater than remembrance—you would lift your eyes from Homer only to see close before you the real Isle of Tenedos.[13]— You would rather read Homer afterwards than remember yourself.[14]— One song of Burns's is of more worth to you than all I could think for a whole year in his native country—His Misery is a dead weight upon the nimbleness of one's quill—I tried to forget it—to drink Toddy without any Care—to write a merry Sonnet—it won't do—he talked with Bitches—he drank with Blackguards, he was miserable—We can see horribly clear in the works of such a man his whole life, as if we were God's spies.[15]—What were his addresses to Jean[16] in the latter part of his life—I should not speak so to you—yet why not—you are not in the same case—you are in the right path, and you shall not be deceived—I have spoken to you against Marriage, but it was general— the Prospect in those matters has been to me so blank, that I have not been unwilling to die—I would not now, for I have inducements to Life—I must see my little Nephews[17] in America, and I must see you marry your lovely Wife[18]—My sensations are sometimes deadened for weeks together—but believe me I have more than once yearne'd for the time of your happiness to come, as much as I could for myself after the lips of Juliet.—From the tenor of my occasional rhodomontade in chitchat, you might have been deceived concerning me in these points—upon my soul, I have been getting more and more close to you every day, ever since I knew you, and now one of the first pleasures I look to is your happy Marriage[19]—the more, since I have felt the

---

[10] Burns's cottage had been functioning as a whiskey shop when Keats visited. Brown recalls: "Not far from this side of the town stood the cottage where Burns was born. Keats had predetermined to write a sonnet under its roof; but its conversion into a whiskey-shop, together with its drunken landlord, went far towards the annihilation of his poetic power" (*Life of Keats*, 50–51).
[11] Burns wrote an unfriendly epitaph for James Humphrey, a mason in Mauchline (who actually died in 1844): "Below thir stanes lie Jamie's banes: / O Death, it's my opinion, / Thou ne'er took such a bleth'rin bitch / Into thy dark dominion." Humphrey, it is said, debated Burns more than was welcome.
[12] The exotically cruel protagonist of William Beckford's gothic tale *Vathek* (1786), set in the Orient and filled with grotesqueries and debauchery. Vathek, the tale concludes, "for the sake of empty pomp and forbidden power, had sullied himself with a thousand crimes." Byron claimed *Vathek* was his Bible.
[13] Located in the northeast Aegean Sea south of the Dardanelles, Tenedos is the ancient name for the island in Turkey called Bozcaada today.
[14] In "Ode on a Grecian Urn" Keats writes: "Heard melodies are sweet, but those unheard / Are sweeter." In both cases "a palpable reality" is subordinate to creative imagination.
[15] In Shakespeare's *King Lear* 5.3.14–17, Lear, addressing Cordelia, projects a time when they will talk together about the news of court: "And we'll talk with them too, / Who loses and who wins, who's in, who's out, / And take upon's the mystery of things / As if we were God's spies."
[16] Jean Armour became Burns's wife in 1788, and survived him (and his notorious infidelity).
[17] George and Georgiana of course had not yet arrived in America. The first of their eight children, a girl, was born in February 1819. Keats dwells here on the question of progeny (in this case his brother's) as an encouragement for living, implying, perhaps, some ambivalence about his own path to immortality; would it come through parenting or poetry?
[18] Reynolds had become engaged to Eliza Drew in 1817, but he did not marry her until August 1822, shortly after he became qualified as a solicitor. Possibly Keats had recently learned of a formal announcement of the engagement. He would certainly have known of the courtship before now.
[19] Keats and Reynolds were close in age, came from similar lower middle-class backgrounds, and grappled with the same problem of weighing practical careers against literary ones. Keats might have found his friend and counterpart's proposal of marriage disturbing, despite claims to the contrary here, as appears from the point he makes above that "the

Prospect in those matters has been to me so blank" and given his appreciation (after George and Georgiana wed) that marriage can signify loss for those left behind.

[20] Reynolds had been ill with rheumatic fever in the spring, with an attack that came on in February 1818 and lasted three months. He was just recovering when Keats began his walking tour. In general, Reynolds was not a healthy man. Keats undermined his resolve to attend to his own health by his rigorous rambles and climbs that summer.

[21] James Rice, Jr., was at this point an acquaintance Keats had met through Reynolds, most likely at Reynolds's home, in 1817. (Keats first mentions him April 17, 1817.) Rice was an attorney; he and Reynolds eventually became partners (see note 7 above). He suffered for a prolonged period from an incurable (though unnamed) disease, and Keats was aware of this all the time he knew Rice. Nevertheless, Rice lived to the age of about seventy-one (his date of birth is not certain). He and Keats became close friends after the tour, spending a month together in Shanklin, on the Isle of Wight during the summer of 1819, when they were *both* ill.

[22] John Taylor, with his partner James Augustus Hessey, was Keats's publisher, replacing Keats's first publishers, Charles and James Ollier, who brought out the 1817 *Poems.* Taylor had been Reynolds's publisher. Posterity has judged Keats fortunate in being taken on by Taylor and Hessey, a distinguished house that published such major figures as Coleridge, DeQuincey, Landor, and Carlyle. Taylor had faith in Keats's abilities and later lent him money and gave him support. After Keats's death Taylor attempted to write a biography but conceded to opposition from Brown and Joseph Severn, another of Keats's friends.

[23] Benjamin Bailey was a friend to Keats, Reynolds, and Rice. See introductory note to Letter 9, which is addressed to Bailey.

pleasure of loving a sister in Law. I did not think it possible to become so much attached in so short a time—Things like these, and they are real, have made me resolve to have a care of my health—you must be as careful.[20]—

The rain has stopped us to day at the end of a dozen Miles, yet we hope to see Loch-Lomond the day after to Morrow;—I will piddle out my information, as Rice[21] says, next Winter at any time when a substitute is wanted for Vingt-un. We bear the fatigue very well.—20 Miles a day in general—A cloud came over us in getting up Skiddaw—I hope to be more lucky in Ben Lomond—and more lucky still in Ben Nevis—what I think you would enjoy is poking about Ruins—sometimes Abbey, sometimes Castle. The short stay we made in Ireland has left few remembrances—but an old woman in a dog-kennel Sedan with a pipe in her Mouth, is what I can never forget—I wish I may be able to give you an idea of her.—

Remember me to your Mother and Sisters, and tell your Mother how I hope she will pardon me for having a scrap of paper pasted in the Book I sent to her. I was driven on all sides and had not time to call on Taylor[22]—So Bailey[23] is coming to Cumberland—well, if you'll let me know where at Inverness, I will call on my return and pass a little time with him—I am glad 'tis not Scotland—Tell my friends I do all I can for them, that is drink their healths in Toddy—Perhaps I may have some lines by and by to send you fresh on your own Letter—Tom has a few to shew you.

Your affectionate friend
John Keats

Letter 7

TO TOM KEATS

The holograph manuscript for Letter 7 is in the British Library. It was postmarked in Glasgow July 14 and was received by Tom in Hampstead on July 17.

[10, 11, 13, 14 July 1818]

Ah! ken ye what I met the day
  Out owre the mountains,
A coming down by craggis grey
  An' mossie fountains?
Ah goud hair'd Marie, yeve I pray
  Ane minute's guessing—
For that I met upon the way
  Is past expressing.
As I stood where a rocky brig
  A torrent crosses,
I spied upon a misty rig
  A troup o' horses—
And as they trotted down the glen
  I sped to meet them,
To see if I might know the men,
  To stop and greet them.
First Willie on his sleek mare came
  At canting gallop—
His long hair rustled like a flame
  On board a shallop.
Then came his brother Rab and then
  Young Peggy's mither,
And Peggy too—adown the glen
  They went togither.
I saw her wrappit in her hood
  Fra wind and raining—
Her cheek was flush wi' timid blood
  'Twixt growth and waning.
She turn'd her dazed head full oft,
  For thence her brithers
Came riding with her bridegroom soft
  An' mony ithers.
Young Tam came up an' eyed me quick
  With reddened cheek—
Braw Tam was daffed like a chick,

He coud na speak.
Ah, Marie, they are all gane hame
　　Through blustring weather,
An' every heart is full on flame
　　An' light as feather.
Ah! Marie, they are all gone hame
　　Fra happy wedding,
Whilst I—Ah is it not a shame?
　　Sad tears am shedding.

Belantree July 10

My dear Tom,
The reason for my writing these lines was that Brown wanted to impose a galloway song upon Dilke[1]—but it wont do—The subject I got from meeting a wedding[2] just as we came down into this place[3]—Where I am afraid we shall be emprisoned awhile by the weather—Yesterday we came 27 Miles from Stranraer—entered Ayrshire a little beyond Cairn,[4] and had our path through a delightful Country. I shall endeavour that you may follow our steps[5] in this walk—it would be uninteresting in a Book of Travels—it can not be interesting but by my

[1] It would have been a good bit of waggery if Keats's ballad had been successfully passed off on their scholarly friend Dilke as an authentic Galloway song, but Keats seems to have judged that his command of Gaelic would not stand up under Dilke's scrutiny. The idea of duping a reading audience with "discoveries" of original Gaelic and Celtic texts was in the air. Newspapers in Belfast and in Ayr were running stories on the disputed authenticity of the ever-popular Ossian poems, published by James Macpherson in 1760 under the title *Fragments of Ancient Poetry Collected in the Highlands of Scotland*. Macpherson claimed to have transcribed poems from an ancient Gaelic bard, Ossian, son of Fingal. Samuel Johnson, among others, doubted the authenticity of Macpherson's research. The *Air Advertiser* and the *Belfast News Letter* carried accounts of a recent paper presented before the society of Scottish antiquarians by Hugh Campbell, Esq., offering proof "sufficient to convince the most incredulous, even Dr. Johnson himself were he in life, that Fingal fought and Ossian sang!" (July 7, 1818).

　Dilke was inclined to be opinionated, and Keats later characterized him as "a Man who cannot feel he has a personal identity unless he has made up his Mind about everything" (*Letters*, 2, 213). Dilke would have taken a strong stand on Keats's Galloway song.

[2] Keats seemed preoccupied with marriage that summer (see Letter 6, composed during the same period as this letter to Tom). The narrator's lament in the last lines of the poem, "Whilst I—Ah is it not a shame? / Sad tears am shedding," might well echo the voice of the poet.

[3] Ballantrae is on the western coast 17½ miles (on today's highway) north of Stranraer. Keats's spelling probably reflects the way the local pronunciation struck his ear. The Ballantrae of Keats's time is still to be seen, at least vestigially. In the hills are the ruins of Ardstinchar Castle, where it is said Mary Queen of Scots stayed and served a banquet of herons. The River Stinchar flows below the castle. A defunct winding bridge (see photo), built from the stones of the castle, is surely the "craggis grey" and "rocky brig" of Keats's ballad.

　Ballantrae is not without its King's Arms, where it is possible Keats stayed and certain that I had tea. On the other hand, perhaps Keats and Brown checked into the new Head Inn, advertised on the front page of the *Air Advertiser* as follows:

　　To Travellers.
　AGNES MILRAITH, in Ballantrae, takes this opportunity of returning her sincere thanks to her Friends, and the Public in general, for the very liberal support she has met with since she entered to the Inn in Ballantrae. And as it will always be her particular study to pay every attention to the comfort and accommodation of those who may stop at her House, she solicits a continuation of that support which she has already received.
　　Travellers may rely upon every accommodation as to good Post Chaises, Horses, and steady drivers.
　　Head Inn, Ballantrae, 3d July 1818.

[4] Keats and Brown reached Ballantrae by way of Cairnryan (also spelled Cairn Ryan), a town peculiar for occupying only one side of the street today, the other "side" being the sea. Cairnryan is an industrial and commercial port, with boats to Larne, Ireland. A large aircraft carrier, the *Eagle*, was being disassembled when I visited.

　The distance Keats mentions ("27 Miles from Stranraer") would be the mileage from Portpatrick to Ballantrae, 25½ miles today, owing to the cut of the highway.

[5] My own efforts to follow their steps along the "green mountainous shore" did not unfold as gracefully as Keats had led me to expect and certainly fell far short of Brown's lyrical description. A major highway (A77) dissevers some of the verdure of Keats's time. I parked in the lot belonging to the Glen Nap Church, left a note of apology for the minister (should he turn up), and, after a consultation with a hunter who would have made Heathcliff seem congenial and clean-cut (he didn't know of any "old" road), I scrambled up a mountainside and trespassed through private fields, all with the happy consequence of gaining some commanding views of what Keats had seen and described so glowingly to Tom. See photo series of route to Ballantrae.

having gone through it—When we left Cairn our Road lay half way up the sides of a green mountainous shore, full of Clefts of verdure and eternally varying—sometimes up sometimes down, and over little Bridges going across green chasms of moss rock and trees—winding about every where. After two or three Miles of this we turned suddenly into a magnificent glen[6] finely wooded in Parts—seven Miles long— with a Mountain Stream winding down the Midst—full of cottages in the most happy Situations—the sides of the Hills covered with sheep—the effect of cattle lowing I never had so finely—At the end we had a gradual ascent and got among the tops of the Mountains whence in a little time I descried in the Sea Ailsa Rock 940 feet hight[7]—it was 15 Miles distant and seemed close upon us—The effect of ailsa with the peculiar perspective of the Sea in connection with the ground we stood on, and the misty rain then falling gave me a complete Idea of a deluge—Ailsa struck me very suddenly—really I was a little alarmed— Thus far had I written before we set out this morning—Now we are at Girvan 13 Miles north of Belantree—Our Walk has been along a more grand shore to day than yesterday—Ailsa beside us all the way—From the heights we could see quite at home Cantire[8] and the large Mountains of Arran one of the Hebrides—We are in comfortable Quarters.[9] The Rain we feared held up bravely and it has been "fu fine this day"[10]—Tomorrow we shall be at Ayr—

To Ailsa Rock

Hearken, thou craggy ocean pyramid,
  Give answer by thy voice, the sea fowls' screams!
  When were thy shoulders mantled in huge streams?
When from the sun was thy broad forehead hid?
How long is't since the mighty power bid
  Thee heave to airy sleep from fathom dreams—
  Sleep in the lap of thunder or sunbeams,
Or when grey clouds are thy cold coverlid?
Thou answer'st not, for thou art dead asleep;
  Thy life is but two dead eternities,
The last in air, the former in the deep—
  First with the whales, last with the eagle skies;
Drown'd wast thou till an earthquake made thee steep—
  Another cannot wake thy giant size!

[6] Glen App.

[7] Ailsa Rock, or Ailsa Craig, as the Scots have it, is a conical rock island whose height is variously represented: 940 feet according to both Keats and Brown, who must have gotten their statistics from a guide book; 1,097 feet in the *Encyclopaedia Britannica*; 1,100 feet in the *Topographical Dictionary of Scotland* (1851); 1,103 in *Black's Picturesque Tourist of Scotland* (1869); 1,114 feet according to Rollins. Ten miles west of Girvan, this granite island was noted in Keats's time and before for its sea fowl. It was one of the spots that produced in early travellers the experience of the sublime. Heron writes, "This imagery was awful and elevating. As it returns upon my imagination, I feel my heart partly tremble for terrour, and partly swell with the conception of sublimity" (*Observations*, 2, 313). Ironically, the name, translated from the Gaelic, means "fairy rock." Brown (Chapter 4) refers to the rental of the island, at fifty pounds a year, double what it was in the time of Heron, who reported it could be rented from the earl of Cassilis for twenty-five pounds a year.

[8] Kintyre.

[9] Even today, the Girvan King's Arms, where they stayed, provides comfortable quarters with amenities of which Keats could not have conceived, including a wide-screen color television and an electric hot-water brewer for tea or coffee. The King's Arms is a large hotel with an annex; it apparently ran to the corner of the street, but according to the elderly night clerk that section burned down between 1940 and 1950. The present entrance to the bar was the entrance to the original hotel. Judging by the large garage area in the rear, formerly the stables, many coaches stopped here, with what business one cannot be entirely sure, for the area had known its share of smugglers and, correspondingly, excisemen. Girvan today has the characteristics of a seaside resort, with amusements, food stalls, a boardwalk, telescopes for viewing Ailsa Craig, and crowds. As I figure it, Keats wrote his sonnet on Ailsa Craig in the evening, after checking into the hotel and dining. I photographed Ailsa at the hour Keats would have been composing.

[10] Several stanzas of Burns's early long poem "The Holy Friar" end with a refrain that sounds like this, though the words vary slightly, and no single refrain says exactly "fu fine this day."

[11] Leaving Girvan the pair would have passed Girvan Old Churchyard with its splendid markers, some dating back to 1716 (the earliest I could make out). Entering Kirkoswald they would have found an old walled cemetery surrounding a ruined church. Tam o' Shanter is buried here, as well as Burns's schoolmaster. Across from the churchyard is a tavern or inn on the grounds of the schoolhouse where Burns, as a teenager living on his uncle's farm in nearby Turnberry, studied mathematics under Hugh Rodger.

[12] The grounds of the first ruin, Crossraguel Abbey, founded in the thirteenth century by Duncas, earl of Carrick, are fairly extensive, and if Keats and Brown did examine them, they would have been involved in the exploration for some time. The tower house of Crossraguel Abbey, with its winding staircase that struck Keats as noteworthy, dates from the sixteenth century and was the residence of the last abbots. The abbey, officially the Cluniac Abbey of Crossraguel, is two miles from Maybole and ten miles south of Ayr. Quite close to it on a hill but not easily accessible is Baltersan Castle, the second ruin Keats came upon that day.

[13] On the outskirts of Glasgow I found, after many abortive attempts and finally an inquiry at the Post Office/licensed store in Fenwick, a quiet farm called Kingswell (no final "s"), owned now, as it has been for several generations, by the Dalziel family. The name Kingswell derives, according to Sheila Dalziel, who showed me around, from the fact that James I of England (James VI of Scotland) had stopped there and drunk from a well in the moors; his horse had gotten bogged down in the process. The Dalziel home, which would have been where Keats stopped, has walls that are virtually 2½ feet thick, and whether Keats spent the night or just held up there to do some letter writing, he was well protected from the elements. Traffic turning off A77, the major road from the south into Glasgow, does not pass there anymore, a new road having diverted it, but the white dividing line down the center of the street of the Dalziel home serves as a reminder of when there were many more passersby. Bushnell experienced some frustration locating Kingswells (it had an "s" in his time), but

This is the only Sonnet of any worth I have of late written—I hope you will like it. 'T is now the 11th of July and we have come 8 Miles to Breakfast to Kirkoswald[11]—I hope the next Kirk will be Kirk-Alloway—I have nothing of consequence to say now concerning our Journey—so I will speak as far as I can judge on the Irish and Scotch—I know nothing of the higher Classes. Yet I have a persuasion that there the Irish are victorious—As to the 'profanum vulgus' I must incline to the Scotch—They never laugh—but they are always comparitively neat and clean—Their constitutions are not so remote and puzzling as the Irish—The Scotchman will never give a decision on any point—he will never commit himself in a sentence which may be referred to as a meridian in his notions of things—so that you do not know him—and yet you may come in nigher neighbourhood to him than to the Irishman who commits himself in so many places that it dazes your head—A Scotchman's motive is more easily discovered than an Irishman's. A Scotchman will go wisely about to deceive you, an Irishman cunningly—An Irishman would bluster out of any discovery to his disadvantage—A Scotchman would retire perhaps without much desire of revenge—An Irishman likes to be thought a gallous fellow—A Scotchman is contented with himself—It seems to me they are both sensible of the Character they hold in England and act accordingly to Englishmen—Thus the Scotchman will become over grave and over decent and the Irishman over-impetuous. I like a Scotchman best because he is less of a bore—I like the Irishman best because he ought to be more comfortable—The Scotchman has made up his Mind within himself in a sort of snail shell wisdom—The Irishman is full of strong headed instinct—The Scotchman is farther in Humanity than the Irishman—there his will stick perhaps when the Irishman shall be refined beyond him—for the former thinks he cannot be improved; the latter would grasp at it for ever, place but the good plain before him.

Maybole—Since breakfast we have come only four Miles to dinner, not merely, for we have examined in the way two Ruins, one of them very fine called Crossragual Abbey. There is a winding Staircase to the top of a little Watch Tower.[12] July 13. *Kingswells*[13]—I have been writing to Reynolds—therefore any particulars since Kirkoswald have escaped me—from said kirk we went to Maybole to dinner—then we set forward to Burnes's town Ayr—the Approach to it is extremely

finally found pretty much what I did—a "hamlet" with only a "substantial farm"—

though he missed the pleasure of an intelligent young woman to guide him.

fine—quite outwent my expectations richly meadowed, wooded, heathed and riveleted—with a grand Sea view terminated by the black Mountains of the isle of Arran. As soon as I saw them so nearly I said to myself 'How is it they did not beckon Burns to some grand attempt at Epic'—The bonny Doon is the sweetest river I ever saw overhung with fine trees as far as we could see—we stood some time on the Brig across it, over which Tam o' Shanter fled—we took a pinch of snuff on the key stone[14]—Then we proceeded to 'auld Kirk Alloway'—As we were looking at it a Farmer pointed out the spots where Mungo's Mither hang'd hersel' and 'drunken Charlie brake's neck's bane'[15]—Then we proceeded to the Cottage he was born in—there was a board to that effect by the door Side—it had the same effect as the same sort of memorial at Stratford on Avon—We drank some Toddy to Burns's Memory with an old Man who knew Burns—damn him—and damn his Anecdotes—he was a great bore—it was impossible for a Southren to understand above 5 words in a hundred—There was something good in his description of Burns's melancholy the last time he saw him. I was determined to write a sonnet in the Cottage—I did—but it is so bad I cannot venture it here[16]—Next we walked into Ayr Town and before we went to Tea, saw the new Brig and the Auld Brig and Wallace tower[17]—Yesterday we dined with a Traveller—We were talking about Kean[18]—He said he had seen him at Glasgow 'in

Scotland. The *Air Advertiser* of July 9, 1818, reports: "Mr. Hazlitt now proceeded to remark on some of Burns's poems. He pointed out the 'Two Dogs' as a very spirited piece of description, and as giving a very vivid idea of the manners of both high and low life. He described the Brigs of Air . . . as being full of the best kind of characteristic and comic painting; but Tam o' Shanter as the masterpiece in this way." Hazlitt, the article continues, concluded his lecture by remarking that old Scottish and English ballads possessed "a still more original cast of thought, and more romantic imagery—a closer intimacy with nature—a firmer reliance on that as the only stock of wealth to which the mind has to resort—a more infantine simplicity of manners—a greater strength of affection—hopes longer cherished, and longer deferred—sighs that the heart dare not leave—and 'thoughts that do often lie too deep for tears.' "

[16] Though Keats did not think well enough of his sonnet "This mortal body of a thousand days" to include it in his letter to Tom, Brown rescued the poem for posterity, probably jotting it down in his journal. I have displayed it separately as it is not legitimately a part of Letter 7.

[17] Keats saw the ancient tower in which Sir William Wallace is said to have been imprisoned. A new tower was built on the same site in 1828 and is also called Wallace Tower.

[18] Edmund Kean (1787–1833) was the dazzling stage actor of Keats's time whose intense, subjective interpretations of Shakespeare's characters were much talked about by theatregoers, many of whom preferred the classical oratorical style of John Phillip Kemble (1757–1823), the other great name on the London stage and Kean's rival.

Kean's interpretation of the role of Othello was highly praised by Hazlitt, who proclaimed that Kean's voice "struck on the heart like the swelling notes of some divine music, like the sound of years of departed happiness" ("Mr. Kean's Othello," *Morning Chronicle*, May 6, 1814). Keats himself had written a review of the actor entitled "Mr. Kean," which was published in the *Champion* (December 21, 1817). Keats admired Kean's passion. He either did not know or did not care that

[14] Keats and Brown commemorate the fate that befell Tam o' Shanter's old gray mare Meg on the keystone of the Brig o' Doon. With the witches from Kirk Alloway chasing him, Tam fled to the keystone of the bridge, since witches could not cross running water, according to superstition. But his horse did not entirely clear the bridge and lost her tail:

> Now, do thy speedy utmost, Meg,
> And win the key-stane of the brig;
> There, at them thou thy tail may toss,
> A running stream they dare na cross!
> But ere the key-stane she could make,
> The fient a tail she had to shake,
> For Nannie, far before the rest,
> Hard upon noble Maggie prest,
> And flew at Tam wi' furious ettle;
> But little wist she Maggie's mettle!
> Ae spring brought off her master hale,
> But left behind her ain grey tail:
> The carlin claught her by the rump,
> And left poor Maggie scarce a stump.
> (ll. 205–224)

The poem's ending urges, "Remember Tam o' Shanter's old grey mare," and Keats and Brown do so with a pinch of snuff.
[15] The farmer points out the site of incidents from "Tam o' Shanter": At night Tam, having drunk a great deal, mounts his horse Meg and charges off to Kirk Alloway where the witches are dancing:

> By this time he was cross the ford,
> Whare in the snaw the chapman smoor'd;
> And past the birks and meikle stane,
> Where drunken Charlie brake's neck-bane;
> And thro' the whins, and by the cairn,
> Whare hunters fand the murder'd bairn;
> And near the thorn, aboon the well,
> Whare Mungo's mither hang'd hersel.
> (ll. 89–96)

In his regard for the poem "Tam o' Shanter," as well as his respect for Burns, Keats reflects the taste of Hazlitt, among others, whose lectures published in *Blackwood's Magazine* were causing a stir in

Kean's personal life was dissolute, besodden, and flamboyantly licentious. By 1818 and the time of Keats's encounter with the confused Scot who claimed to have seen Kean in Glasgow, Kean was in Paris, having difficulty with his career, for he had alienated both employers and supporters. Rollins indicates that Kean performed in Glasgow in 1815 during Passion Week.

[19] Glasgow Cathedral, the church of Saint Kentigern, apostle and bishop of the early Celtic church and more commonly known as Saint Mungo (meaning "Dear One"), is built high on a hill. One sees it best approaching the bridge onto High Street, which leads to the Cathedral. Saint Mungo is buried under the Cathedral. The church is a two-story building, with the choir separated in the upper story and the first story referred to as the Lower Church. Keats may have had this distinction in mind, as well as the elevated situation of the Cathedral, in his pun "High Kirk."
[20] See Introduction: The Emigration of the George Keatses.

Othello in the Jew, I me an er, er, er, the Jew in Shylock.' He got bother'd completely in vague ideas of the Jew in Othello, Shylock in the Jew, Shylock in Othello, Othello in Shylock, the Jew in Othello &c &c &c he left himself in a mess at last—Still satisfied with himself he went to the Window and gave an abortive whistle of some tune or other—it might have been Handel. There is no end to these Mistakes—he'll go and tell people how he has seen 'Malvolio in the Countess' 'Twelfth night in 'Midsummer nights dream—Bottom in much ado about Nothing—Viola in Barrymore—Antony in Cleopatra—Falstaff in the mouse Trap.—July 14. We entered Glasgow last Evening under the most oppressive Stare a body could feel—When we had crossed the Bridge Brown look'd back and said its whole population had turned to wonder at us—we came on till a drunken Man came up to me—I put him off with my Arm—he returned all up in Arms saying aloud that, 'he had seen all foreigners bu-u-u-t he never saw the like o' me—I was obliged to mention the word Officer and Police before he would desist—The City of Glasgow I take to be a very fine one—I was astonished to hear it was twice the size of Edinburgh—It is built of Stone and has a much more solid appearance than London—We shall see the Cathedral this morning—they have devilled it into a 'High Kirk'[19]—I want very much to know the name of the Ship George is gone in—also what port[20] he will land in—I know nothing about it—I hope you are leading a quiet Life and gradually improving—Make a long lounge of the whole Summer—by the time the Leaves fall I shall be near you with plenty of confab—there are a thousand things I cannot write—Take care of yourself—I mean in not being vexed or bothered at any thing—God bless you!

John—

Letter 8

TO TOM KEATS

[17, 18, 20, 21 July 1818]

Cairn-something July 17th

My dear Tom,

Here's Brown going on so that I cannot bring to Mind how the two last days have vanished—for example he says 'The Lady of the Lake went to Rock herself to sleep on Arthur's seat and the Lord of the Isles coming to Press a Piece and seeing her Assleap remembered their last meeting at Cony stone Water so touching her with one hand on the Vallis Lucis while the other un-Derwent her Whitehaven, Ireby stifled her clack man on, that he might her Anglesea and give her a Buchanan and said.'[1] I told you last how we were stared at in Glasgow—we are not out of the Crowd yet—Steam Boats on Loch Lomond and Barouches[2] on its sides take a little from the Pleasure of such romantic chaps as Brown and I—The Banks of the Clyde are extremely beautiful—the north End of Loch Lomond grand in excess—the

[1] Much vulgar mischief is attributed to friend Brown by Keats here. Punning with place names and using slang that refers to sexual intercourse and both male and female genitalia, Brown, claims Keats, spoofs the King Arthur legend. Keats's biographer Robert Gittings has identified the sexual slang in the passage rather specifically, providing the following key: "*Piece*, prostitute; *Ass*, arse; *Cony*, the female pudendum; *stone*, testes; *Water*, semen; *Vallis Lucis*, sluices, the female pudendum; *Stifled*, choked, sexually occupied; *Clack*, the clack-valve of a pump, pump and pump-handle being commonplaces of sexual slang" (*John Keats*, appendix, 452). Gittings notes that in Rollins's text of the letter the word "Cony" has been misrepresented as "Corry." I have used Gittings's corrected reading. *Cony* (Coniston Water) accords with my own position that place names of the Lake District are dominant in this passage.

There is a place called Arthur's Seat, a high hill in Holyrood Park in Edinburgh, although King Arthur is not the source of the name. (The two did not visit Edinburgh but

Brown must have talked about the possibility, perhaps for the return trip.) Keats may also have had an association in his mind with a spot in the Lake District called Arthur's Round Table, a circular embankment near Brougham Castle. The passage contains fragmentary allusions to other places: Derwentwater; Ireby; Whitehaven, a seaport town in Cumberland and Lowther territory; and Coniston Water, in the Lake District. It is possible that Vallis Lucis was a play on Lucy's valley, or the valley of the Lucy poems of Wordsworth.

George Buchanan (1506–1582) was a Scottish reformer, humanist, Latin scholar, and poet whose ode *Calen lae Maiae* was much admired by Wordsworth, who mentions him and "his beautiful Ode to the First of May" in a discussion of climate and atmosphere around Rydal (*Guide to the Lakes*, 47).

[2] The steam boat was new on the scene; a barouche was a four-wheeled carriage with two seats facing each other. Tourism had grown, and Loch Lomond was already becoming congested.

The holograph manuscript for Letter 8 is in the Keats Museum in Hampstead. The letter was written between July 17 and 21. It is postmarked in Glasgow 23 July and arrived in Hampstead at 10:00 A.M. (FN[n], or forenoon) on July 30, with ½ pence due.

Cairndow, a very tiny town at the northern tip of Loch Fyne, served to break up the trip for travellers between Tarbet (and nearby Arrochar), at the top of Loch Lomond, and Inverary. When Robert Heron made his tour of Scotland in 1793 he stopped in Cairndow, staying at the Cairndow Inn, which, he said, was "intended as a post half-way house, to divide the long stage between Arrochar and Inverness." Heron was quite pleased with the inn ("small, snug, and neat"), the landlord ("one of the most obliging men"), and even the dinner (a "comfortable" dinner). The stables, he observed, were "narrow in proportion to the smallness of the house" (*Observations*, 1, 334). Dorothy Wordsworth and her brother arrived at the Cairndow Inn late at night on August 29, 1803, and were "well received, and sate down in a neat parlour with a good fire" (*Recollections*, 124). They breakfasted on the superior herring from Loch Fyne recommended by their landlord. Southey stayed at the inn in 1819, on his tour with Thomas Telford, and it seems to have been one of the few places that measured up to his standards. It was, he said, "a single house, small, but very comfortable. Some magazines and other books were in the room, a Prayer Book among them, and a volume of Tillotson's *Sermons*" (*Journal of a Tour*, 245). Today the stables have been converted into a restaurant and the whole operation is called the Cairndow Stagecoach Inn and Stables Restaurant. I was fascinated by the Kilmorich Church in Cairndow because it was dated 1816 and would have seemed new to Keats.

Though Keats writes "Cairn-something" at the top of his letter, he could not have been confused about the spelling. It was too easy. He is posturing, pretending an urbane weariness of Scottish place names containing "cairn."

entrance at the lower end to the narrow part from a little distance is precious good—the Evening was beautiful nothing could surpass our fortune in the weather—yet was I worldly enough to wish for a fleet of chivalry Barges with Trumpets and Banners just to die away before me into that blue place among the mountains—I must give you an outline as well as I can.[3]

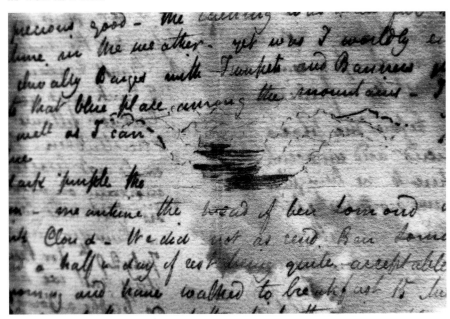

Not B[4]—the Water was a fine Blue silverd and the Mountains a dark purple the Sun setting aslant behind them—meantime the head of ben Lomond was covered with a rich Pink Cloud—We did not ascend Ben Lomond—the price being very high and a half a day of rest being quite acceptable—We were up at 4 this morning and have walked to breakfast 15 Miles through two tremendous Glens[5]—at the end of the first there is a place called rest and be thankful which we took for an Inn—it was nothing but a Stone[6] and so we were cheated into 5 more Miles to Breakfast—I have just been bathing in Loch fine a saltwater Lake opposite the Window—quite pat and fresh but for the

---

[3] Keats makes an ink sketch for Tom with simple, clean strokes. See the photograph of this portion of the letter.

[4] Nota bene is the Latin for "note well." Keats also uses the more common abbreviation, N. B.

[5] Glen Croe and Glen Kinglas.

[6] Exactly what Keats and Brown found at the top of the pass, after tromping through the very dramatic, steep, moody valley of Glen Croe across the road probably built by General Wade is a puzzlement. Keats said it was a "Stone," and that is exactly what I found—a stone about the size of a milestone that read:

REST & BE THANKFUL
MILITARY ROAD REP[D]
BY 93RD REG[T] 1768
TRANSFERRED TO COMMR: FOR H.R.H. ? H
IN THE YEAR 1814
AD

This would have satisfied me and I would have dropped the matter had I not been attempting to match this evidence with what Brown wrote to Dilke (see Letter 13): "'Rest and be thankful' was not an Inn, but a stone seat!" If the stone I found had been a seat, it must have been intended for an elf. Stoddart (1801) had identified "a green seat, near the twenty-ninth milestone" (*Remarks*, 250). From Dorothy Wordsworth's journal I learned that something seat-like was there in 1803: "At the top of the hill we came to a seat with the well-known inscription, 'Rest and be thankful.' On the same stone it was recorded that the road had been made by Col. Wade's regiment. The seat is placed so as to command a full view of the valley, and the long, long road, which, with the fact recorded, and the exhortation, makes it an affecting resting-place" (*Recollections*, 123). When Southey came to this spot in 1819 he found, "On the summit is a seat in the green bank, looking down Glencroe, and by it the stone bearing the beautiful inscription which all travellers have noticed—'Rest, and be thankful'" (*Journal of a Tour*, 245–246). Beattie (1838) speaks of a "semicircular stone seat, erected at the summit of the pass, bearing the inscription, 'Rest, and be thankful'" (*Scotland, Illustrated*, 2, 112). A century later Bushnell, to some extent *my* guide, "arrived at a clumsy stone bench: Rest and be Thankful." De-romanticizing further, Bushnell noted: "There was nothing else but a monument, also stone" (*Walk*, 178–179).

It is a humbling experience to attempt to reconcile the "data" in accounts of travellers from 1801 to the present. If the discrepancies of companion travellers like Keats and Brown have made me wish for a rest for which I could be thankful, I suppose I have also learned something about what travellers see and what they half create in the telling of their adventures.

cursed Gad flies—damn 'em they have been at me ever since I left the Swan and two necks[7]—

All gentle folks who owe a grudge[8]
  To any living thing,
Open your ears and stay your trudge
  Whilst I in dudgeon sing.

The gadfly he hath stung me sore—
  O may he ne'er sting you!
But we have many a horrid bore
  He may sting black and blue.

Has any here an old grey mare
  With three legs all her store?
O put it to her buttocks bare
  And straight she'll run on four.

Has any here a lawyer suit
  Of 1743?
Take lawyer's nose and put it to't
  And you the end will see.

Is there a man in Parliament
  Dumfounder'd in his speech?
O let his neighbour make a rent
  And put one in his breech.

O Lowther, how much better thou
  Hadst figur'd t' other day,
When to the folks thou mad'st a bow
  And hadst no more to say,

If lucky gadfly had but ta'en
  His seat upon thine a—e,
And put thee to a little pain
  To save thee from a worse.

Better than Southey it had been,
  Better than Mr. D——,
Better than Wordsworth too, I ween,
  Better than Mr. V——.[9]

[7] The Swan with Two Necks was one of the best-known coaching inns of the era, located on Lad Lane, a street which no longer exists but which can be mentally superimposed upon a modern map near Gresham Street just east of St. Martin's Le Grand, north of St. Paul's Cathedral. Its odd name is said to have its source in the practice of making nicks on the bills of swans to show ownership. The Vintner's Company used two nicks. The "nicks" had become "necks" well before Keats's time (Robinson, *British Post Office*, 138n; *Letters*, 1, 295n).

[8] See discussion of the poem in Introduction: The Westmorland Elections.

[9] Maurice Buxton Forman speculates, "Mr. V—— would doubtless be the then Chancellor of the Exchequer, Nicholas Vansittart, first Baron Bexley (1766–1851); and Mr. D—— may perhaps have been Robert Saunders Dundas, second Viscount Melville (1771–1851), who held office in a previous ministry; but this last name rests upon mere conjecture" (*Poetical Works*, 4, 145). But Dundas and Vansittart were not in the news (local or otherwise) at the time Keats was writing this poem, and they had nothing to do with the Westmorland election. There is no reason they should have been on his mind. Jack Stillinger makes a more plausible suggestion: "References may be to Joseph Dykes Ballentyne Dykes (d. 1830) and Sir Frederick Fletcher Vane (1760–1832), property owners who were active in the Westmorland election of July 1818" (*Complete Poems*, 448).

Wordsworth appears in this stanza because he was, as I have indicated above, an energetic supporter of the Lowther candidates, and like Southey, had converted to conservative politics.

Forgive me pray, good people all,
    For deviating so;
In spirit sure I had a call—
    And now I on will go.

Has any here a daughter fair
    Too fond of reading novels,
Too apt to fall in love with care
    And charming Mister Lovels?[10]

O put a gadfly to that thing
    She keeps so white and pert—
I mean the finger for the ring—
    And it will breed a wert.

Has any here a pious spouse
    Who seven times a day
Scolds as King David pray'd, to chouse
    And have her holy way?

O let a gadfly's little sting
    Persuade her sacred tongue
That noises are a common thing
    But that her bell has rung.

And as this is the summum bo-
    Num of all conquering,
I leave withouten wordes mo
    The gadfly's little sting.

[Cladich, July 18]

Last Evening we came round the End of Loch Fine to Inverary—the Duke of Argyle's Castle[11] is very modern magnificent and more so from the place it is in—the woods seem old enough to remember two or three changes in the Crags about them—the Lake was beautiful and there was a Band at a distance by the Castle. I must say I enjoyed two or three common tunes—but nothing could stifle the horrors of a solo on the Bag-pipe—I thought the Beast would never have done—Yet was I doomed to hear another—On entering Inverary we saw a Play Bill—Brown was knock'd up from new shoes—so I went to the Barn alone where I saw the Stranger accompanied by a Bag pipe—There they went on about 'interesting creaters' and 'human nater'—till the Curtain fell and then Came the Bag pipe—When Mrs Haller fainted

[10] Again Forman proposes an "indubitable" identification here: "The reference is doubtless to the hero of Scott's novel *The Antiquary*, properly the Honourable William Geraldin, heir to the Earl of Glenallan, but known throughout the book as Mr. Lovel" (*Poetical Works*, 4, 145). The Quaker poet Robert Lovell, brother-in-law to both Southey and Coleridge, seems to me another possibility, since he belongs to the Lake District scenario which is so much a part of this poem and of the beginning of the letter containing it. There is no evidence of his charm, however.

[11] A present-day visitor would probably know this castle as Inverary Castle, though in Keats's time tourists were careful to note the distinction between the remains of the fifteenth-century edifice and the one they beheld set back from the village, the elaborate eighteenth-century structure Dorothy Wordsworth describes as "a stately turreted mansion, but with a modern air, standing on a lawn, retired from water, and screened behind by woods covering the side of high hills to the top, and still beyond, by bare mountains" (*Recollections*, 126). The castle Keats saw belonged to the sixth duke of Argyll, George William Campbell.

down went the Curtain and out came the Bagpipe—at the heartrending, shoemending reconciliation the Piper blew amain—I never read or saw this play before; not the Bag pipe, nor the wretched players themselves were little in comparison with it—thank heaven it has been scoffed at lately almost to a fashion[12]—

> Of late two dainties were before me plac'd,
>   Sweet, holy, pure, sacred, and innocent,
>   From the ninth sphere to me benignly sent
> That gods might know my own particular taste.
> First the soft bag-pipe mourn'd with zealous haste;
>   The Stranger next with head on bosom bent
>   Sigh'd; rueful again the piteous bag-pipe went;
> Again the Stranger sighings fresh did waste.
> O bag-pipe, thou didst steal my heart away;
>   O Stranger, thou my nerves from pipe didst charm;
> O bag-pipe thou didst reassert thy sway;
>   Again thou Stranger gav'st me fresh alarm—
> Alas! I could not choose. Ah! my poor heart,
> Mumchance art thou with both obliged to part.

I think we are the luckiest fellows in Christendom—Brown could not proceed this morning on account of his feet and lo there is thunder and rain—

          [Ford]

July 20th For these two days past we have been so badly accomodated more particularly in coarse food that I have not been at all in cue to write. Last night poor Brown with his feet blistered and scarcely able to walk, after a trudge of 20 Miles down the Side of Loch Awe had no supper but Eggs and Oat Cake—we have lost the sight of white bread entirely—Now we had eaten nothing but Eggs all day—about 10 a piece and they had become sickening—.

To day we have fared rather better—but no oat Cake wanting—we had a small Chicken and even a good bottle of Port—but all together the fare is too coarse—I feel it a little—another week will break us in—I forgot to tell you that when we came through Glencroe[13] it was

critic's ink Keats must have welcomed an opportunity to rate a production in Inverary, in the middle of his walking tour; Brown, as a playwright, would have had something to say too had he not been laid up that night.

The play, entitled *Menschenhass und Rue* (Misanthropy and Remorse) in the original German, concerns a problem between the Count and Countess Waldbourg. The young wife, having been seduced by her husband's friend, leaves her husband and children; when she realizes that her seducer had lied to her about her husband's fidelity, she leaves him as well. Filled with remorse, she assumes the name of Mrs. Haller and takes employment as companion to a Countess Wintersen. When the play opens, Mrs. Haller has been living in the Wintersen castle for three years. A reclusive misanthrope who "hates the whole human race, but women particularly," according to his servant, lives in a lodge near the Wintersen estate. Known only as the Stranger, he nurses his mysterious grievance. On one occasion, however, he saves Count Wintersen's son from drowning and is subsequently persuaded to appear at the castle to be thanked. Here he is introduced to Mrs. Haller and in a climactic moment the estranged husband and wife recognize each other. Mrs. Haller (Countess Waldbourg) faints, whereupon the Stranger (Count Waldbourg) rushes from the room. In the play's final scene the husband forgives his repentant wife for dishonouring him and, with the appearance of their two children as catalyst, the couple fly into a reconciling embrace.

Written in 1787, the play had been very popular in Europe and America, and the last scene, with its apparent endorsement of a wife's infidelity, was controversial.

[12] Keats's critical awareness of the play *The Stranger*, written by August von Kotzebue, translated from the German for the British stage, probably came from the fact that his good friend Reynolds had panned it in a review for the *Champion* (March 2, 1817) and that Reynolds was one of the many to do so. In the winter Keats himself tried his hand at theatre criticism, substituting for Reynolds in the *Champion* on December 21 and early in January (Jones, *Life of Reynolds*, 132; Gittings, *Keats*, 172–173). Having dipped his pen in

[13] Keats backtracks in his letter to give a brief glimpse of the glen he and Brown had trudged through believing they were to have breakfast at an inn called Rest and Be Thankful at the top. Glen Croe was someplace no traveller would fail to write home about. Most whose journals and accounts we still read today did so at length, emphasizing the arduousness of the 860-foot ascent and descent, the sublime ruggedness of the steep hills from the perspective of a traveller in the bottom of the valley, and the scarcity of population. Keats

bows to convention, but with his image of the dogs among the crags, he takes a decidedly nonconformist tack.

[14] The walk was along what is now referred to as the old road, which is somewhat elevated and provides good views of the long, narrow lake, whose name means "dark lake." The area was quite remote for an Englishman.
[15] No doubt Innischonnel Castle, dating from as early as the twelfth century, and, visible about one mile west on Keats's path, the remains of a chapel, with its surrounding walled-in graveyard, on Innish Errich.
[16] Keats meant Luing Island. Actually, as "luing" is the Scottish for "long," Keats has simply translated.

[17] After the Battle of Culloden and the final overthrow of the Jacobites in 1746, Highland dress was banned.
[18] There are no inns in Ford today. I stopped at the Post Office to inquire where one might have been in 1818 and was sent down the street to a white house with what I thought were much better than "tolerable windows," given all the books they revealed within. A sophisticated young couple, graduates of the University of Edinburgh who had lived in the Lake District for many years, own the house now. Ralph and Lucy Clough, with their three children, retreated from inflation to this place, taking all their wit and ingenuity with them. Mr. Clough had the idea that Great Britain could remain a world power if it would stop trying to progress and simply devote all energies to preserving the nineteenth century, announcing to the world, "We are open from May to October!" What a good story to cheer up Tom, I thought on Keats's behalf, losing track of a century or so.

early in the morning and we were pleased with the noise of Shepherds Sheep and dogs in the misty heights close above us—we saw none of them for some time, till two came in sight creeping among the Craggs like Emmets, yet their voices came quite plainly to us—The Approach to Loch Awe was very solemn towards nightfall—the first glance was a streak of water deep in the Bases of large black Mountains—We had come along a complete mountain road, where if one listened there was not a sound but that of Mountain Streams. We walked 20 Miles by the side of Loch Awe[14]—every ten steps creating a new and beautiful picture—sometimes through little wood—there are two islands on the Lake each with a beautiful ruin[15]—one of them rich in ivy—We are detained this morning by the rain. I will tell you exactly where we are—We are between Loch Craignish and the Sea just opposite Long Island[16]—Yesterday our walk was of this description—the near Hills were not very lofty but many of their Steeps beautifully wooded—the distant Mountains in the Hebrides very grand the Saltwater Lakes coming up between Crags and Islands fulltided and scarcely ruffled—sometimes appearing as one large Lake, sometimes as three distinct ones in different directions—At one point we saw afar off a rocky opening into the main Sea—We have also seen an Eagle or two. They move about without the least motion of Wings when in an indolent fit—I am for the first time in a country where a foreign Language is spoken—they gabble away Gaelic at a vast rate—numbers of them speak English—There are not many Kilts in Argylshire[17]—At Fort William they say a Man is not admitted into Society without one—the Ladies there have a horror at the indecency of Breeches. I cannot give you a better idea of Highland Life than by describing the place we are in—The Inn or public is by far the best house in the immediate neighbourhood[18]—It has a white front with tolerable windows—the table I am writing on suprises me as being a nice flapped Mehogany one; at the same time the place has no watercloset nor anything like it. You may if you peep see through the floor chinks into the ground rooms. The old Grandmother of the house seems intelligent though not over clean. N.B. No snuff being to be had in the village, she made us some. The Guid Man is a rough looking hardy stout Man who I think does not speak so much English as the Guid wife who is very obliging and sensible and moreover though stockingless, has a pair of old Shoes—Last night some Whisky Men sat up clattering Gaelic till I am sure one o'Clock to our great annoyance—There is a Gaelic testament on the Drawers in the next room—White and blue China ware has crept all about here—Yesterday there passed a Donkey laden with tin-pots—opposite the Window there are hills in a Mist—a few Ash trees and a mountain stream at a little distance—They possess a few head of Cattle—If you had gone round to the back of the House just now—you would have seen more hills in a Mist—some dozen wretched black Cottages scented of peat smoke which finds its way by the door or a hole in the roof—a girl here and there barefoot. There was one little thing driving Cows down a slope like a mad thing—there was another standing at the cowhouse door rather pretty fac'd all up to the ankles in dirt—

[Oban]

We have walk'd 15 Miles in a soaking rain to Oban opposite the Isle of Mull which is so near Staffa we had thought to pass to it—but the expense is 7 Guineas and those rather extorted—Staffa you see is a fashionable place and therefore every one concerned with it either in this town or the Island are what you call up—'t is like paying sixpence for an apple at the playhouse—this irritated me and Brown was not best pleased—we have therefore resolved to set northward for fort William tomorrow morning—I fell upon a bit of white Bread to day like a Sparrow—it was very fine—I cannot manage the cursed Oatcake—Remember me to all and let me hear a good account of you at Inverness—I am sorry Georgy had not those Lines.[19] Good bye.

Your affectionate Brother
John—

[19] This has been taken to be a reference to the letter Keats wrote to George (Letter 1) that never reached him, but it seems to me more sensible that "a good account of you" is what Keats meant (i.e., too bad George couldn't have heard before departing that you are well).

The holograph manuscript for Letter 9 is in the Houghton Library at Harvard. It is addressed to M[r] B. Bailey at his father's home (J. Bailey Esq[re]) at Thorntey Abbey, Peterborough. It was then readdressed to M[r] Fairbairn's, Cant Square, Carlisle. Letter 9 was postmarked Glasgow 31 Jul 1818 at 4:05. (The arrival time is not clear.)

Benjamin Bailey figured importantly in the circle of Keats's friends that included Rice and Reynolds. Keats and Bailey met through Reynolds in the spring of 1817, and their friendship ripened in the summer of that year. In the fall, Keats spent the month of September and part of October in Oxford sharing Bailey's college rooms at Magdalen Hall. While there Keats composed the third book of *Endymion*. The visit to Stratford-on-Avon alluded to in Letters 6 and 8 occurred during this period.

At the time of the walking tour Bailey was twenty-seven years old, had been ordained as an Anglican priest, and had just been given a curacy near Carlisle. In May and June, Bailey, disturbed by the Cockney School attacks, had written in Keats's defence in an Oxford newspaper. During the period of this letter, Bailey took a trip to Scotland to a point some thirty-five miles north of Edinburgh to visit Bishop Gleig, who was to become his father-in-law. There, in the Bishop's Chapel, he preached his maiden sermon. On this Scottish journey he talked with John Lockhart, one of the two vicious writers for *Blackwood's*, and tried to persuade him of Keats's worth.

[1] Tom had been sending Keats's letters to the Reynoldses, as Keats had requested. The first letter apparently prompted Reynolds to write to Keats to tell him that Bailey had received a curacy near Carlisle, in Cumberland. Keats would have stopped in Cumberland to see Bailey on his way back to London.
[2] The myth of Ceres and her daughter Proserpina (Persephone), who was carried off by Dis, god of the underworld, while picking flowers, is recounted by Milton in the fourth book of *Paradise Lost*:

> Not that fair field
> Of *Enna*, where *Proserpin* gath'ring flow'rs
> Herself a fairer Flow'r by gloomy *Dis*
> Was gather'd, which cost *Ceres* all that pain
> To seek her through the world. (ll. 268–272)

Letter 9

TO BENJAMIN BAILEY

[18, 22 July 1818]

Inverary July 18th

My dear Bailey,
The only day I have had a chance of seeing you when you were last in London I took every advantage of—some devil led you out of the way—Now I have written to Reynolds to tell me where you will be in Cumberland[1]—so that I cannot miss you—and when I see you the first thing I shall do will be to read that about Milton and Ceres and Proserpine[2]—for though I am not going after you to John o' Grotts[3] it will be but poetical to say so. And here Bailey I will say a few words written in a sane and sober Mind, a very scarce thing with me, for they may hereafter save you a great deal of trouble about me, which you do not deserve, and for which I ought to be bastinadoed. I carry all matters to an extreme—so that when I have any little vexation it grows in five Minutes into a theme for Sophocles—then and in that temper if I write to any friend I have so little selfpossession that I give him matter for grieving at the very time perhaps when I am laughing at a Pun. Your last Letter made me blush for the pain I had given you—I know my own disposition so well that I am certain of writing many times hereafter in the same strain to you—now you know how far to believe in them—you must allow for imagination—I know I shall not be able to help it. I am sorry you are grieved at my not continuing my visits to little Britain[4]—yet I think I have as far as a Man can do who has Books to read and subjects to think upon—for that reason I have been no where else except to Wentworth place[5] so nigh at hand—moreover I

[3] John o' Groats, at the northern extremity of Great Britain's mainland, was Keats's and Brown's destination. "Going to John o' Groats" was a popular metaphor for going to land's end. For those today who like to put a fine point on geographical matters, John o' Groats is not the northern*most* extremity of Scotland: Dunnets Head is. John o' Groats is named for a Dutch ferryman named John de Groot who settled there during the reign of James IV and built a curious eight-sided house with eight doors. One contemporary map lists the village as John o' Groats House.
[4] Little Britain was the street in London just north of St. Paul's Cathedral where the family of John Hamilton Reynolds lived. The street derives its name from the fact that the duke of Brittany had a house there. In the nineteenth century Little Britain was the center of the book publishing business. Readers of Dickens will remember that Mr. Jaggers, the lawyer in *Great Expectations*, had his offices on Little Britain.
[5] Wentworth Place was the house Dilke and

have been too often in a state of health that made me think it prudent not to hazard the night Air—Yet further I will confess to you that I cannot enjoy Society small or numerous—I am certain that our fair friends[6] are glad I should come for the mere sake of my coming; but I am certain I bring with me a Vexation they are better without—If I can possibly at any time feel my temper coming upon me I refrain even from a promised visit. I am certain I have not a right feeling towards Women—at this moment I am striving to be just to them but I cannot—Is it because they fall so far beneath my Boyish imagination? When I was a Schoolboy I thought a fair Woman a pure Goddess, my mind was a soft nest in which some one of them slept though she knew it not—I have no right to expect more than their reality. I thought them etherial above Men—I find them perhaps equal—great by comparison is very small—Insult may be inflicted in more ways than by Word or action—one who is tender of being insulted does not like to think an insult against another—I do not like to think insults in a Lady's Company—I commit a Crime with her which absence would have not known—Is it not extraordinary? When among Men I have no evil thoughts, no malice, no spleen—I feel free to speak or to be silent—I can listen and from every one I can learn—my hands are in my pockets I am free from all suspicion and comfortable. When I am among Women I have evil thoughts, malice spleen—I cannot speak or be silent—I am full of Suspicions and therefore listen to no thing—I am in a hurry to be gone—You must be charitable and put all this perversity to my being disappointed since Boyhood—Yet with such feelings I am happier alone among Crowds of men, by myself or with a friend or two—With all this trust me Bailey I have not the least idea that Men of different feelings and inclinations are more short sighted than myself—I never rejoiced more than at my Brother's Marriage and shall do so at that of any of my friends[7]—. I must absolutely get over this—but how? The only way is to find the root of evil, and so cure it "with backward mutters of dissevering Power."[8] That is a difficult thing; for an obstinate Prejudice can seldom be produced but from a gordian complication of feelings, which must take time to unravell and care to keep unravelled—I could say a good deal about this but I will leave it in hopes of better and more worthy dispositions—and also content that I am wronging no one, for after all I do think better of Womankind than to suppose they care whether Mister John Keats five feet hight likes them or not. You appear to wish to avoid any words on this subject—don't think it a bore my dear fellow—it shall be my Amen—

[6] Brown built and shared in Hampstead. It was roughly a quarter of a mile from Well Walk, where Keats and Tom lived, and the Keats brothers frequently visited the Dilkes and Brown. Wentworth Place became Keats's home less than a year later, when Brown invited him to move in after Tom's death. It is now (as "Keats House") a museum and library.
[6] Keats scholars concur that this refers to the Reynolds sisters: Jane, Marianne, Eliza, and Charlotte, all of whom were unmarried at the time of Keats's letter. Marianne had been the object of Bailey's attention. Indeed, he had proposed to her but been rejected by September 1818. Keats at this point must have been under the impression that Marianne and Bailey were engaged.

[7] Marriage was a sensitive topic for Keats that summer. It seemed to be either accomplished or forthcoming for everyone but himself. When Bailey married Hamilton Gleig on April 20, 1819, however, Keats did not rejoice: he wrote to his brother George (February 19, 1819) expressing disapproval. Bailey had scarcely been rejected by Marianne Reynolds before he committed himself (strategically) to the daughter of the bishop he'd met in Sterling, and Keats judged that "his so quickly taking to miss Gleig can have no excuse—except that of a Ploughmans who wants a wife—" (Letters, 2, 67).
[8] Keats quotes Milton's Comus. Milton, in turn, recalls both Ovid and Spenser in this image, which has to do with breaking a spell or enchantment by reciting a formula of words backward.

I should not have consented to myself these four Months[9] tramping in the highlands but that I thought it would give me more experience, rub off more Prejudice, use me to more hardship, identify finer scenes load me with grander Mountains, and strengthen more my reach in Poetry, than would stopping at home among Books even though I should reach Homer—By this time I am comparitively a mountaineer—I have been among wilds and Mountains too much to break out much about their Grandeur. I have fed upon Oat cake—not long enough to be very much attached to it—The first Mountains I saw, though not so large as some I have since seen, weighed very solemnly upon me. The effect is wearing away—yet I like them mainely—We have come this evening with a Guide, for without was impossible, into the middle of the Isle of Mull,[10] pursuing our cheap journey to Iona and perhaps staffa—We would not follow the common and fashionable mode[11] from the great imposition of expense. We have come over heath and rock and river and bog to what in England would be called a horrid place[12]—yet it belongs to a Shepherd pretty well off perhaps—The family speak not a word but gaelic and we have not yet seen their faces for the smoke which after visiting every cranny, (not

[9] Keats apparently anticipated that the entire walking tour, round-trip, would take four months, which would have brought him back to Hampstead in October.

[10] Keats and Brown made affordable arrangements after all, which paralleled the fashionable travelling route to Iona and Staffa by way of Mull. They ferried from the mainland at Gallanach, two miles south of Oban, to the Isle of Kerrera, walked across Kerrera, probably to Barr-nam-Boc Bay, and then crossed by boat to Mull, landing at an islet of the Firth of Lorne at either Grasspoint or, heading inward a little further, at Lochdonhead. (Bushnell is inclined to accept Lochdonhead; I, after three different visits to Mull in an attempt to recreate Keats's experience, opt for Grasspoint, for there has been since Bushnell's time some reconstruction of the old Drover's Inn at Grasspoint and along with it some exposure of local history to which Bushnell would not have had access.) The main structure of the Drover's Inn (also called the Old Ferry Inn) was built in the eighteenth century as a residence. In the nineteenth century it was used as an inn for cattlemen. Stepping ashore at Grasspoint Keats would have found himself only a few yards from the inn, and possibly some noisy guests. Lionel Leslie, an ex-Army officer, who with his wife, Barbara, began to renovate the inn in 1946, produced a book describing the structure and setting of the inn in terms that linked it quite satisfyingly, in my mind, to Keats's experience: "On the rim of the sea overlooking the jetty stood the house. It was a derelict [in 1945] with walls of undressed stone . . . and the slated roof torn off by the winter hurricanes. . . . A road led to it across the bog and over the brae, winding between great boulders, pebbles filling the ruts and grass sprouting in the centre. . . . But the house was still known as the Inn. Back in the last century in its heyday the cattle drovers— wild fellows who tramped the glens with their beasts, a bag of oatmeal strapped to their belts with a bottle of whisky to moisten it —used to wait here for the boats to carry them with their cattle to the mainland. Here they rested and sang their wild songs, punctuated by Gaelic oaths as strong as their liquor" (Drover's Inn).

The road, which came to be called the Drover's Road, was used in earlier times by pilgrims making their way to Iona. Leading toward Lochdonhead, and then across the island, the road is alternately known as the Pilgrim's Road. It was by way of the Drover's Road, I believe, that Keats, Brown, and the guide came to "the middle of the Isle of Mull," where they stayed in the shepherd's hut.

[11] The fashionable way to go would have been to sail from Oban to either Ach-na-craig (Achnacroish, near Craignure) or Aros, and then to hire a guide and ponies to see the island. Mrs. Murray's 1810 guide book tells us:

"I should not like to take the voyage from Oban to Aros in a small boat, (although many gentlemen do it,) particularly if it should be at spring tide: for then, when you get between the island of Lismore, and the point of Mull where Duart Castle stands, you will find the conflux of the currents, from almost every point, occasion great swells and agitations, not very pleasant, particularly should it be a blowing day.

"As the route from Oban to Aros is rather the oftenest taken, I will begin with that. It is a voyage of about nine leagues. A boat owner asked me a guinea to convey me from Oban to Aros" (Companion, 2, 32).

As for the route from Oban to Ach-na-craig: "That directly from Oban to Ach-na-craig, in a very good sailing boat, is six shillings, and you may, if you please, add a shilling for the boatmen to drink your health. The distance is about five leagues" (2, 32). Today the customary route is by ferry from Oban to Craignure, and once on the island, by bus to other destinations.

[12] The shepherd's hut Keats describes is typical. John Leyden in 1800 described living conditions that hadn't changed by 1818: "The huts of the peasants in Mull are most deplorable. Some of the doors are hardly four feet high, and the houses themselves, composed of earthen sods in many instances, are scarcely twelve. There is often no other outlet of smoke but at the door, the consequence of which is that the women are more squalid and dirty than the men, and their features more disagreeable" (Tour in the Highlands, 34–35).

excepting my eyes very much incommoded for writing), finds its way out at the door. I am more comfortable than I could have imagined in such a place, and so is Brown—The People are all very kind. We lost our way a little yesterday and enquiring at a Cottage, a young Woman without a word threw on her cloak and walked a Mile in a missling rain and splashy way to put us right again. I could not have had a greater pleasure in these parts than your mention of my Sister—She is very much prisoned from me[13]—I am affraid it will be some time before I can take her to many places I wish—I trust we shall see you ere long in Cumberland—at least I hope I shall before my visit to America more than once I intend to pass a whole year with George if I live to the completion of the three next[14]—My sisters well-fare and the hopes of such a stay in America will make me observe your advice—I shall be prudent and more careful of my health than I have been—I hope you will be about paying your first visit to Town after settling when we come into Cumberland—Cumberland however will be no distance to me after my present journey—I shall spin to you in a minute—I begin to get rather a contempt for distances. I hope you will have a nice convenient room for a Library. Now you are so well in health do keep it up by never missing your dinner, by not reading hard and by taking proper exercise. You'll have a horse I suppose so you must make a point of sweating him. You say I must study Dante—well the only Books I have with me are those three little Volumes.[15] I read that fine passage you mention a few days ago. Your Letter followed me from Hampstead to Port Patrick and thence to Glasgow—you must think me by this time a very pretty fellow—One of the pleasantest bouts we have had was our walk to Burns's Cottage, over the Doon and past Kirk Alloway—I had determined to write a Sonnet in the Cottage. I did but lauk it was so wretched I destroyed it—howev[r] in a few days afterwards I wrote some lines cousin-german to the Circumstance which I will transcribe or rather cross scribe in the front of this—Reynolds's illness has made him a new Man—he will be stronger than ever—before I left London he was really getting a fat face—Brown keeps on writing volumes of adventures to Dilke—when we get in of an evening and I have perhaps taken my rest on a couple of Chairs he affronts my indolence and Luxury by pulling out of his knapsack 1st his paper—2[ndy] his pens and last his ink—Now I would not care if he would change about a little—I say now, why not Bailey take out his pens first sometimes—But I might as well tell a hen to hold up her head before she drinks instead of afterwards—Your affectionate friend

John Keats—

[13] Fanny Keats, fifteen and in the guardianship of Richard Abbey. See Introduction: A Time to Travel.

[14] The conditional mode of this statement makes it tragically ironic, for Keats *did* live only three more years. What precognition he may have had of a foreshortened life is hard to fathom. More to the point, what sense he may have had at the time of writing this letter that his health had been jeopardized is disturbing to consider.

[15] Keats had told Bailey, in a letter to him on June 10, that "if I take any book with me it shall be those minute volumes of carey for they will go into the aptest corner." Taylor and Hessey had published Cary's translation of the *Divine Comedy* in 1814. The size, 32mo, made the three volumes eminently portable but, it seems to me, impossible to read in a smoke-filled shepherd's hut, or even by candlelight in a better place. As a matter of fact, Keats gives no evidence of reading or thinking about Dante in his letters and journal; Milton has been on his mind. He is perhaps only being polite in telling Bailey that Dante is the only reading material he took with him.

There is a joy in footing slow across a silent plain,
Where patriot battle has been fought, when glory had the gain;
There is a pleasure on the heath where Druids old have been,
Where mantles grey have rustled by and swept the nettles green:
There is a joy in every spot made known by times of old,
New to the feet, although the tale a hundred times be told:
There is a deeper joy than all, more solemn in the heart,
More parching to the tongue than all, of more divine a smart,
When weary feet forget themselves upon a pleasant turf,
Upon hot sand, or flinty road, or sea shore iron scurf,
Toward the castle or the cot where long ago was born
One who was great through mortal days and died of fame
   unshorn.
Light hether-bells may tremble then, but they are far away;
Woodlark may sing from sandy fern,—the sun may hear his lay;
Runnels may kiss the grass on shelves and shallows clear,
But their low voices are not heard, though come on travels drear;
Blood-red the sun may set behind black mountain peaks;
Blue tides may sluice and drench their time in caves and
   weedy creeks;
Eagles may seem to sleep wing-wide upon the air;
Ring doves may fly convuls'd across to some high cedar'd lair;
But the forgotten eye is still fast wedded to the ground—
As palmer's that with weariness mid-desert shrine hath found.
At such a time the soul's a child, in childhood is the brain;
Forgotten is the worldly heart—alone, it beats in vain.
Aye, if a madman could have leave to pass a healthful day,
To tell his forehead's swoon and faint when first began decay,
He might make tremble many a man whose spirit had gone forth
To find a bard's low cradle place about the silent north.
Scanty the hour and few the steps beyond the bourn of care,
Beyond the sweet and bitter world—beyond it unaware;
Scanty the hour and few the steps, because a longer stay
Would bar return and make a man forget his mortal way.
O horrible! to lose the sight of well remember'd face,
Of brother's eyes, of sister's brow, constant to every place;
Filling the air, as on we move, with portraiture intense,
More warm than those heroic tints that fill a painter's sense,
When shapes of old come striding by and visages of old,
Locks shining black, hair scanty grey, and passions manifold.
No, no, that horror cannot be—for at the cable's length

Man feels the gentle anchor pull and gladdens in its strength.
One hour, half ideot, he stands by mossy waterfall,
But in the very next he reads his soul's memorial:
He reads it on the mountain's height, where chance he may sit
    down
Upon rough marble diadem, that hill's eternal crown.
Yet be the anchor e'er so fast, room is there for a prayer
That man may never lose his mind on mountains bleak and bare;
That he may stray league after league some great birthplace
    to find,
And keep his vision clear from speck, his inward sight unblind.

The holograph manuscript for Letter 10 is in the Houghton Library at Harvard. It is addressed to Mr Thos Keats at Well Walk in Hampstead, Middlesex. Its Scottish postmark (GLASGOW 31 Jul 1818 4:05) suggests it was put in the same mail as Letter 9, to Bailey. Keats most likely saved both until he was on the mainland in Oban, from which point the mail was carried by horse or gig to Glasgow, where there was centralized postal service. The letter arrived at 10·00 A.M. August 3, with ½ pence due. Tom marked it received and answered on the same date.

Derry-na-Cullen (also spelled without the hyphens) translated from the Gaelic means "house under the waterfall." It was so well-built a house that Keats called it a mansion. In my own efforts to locate it I inquired among local residents and the term *mansion* triggered responses; it must have been referred to by that epithet down to the present. Learning its approximate location in Glen More and finding it were two entirely different matters. It took three attempts. Finally, without a guide but with the characteristic obstinacy that had taken me this far in the walking tour, I tromped through the quite desolate, damp glen and found the ruined house under the waterfall—though the waterfall proved to be somewhat in the distance. The fallen slate of the roof, which had probably come from nearby Luing Island, where slate has for a long time been the primary industry, and the exposed architectural design of the residence suggested that Derry-na-Cullen had been the residence of someone privileged on Mull—perhaps, I speculated, one of the clan of McLaen who were so well known in these parts. Keats and Brown would have felt indulged taking their breakfast here after the previous night in a smoke-filled shepherd's hut.

The site of the mansion is identified as Derrynaculen (no hyphens, and one "l") on a modern Bartholomew map. One can reach it, as I did, by following a combination of a perilous footpath, the flow of the Coladoir River, and personal instinct. It is about a mile and a quarter from a small inlet of Loch Scridain, which becomes Loch Beg where the Coladoir meets it at the midwestern end of Mull. Using automobile routes, it is slightly less than a mile and a quarter from the

Letter 10

TO TOM KEATS

[23, 26 July 1818]

Dun an cullen

My dear Tom,

Just after my last had gone to the Post in came one of the Men with whom we endeavoured to agree about going to Staffa—he said what a pitty it was we should turn aside and not see the Curiosities. So we had a little talk and finally agreed that he should be our guide across the Isle of Mull—We set out, crossed two ferries, one to the isle of Kerrara of little distance, the other from Kerrara to Mull 9 Miles across—we did it in forty minutes with a fine Breeze—The road through the Island, or rather the track is the most dreary you can think of—between dreary Mountains—over bog and rock and river with our Breeches tucked up and our Stockings in hand[1]—About eight o Clock we arrived at a shepherd's Hut into which we could scarcely get for the Smoke through a door lower than my shoulders—We found our way into a little compartment with the rafters and turf thatch blackened with smoke—the earth floor full of Hills and Dales—We had some white Bread with us, made a good Supper and slept in our clothes in some Blankets, our Guide snored on another little bed about an Arm's length off—This morning we came about six Miles to Breakfast by rather a better path and we are now in by comparison a Mansion—Our Guide is I think a very obliging fellow—in the way this morning he sang us two Gaelic songs—one made by a Mrs Brown on her husband's being drowned the other a jacobin one on Charles Stuart.

intersection of A849 and B8035. Derry-na-Cullen (or Derrynaculen) is less than half-way to Bunessan, where Keats and Brown caught a boat to Iona and Staffa.

[1] The pair took a winding, treacherous route that is now by and large the path of A849, the principal, and shortest, road across Mull for tourists heading toward Iona and Staffa. When Johnson journeyed to Mull in 1773, he and Boswell made their way in a more conventional manner for gentlemen travellers, trekking on ponies on the northern side of Mull. Johnson found the territory "a dreary country," and when Boswell begged to differ, Johnson added, "O, sir . . . a most dolorous country!" The trials of making their way across Mull were as real for Johnson, Boswell (with no bridle for his sheltie), and guide Joseph (with no saddle on his pony) as they were for Keats, Brown, and their nameless guide. Boswell recorded for October 16, 1773: "At one place, a loch having swelled over the road, we were obliged to plunge through pretty deep water. Dr. Johnson observed, how helpless a man would be, were he travelling here alone, and should meet with any accident" (*Boswell's Journal*, 309). What put Johnson particularly out of humour, however, was that he lost the large oak walking stick he had brought with him from London.

For some days Brown has been enquiring out his Genealogy here—he thinks his Grandfather came from long Island—he got a parcel of people about him at a Cottage door last Evening—chatted with ane who had been a Miss Brown and who I think from a likeness must have been a Relation—he jawed with the old Woman—flatterd a young one—kissed a child who was affraid of his Spectacles and finally drank a pint of Milk—They handle his Spectacles as we do a sensitive leaf—.

[From the mainland][2]

July 26th Well—we had a most wretched walk of 37 Miles across the Island of Mull and then we crossed to Iona or Icolmkill from Icolmkill we took a boat at a bargain to take us to Staffa and land us at the head of Loch Nakgal[3] whence we should only have to walk half the distance to Oban again and on a better road[4]—All this is well pass'd and done with this singular piece of Luck that there was an intermission in the bad Weather just as we saw Staffa at which it is impossible to land but in a tolerable Calm Sea[5]—But I will first mention Icolmkill[6]—I know

[2] Keats's whereabouts are difficult to pin down for most of the period after he left Derry-na-Cullen. He continued to walk to Bunessan, where he probably spent the night. From that point he either sailed to Iona (as apparently Mrs. Murray had done some some years earlier), or he continued his westward walk to Fionnphort, at the western extremity of Mull, and took a ferry the one mile to Iona. He and Brown would have remained on this small island just long enough to see the sights. Then, according to Brown: "We hired a Boat at Iona to take us to Staffa" (Letter 14). They would not have remained on Staffa more than a few hours, and Keats's mention of the head of Loch Na Keal (he wrote Loch Nakgal) gives a clue as to how the return to Mull ran: from Staffa past the island called Little Colonsay, along the southern coast of Ulva, into the Sound of Ulva to a port at Oskamull. From that point they would have been on a path to Salen (Aros), not far from Aros Castle. They would have been tired enough to want to spend the night in Salen. They very likely caught one of the fashionable ferries from Salen to Oban the next day, where, Keats told Tom, "it [is] best to stay a day or two." It is from Oban or nearby (accommodations were

expensive and few in the small city, which tended then, as it does today, to overflow with tourists in the summer months) that Keats wrote to Tom.
[3] Loch Na Keal, a large basin of the Atlantic reaching into Mull at its neck between the north and south of the island. In travel literature of the late eighteenth and early nineteenth centuries, the name occurs spelled with several slight variations.
[4] It is only about eight miles from Oskamull, now generally called Ulva Ferry, to Aros (or Salen), and these were well-worn miles.
[5] Nature has not changed. Where the weather is concerned, it is still a risky business to visit Staffa. Approaching it with a budget mentality, just as Keats and Brown had, I made arrangements through a private service on Mull known to my bed and breakfast hostess and was told that I should appear at Ulva Ferry at 8:00 A.M., and if enough people subscribed that day we would head out. There was a handful of us, just enough to fill a very small motor boat with a pilot and an all-purpose mate. We were given yellow slickers to protect against the drenching spray, a photographer's nightmare. The waves around the island were high and foamy. Not a word of

tourist information passed our captain's lips, and we were deposited most unceremoniously on what he construed to be a landing, warned to be cautious on the island, and told to be back at the landing (if we could recognize it) for departure on time, without fail! The warning had to do with a palpable reality: when the tides changed, the trip back to Mull in a small vessel would be dangerous, if not impossible.
[6] Keats's lengthy description of Iona, or Icolmkill, betrays no irritation with what must certainly have annoyed him: this sacred island was now a fashionable tourist attraction. His detailed account to Tom contains a vast amount of information, rather fortunately gleaned from either the well-informed (albeit short!) local school teacher or some guide book, of which there would have been many.

To flesh out and update all of Keats's notes on Iona would be to digress into another book. But pausing at the Nunnery is a tradition worth honouring here. It was built before 1200 and occupied by Benedictine nuns, the original twelve of whom were the daughters of Highland chiefs. The women from the island and nearby were buried in the Nunnery, and the reason for this practice presented Mrs. Murray, our early nineteenth-century tour guide, with the problem of putting down an unfortunate story about Saint Columba: he did not like women and isolated them even in burial. Mrs. Murray explains to her readers: "It is reported, and written too, that the holy Saint had an aversion to women; I will endeavour to clear his reputation on that subject and vindicate the honour of the female sex by a query. If the females had been all banished from I-Ona, why did Saint Columba erect a beautiful edifice, called the nunnery? . . . Besides, if in process of time a great town rose at the very gates of the monastery, how could that town be peopled without women?" (Companion, 2, 216–217).

Her argument would not go far with a modern feminist, for she tries to polish the saint's record by claiming that he banished women to the island called Nun's Island (Eilean Nam Bar in Gaelic) because "during the time the foreign colony of holymen were erecting the buildings" there was concern "lest their [the women's] charms and allurements should, by rendering the men less industrious, impede the great work." The women hadn't been banished for life but only during the duration of the construction, she supposed, or perhaps more correctly, hoped, for she adds that having seen the Island of Women, "I lament the horrible state the poor females must have been in" (2, 217).

Mrs. Murray's claim for the Nunnery was probably a reaction to her predecessor, Pennant, who used Saint Columba's alleged distaste for women to make the opposite argument: "This nunnery could not have been founded (as some assert) in the days of Saint Columba, who was no admirer of the fair sex; in fact he held them in such abhorrence, that he detested all cattle on their account, and would not permit a cow to come within sight of the sacred walls; because . . . 'Where there is a cow, there must be a woman; and where there is a woman, there must be mischief'" (*Pennant's Second Tour*, 296).

Pennant noticed cows in and about the Nunnery when he visited, as did Boswell and Johnson in 1773, who remarked that the cows had made their home there. The irony of their bovine presence would have struck all three men. Keats does not mention cows in his letter, but he would certainly have heard of Saint Columba's rumoured aversion to women.

The duke of Argyll made a gift of the ruins of the Nunnery to the Church of Scotland in 1899, and they were partly restored in 1923. Today the grounds, and indeed all of the sacred grounds of Iona, are maintained by the Iona Cathedral Trust, called on the island the Iona Community.

[7] In Keats's time and until 1842, there was a wide path paved with large red stones leading from the Nunnery to the Abbey of Iona. The path was buried to make a more passable road (for the growing number of tourists no doubt), but the Iona Community opened up a section of the old stone road, called the Street of the Dead, in 1962 (see photo). John Mackenzie Semple, of the Iona Community, gives its history: "In ancient and mediaeval times, between the Nunnery and the Abbey, there was a town named Sodora, and its main street was called the 'Street of the Dead' because along it passed, in those days, the great funeral processions of the early Kings, of the Lords of the Isles, and of the local Chiefs (MacLeans,

not whether you have heard much about this Island, I never did before I came nigh it. It is rich in the most interesting Antiquities. Who would expect to find the ruins of a fine Cathedral Church, of Cloisters, Colleges, Monastaries and Nunneries in so remote an Island? The Beginning of these things was in the sixth Century under the superstition of a would-be Bishop-saint who landed from Ireland and chose the spot from its Beauty—for at that time the now treeless place was covered with magnificent Woods. Columba in the Gaelic is Colm signifying Dove—Kill signifies church and I is as good as Island—so I-colm-kill means the Island of Saint Columba's Church—Now this Saint Columba became the Dominic of the barbarian Christians of the north and was famed also far south—but more especially was reverenced by the Scots the Picts the Norwegians the Irish. In a course of years perhaps the Iland was considered the most holy ground of the north, and the old kings of the afore mentioned nations chose it for their burial place[7]—We were shown a spot in the Churchyard where they say 61 kings are buried 48 Scotch from Fergus 2nd to Macbeth[8] 8 Irish 4 Norwegian and 1 french—they lie in rows compact—Then we were shown other matters of later date but still very ancient—many tombs of Highland Chieftains—their effigies in complete armour face upwards[9]—black and moss covered—Abbots and Bishops of the island always of one of the chief Clans—There were plenty Macleans and Macdonnels, among these latter the famous Macdonel Lord of the Isles—There have been 300 Crosses in the Island but the Presbyterains destroyed all but two, one of which[10] is a very fine one and completely covered with a shaggy coarse Moss—The old Schoolmaster an ignorant little man but reckoned very clever, showed us these things—He is a Macklean and as much above 4 foot as he is under 4 foot 3 inches—he stops at one glass of whiskey unless you press another and at the second unless you press a third. I am puzzled

MacKinnons, and MacQuarries). The funerals proceeded from the Mound of Lamentation on Martyrs' Bay, up past the Nunnery's west wall, and on to the Abbey—priests and monks, bodyguard and banner, harpers and pipes, a host of kinsmen and the heir, escorting the body exposed on its bier" (*Nunnery and Tombs of the Kings*, 4).

[8] Both Duncan, whom Macbeth murdered, and Macbeth were buried here, in 1040 and 1057, respectively.

[9] I wondered why I was not as impressed as Keats had been by the sacred cemetery where

all the kings had been buried face upward when I visited on August 2, 1979. The kings were missing! I soon discovered that all the stones had been moved to what the local people called a museum but was really a dark, cool room in the Abbey which they named "museum."

[10] If it was not the one I photographed, St. John's (see photo), it was one much like it. St. John's Cross was restored from fragments in 1926. St. Martin's Cross is probably the second of the two not destroyed when Keats visited.

how to give you an Idea of Staffa.[11] It can only be represented by a first rate drawing[12]—One may compare the surface of the Island to a roof—this roof is supported by grand pillars of basalt[13] standing together as thick as honey combs. The finest thing is Fingal's Cave[14]—it is entirely a hollowing out of Basalt Pillars. Suppose now the Giants who rebelled against Jove had taken a whole Mass of black Columns and bound them together like bunches of matches—and then with immense Axes had made a cavern in the body of these columns—of course the roof and floor must be composed of the broken ends of the Columns—such is fingal's Cave except that the Sea has done the work of excavations and is continually dashing there—so that we walk along the sides of the cave on the pillars which are left as if for convenient Stairs—the roof is arched somewhat gothic wise and the length of some of the entire side pillars is 50 feet—About the island you might seat an army of Men each on a pillar—The length of the Cave is 120 feet and from its extremity the view into the sea through the large Arch at the entrance—the colour of the columns is a sort of black with a lurking gloom of purple therin—For solemnity and grandeur it far surpasses the finest Cathedrall—At the extremity of the Cave there is a small perforation into another cave, at which the waters meeting and buffetting each other there is sometimes produced a report[15] as of a cannon heard as far as Iona which must be 12 Miles—As we approached in the boat there was such a fine swell of the sea that the pillars appeared rising immediately out of the crystal—But it is impossible to describe it[16]—

[11] Visitors to the island from the latter part of the eighteenth century on almost always gave an idea of Staffa by reporting its measurements and geological makeup, and they never failed to comment on the hazards of approaching the island. Faujas St. Fond, a professor of geology at the museum of natural history in Paris, visited Staffa in 1784 and measured Fingal's Cave in what he regarded as exact dimensions: the breadth at the entrance, the height from sea level, and so on (*Travels*, 61). His figures do not correspond to Keats's or to those of contemporary travel pamphlets, but they seem to have started the trend of scientific precision in commentaries on Fingal's Cave. Mrs. Murray writes about Staffa extensively, reminding us that in 1800 she was only the ninth woman ever to visit and emphasizing that the others had travelled more luxuriously than she. Pennant, she says, did much to invite attention to Staffa, which had before 1770 been consciously avoided, though he, like Dr. Johnson, never actually set foot on the island. Staffa was first noticed as a significant geological phenomenon by Sir Joseph Banks, an explorer on his way to Iceland in 1772. Keats is exceptional among early travellers in writing about the island metaphorically.

[12] Staffa had been represented in guide books by drawings done by Sir Joseph Banks (or his draftsmen).

[13] The surface of Staffa is indeed quite flat and roof-like (see photo). An aesthetic and structural question in Mrs. Murray's time was whether the surface was too heavy for the supporting pillars. "Some visitors to Staffa have thought its crown, in appearance, too heavy for its supporters; so do the commonality of the isles; who allege that the weight of Staffa's head is too heavy for its legs, having bent them on the east side of Fingal's Cave" (*Companion*, 2, 168).

[14] Far and away the most dazzling attraction on Staffa is a cave hollowed out by the sea and formed by basalt pillars. It is a high, deep, vaulted cavern: the Staffa marine literature gives the dimensions as 230 feet deep, 60 feet high (above water level), and 50 feet wide (at the entrance). The pillars, like the ones of the Giant's Causeway in Ireland (which Keats and Brown never reached), were formed by the slow cooling of lava after volcanic eruptions. The cave is named for the Celtic warrior-chief Fingal, father of the bard Ossian, whose poems were made famous by James Macpherson. The hills of Morven and all the area near Staffa were filled with Ossianic lore, and Keats could not have failed to be conscious that in Fingal's Cave he stood within the gigantic influence of a poet's father. The story he weaves for Tom about Jove and the Giants is on a scale with Fingal's "history."

[15] Keats's appreciation of the hardness rather than the melodiousness of the sound of the water buffeting and echoing is unusual. Early travellers always wrote about the music to be heard in Fingal's Cave. Leyden writes: "The Cave of Fingal, termed in Gaelic An-ua-vine, or *the melodious cave*, is grand almost beyond imagination" (*Tour in the Highlands*, 40). And no travel literature after the nineteenth century fails to tell us that Mendelssohn, who visited Staffa in 1829, heard the first bars of his Hebrides Overture in Fingal's Cave.

[16] Rather than attempt to describe the cave Keats writes a poem, a fragment, according to Brown ("I never could induce him to finish"). Concerned with the "cathedral of the sea," the poem grows out of the Staffa experience, with perhaps a reference to the Iona visit as well ("St. John in Patmos' isle" associates Saint Columba with the cross of Saint John on Iona). Throughout, Christian and classical figures and beliefs are conjoined, just as people in the Hebrides fuse Christian and Celtic history. The last lines decry the transgression of fashionable tourists on the setting of the cave/cathedral.

[17] The Dee is a river in Scotland that runs through Kirkcudbright, which Keats had visited, as well as Edinburgh and Wales. Thomas Telford created an amazing aqueduct over it in 1805, and Telford, whose reputation was particularly brilliant in northern Scotland in connection with his Caledonian Canal, a major engineering feat under construction in 1818, may be meant for the Wizard of the Dee, who could never have dreamed of such a structure as Fingal's Cave.

[18] The subject of Milton's pastoral monody. Milton's poem celebrates Edward King (Lycidas), a friend and Fellow of Christ College, Cambridge, drowned in a shipwreck on August 10, 1637. Keats was probably remembering especially the lines:

> Ay me! Whilst thee the shores, and
>   sounding Seas
> Wash far away, wher'er thy bones are
>   hurl'd
> Whether beyond the stormy *Hebrides*,
> Where thou perhaps under the whelming
>   tide
> Visit'st the bottom of the monstrous world;
> Or whether thou to our moist vows denied,
> Sleep'st by the fable of *Bellerus* old,
> Where the great vision of the guarded
>   Mount
> Looks toward *Namancos* and *Bayona's* hold;
> Look homeward Angel now, and melt with
>   ruth:
> And, O ye *Dolphins*, waft the hapless
>   youth.   (ll. 154–164)

Milton's poem, like Keats's, combines Christian and classical imagery.

Not Aladdin magian
Ever such a work began;
Not the Wizard of the Dee[17]
Ever such a dream could see;
Not St. John in Patmos' isle,
In the passion of his toil,
When he saw the churches seven,
Golden aisled, built up in heaven,
Gazed at such a rugged wonder.
As I stood its roofing under,
Lo! I saw one sleeping there
On the marble cold and bare,
While the surges washed his feet
And his garments white did beat
Drench'd about the sombre rocks;
On his neck his well-grown locks,
Lifted dry above the main,
Were upon the curl again.
"What is this and what art thou?"
Whisper'd I and touched his brow.
"What art thou and what is this?"
Whisper'd I and strove to kiss
The spirit's hand to wake his eyes.
Up he started in a trice.
"I am Lycidas,"[18] said he,
"Fam'd in funeral minstrelsy.
This was architected thus
By the great Oceanus;
Here his mighty waters play
Hollow organs all the day;
Here by turns his dolphins all,
Finny palmers great and small,
Come to pay devotion due—
Each a mouth of pearls must strew.
Many a mortal of these days
Dares to pass our sacred ways,
Dares to touch audaciously
This cathedral of the sea.
I have been the pontif priest
Where the waters never rest,
Where a fledgy sea bird choir

Soars for ever; holy fire
I have hid from mortal man;
Proteus[19] is my sacristan.
But the stupid eye of mortal
Hath pass'd beyond the rocky portal;
So for ever will I leave
Such a taint, and soon unweave
All the magic of the place.
'Tis now free to stupid face,
To cutters and to fashion boats,
To cravats and to petticoats.
The great sea shall war it down,
For its fame shall not be blown
At every farthing quadrille dance."
So saying with a spirit's glance
He dived—

I am sorry I am so indolent as to write such stuff as this—it cant be help'd—The western coast of Scotland is a most strange place—it is composed of rocks Mountains, mountainous and rocky Islands intersected by Lochs—you can go but a small distance any where from salt water in the highlands.

I have a slight sore throat[20] and think it best to stay a day or two at Oban.[21] Then we shall proceed to Fort William and Inverness— Where I am anxious to be on account of a Letter from you—Brown in his Letters puts down every little circumstance I should like to do the same but I confess myself too indolent and besides next winter every thing will come up in prime order as we verge on such and such things. Have you heard in any way of George? I should think by this time he must have landed—I in my carelessness never thought of knowing where a letter would find him on the other side—I think Baltimore but I am affraid of directing to the wrong place—I shall begin some chequer work for him directly and it will be ripe for the post by the time I hear from you next after this—I assure you I often long for a seat and a Cup o' tea at well Walk—especially now that mountains, castles and Lakes are becoming common to me—yet I would rather summer it out for on the whole I am happier than when I have time to be glum—perhaps it may cure me—Immediately on my return I shall begin studying hard with a peep at the theatre now and then—and depend upon it I shall be very luxurious—With respect to Women I think I shall be able to conquer my passions hereafter better than I

[19] A sea god who could change his shape at will, Proteus was a prophet who lived in an enormous cave. He was Neptune's herdsman.

[20] Keats minimizes the severity of his illness for Tom's sake. This is the sore throat from which he was never fully to recover, however.
[21] Where Keats stayed and indeed how long is not known. The town of Oban is small. At the peak of the tourist season, from Mrs. Murray's time (she found the inn full and had to locate private accommodation) to mine (the situation was so hopeless I ended up sleeping in the back seat of my small car), visitors can only find rooms at the highest expense. Keats and Brown may have rested at the little old inn that still stands on the north side of the harbour on George Street.

have yet done—You will help me to talk of george next winter and we will go now and then to see Fanny—Let me hear a good account of your health and comfort telling me truly how you do alone—

Remember me to all including M^r and Mrs Bentley—

Your most affectionate Brother
John—

Letter 11

TO TOM KEATS

[3, 6 August 1818]

Letter Findlay August 3rd

My dear Tom,   Ah mio Ben.

We have made but poor progress Lately,[1] chiefly from bad weather for my throat is in a fair way of getting quite well, so I have had nothing of consequence to tell you till yesterday when we went up Ben Nevis, the highest Mountain in Great Britain—On that account I will never ascend another in this empire—Skiddaw is no thing to it either in height or in difficulty. It is above 4300 feet from the Sea level[2] and Fortwilliam stands at the head of a Salt water Lake,[3] consequently we took it completely from that level. I am heartily glad it is done—it is almost like a fly crawling up a wainscoat—Imagine the task of mounting 10 Saint Paul's without the convenience of Stair cases. We

The holograph manuscript for Letter 11 is in the Houghton Library at Harvard. It is addressed to Mr Thos Keats at Well Walk, Hampstead, Middlesex, and marked Single. It was postmarked Inverness, 6 Aug 1818, 6:37 Evening, and then marked Too Late, apparently for the mail coach to Edinburgh. It might have taken the postal route by foot post or horse post down the side of Loch Ness to Oban, Inverary, Dumbarton, and Glasgow. In any case, it arrived the morning of August 12, with a half pence due.

The tiny hamlet of Letterfinlay some fifteen or sixteen miles north of Fort William near Laggan at the north end of Loch Lochy is no longer mentioned on maps. There was in Keats's time an inn, cited by both Stoddart and Mrs. Murray, called Letter Findlay (with a "d"). Stoddart speaks of it as "a poor inn, which serves as a stage-house between Forts William and Augustus" (*Remarks*, 60). Mrs. Murray found the inn and its location much more charming: "The road again mounts a shelf hanging over the lake, and at about the mid-way of it I found Letter Findlay inn, close on the edge of the lake, screened at the back by high mountains, and very much shaded by wood. At the door of the inn is a small green patch, bordered by birch and alders; rushes, bushes, and shrubs creeping down to the water. On this fairy green I had the chaise turned that I might face the grand scenery of the lake" (*Companion*, 1, 277). When Southey and his touring companion Thomas Telford stopped there in 1819, Southey, whose standards were those of an English country gentleman, complained: "Halted at Letter-Findlay, a single house, which is said to have been much improved of late; it is not easy to believe that it can ever have been dirtier or more uncomfortable than it is now: however, we made a good fire, and got biscuits, cheese, milk and whiskey" (*Journal of a Tour*, 201).

When I visited, Letterfinlay had lost the "d" and was located virtually on the highway, which itself was on the line of General Wade's military road. The house which had been the inn was so close to the water that I risked falling into the lake to photograph it. Loch Lochy widened after dams and locks had been built as part of the Caledonian Canal project. There was an old oak tree on the water which could never be cut down because it is so deeply rooted. In fact, it is so well anchored that during World War I, when Loch Lochy was a testing area for submarines, the tree was used for mooring them. James McKerracher, for whom the old inn is now a private residence, filled me in on a bit more of the history, somewhat hastily, because he was headed off to shop for groceries when I stopped him. Mr. McKerracher's late wife's mother had been born in that house, and was the third generation to call it home. According to stories passed down to McKerracher, Keats had stopped there more than once (an idea I couldn't reconcile with any of the data of Keats's letters or Bushnell's reconstruction of the walking tour). Bonnie Prince Charlie, he said, had also stayed at the inn, hiding in a cellar where illegal wine and whiskey were made. Mrs. Murray wrote about Prince Charles Stuart's skulking in the neighbourhood after the Battle of Culloden. A Donald Cameron of Glenpean escorted him to shelter. The tales of Prince Charles abound even today in this area. It is curious that Keats makes no mention of the local tales when he writes from Letterfinlay. He does, however, invoke the Cameron name in his comic poem about Ben Nevis.

[1] They had walked 52½ miles from Oban to Fort William, crossing the Lynn of Lorne at Connel, passing through part of the Balcardine Forest area, travelling along Loch Linnhe, ferrying at Ballachulish, going through Glenrigh Forest along the narrow portion of Linnhe, until they reached Fort William. The pair stayed there, or nearby, at an unknown resting place, in order to climb Ben Nevis. Then they walked to Spaen Bridge, called in Keats's time High Bridge, built by General Wade in 1736. (In ruins today, it is remembered because the first shots of the 1745 Jacobite uprising were fired here.) Mrs. Murray complains: "The eight miles from High Bridge to Fort William, is the most dreary, though not the ugliest, space I had travelled in Scotland" (*Companion*, 1, 283–284). It was another 15½ miles through a forested area back along Loch Linnhe to Letterfinlay. As to the dates, Bushnell's reckoning (see Itinerary) seems altogether sound, though, of course, unverifiable.
[2] Figures differ: 4,370 in Leyden, Stoddart, and Mrs. Murray; from 4,406 to 4,418 in modern maps and guide books.
[3] Loch Linnhe, which opens into the Atlantic. It was the focus of much interest because it figured critically in the construction of the Caledonian Canal.

203

set out about five in the morning with a Guide in the Tartan and Cap and soon arrived at the foot of the first ascent which we immediately began upon—after much fag and tug and a rest and a glass of whiskey apiece we gained the top of the first rise and saw then a tremendous chap above us which the guide said was still far from the top—After the first Rise our way lay along a heath valley in which there was a Loch—after about a Mile in this Valley we began upon the next ascent more formidable by far than the last and kept mounting with short intervals of rest untill we got above all vegetation, among nothing but loose Stones which lasted us to the very top—the Guide said we had three Miles of a stony ascent[4]—we gained the first tolerable level after the valley to the height of what in the Valley we had thought the top and saw still above us another huge crag which still the Guide said was not the top—to that we made with an obstinate fag and having gained it there came on a Mist, so that from that part to the verry top we walked in a Mist.[5] The whole immense head of the Mountain is composed of large loose stones[6]—thousands of acres—Before we had got half way up we passed large patches of snow and near the top there is a chasm some hundred feet deep completely glutted with it— Talking of chasms[7] they are the finest wonder of the whole—they appear great rents in the very heart of the mountain though they are not, being at the side of it, but other huge crags arising round it give the appearance to Nevis of a shattered heart or Core in itself—These Chasms are 1500 feet in depth and are the most tremendous places I have ever seen—they turn one giddy if you choose to give way to it—We tumbled in large stones and set the echoes at work in fine style. Sometimes these chasms are tolerably clear, sometimes there is a misty cloud which seems to steam up and sometimes they are entirely smothered with clouds—

After a little time the Mist cleared away but still there were large Clouds about attracted by old Ben to a certain distance so as to form as it appeard large dome curtains which kept sailing about, opening and shutting at intervals here and there and everrywhere; so that although we did not see one vast wide extent of prospect all round we saw something perhaps finer—these cloud-veils opening with a dissolving motion and showing us the mountainous region beneath as through a loop hole—these Mouldy loop holes ever varrying and discovering fresh prospect east, west north and South—Then it was misty again and again it was fair—then puff came a cold breeze of wind and bared a craggy chap we had not yet seen though in close neighbourhood— Every now and then we had over head blue Sky clear and the sun

[4] Those early travellers who ventured to the top of Ben Nevis ("There are but few who attain so high a station, it being a very laborious journey to climb that mountain to the top," says Mrs. Murray, *Companion*, 1, 292) never fail to mention the stony ascent. Leyden (who *did* make it) told of finding "nothing but yellow moss and gray stones, which occupied the whole side of the mountain and rendered it exceedingly difficult to advance" (*Tour in the Highlands*, 184).

[5] The mist Keats speaks of was one I came to know well. Through all of my own climb I was in a mist, sometimes a very heavy one. The visibility was for me, as it had been for Bushnell, no more than a hundred yards at best. Higher up, on a rocky path, I was usually upright, and it was eerie to look into deep chasms and see only fog, or, worse, to hear pounding water and a rushing stream but not to see the waterfall.

[6] Leyden noted: "The top of the mountain is of considerable extent, and entirely covered with loose stones, chiefly granitine" (*Tour in the Highlands*, 186). Mrs. Murray had heard that at the top "is a bed of white pebbles, some of them beautiful" (*Companion*, 1, 291– 292). In this instance her lack of firsthand experience left her guidebook material a little short of authenticity.

[7] Leydon notes the chasms, as well as the snow in them, but not with as much enthusiasm as Keats, who seems genuinely pleased with himself for tackling the climb when other inveterate travellers (like Stoddart and Murray) had or could not.

pretty warm. I do not know whether I can give you an Idea of the prospect[8] from a large Mountain top—You are on a stony plain which of course makes you forget you are on any but low ground—the horison or rather edges of this plain being above 4000 feet above the Sea hide all the Country immediately beneath you, so that the next objects you see all round next to the edges of the flat top are the Summits of Mountains of some distance off—as you move about on all sides you see more or less of the near neighbour country according as the Mountain you stand upon is in different parts steep or rounded—but the most new thing of all is the sudden leap of the eye from the extremity of what appears a plain into so vast a distance. On one part of the top there is a handsome pile of stones done pointedly by some soldiers of artillery,[9] I climed onto them and so got a little higher than old Ben himself. It was not so cold as I expected—yet cold enough for a glass of Wiskey now and then—There is not a more fickle thing than the top of a Mountain—what would a Lady give to change her head-dress as often and with as little trouble!—There are a good many red deer upon Ben Nevis we did not see one—the dog we had with us kept a very sharp look out and really languished for a bit of a worry—I have said nothing yet of our getting on among the loose stones large and small sometimes on two sometimes on three, sometimes four legs—sometimes two and stick, sometimes three and stick, then four again, then two, then a jump, so that we kept on ringing changes on foot, hand, Stick, jump boggle, stumble, foot, hand, foot, (very gingerly) stick again, and then again a game at all fours.[10] After all there was one M[rs] Cameron[11] of 50 years of age and the fattest woman in all

15th August 1957."

I wondered what soldiers of artillery had erected the mound Keats found. General Wade had no business at the top of this mountain; he was too busy with roads. The uprisings of 1715 and 1745 had already been commemorated in many other places in the area. Perhaps the Highlanders who had died in the Battle of Waterloo had been remembered here, as they were in Kincraig, with a cairn. Bushnell, once a military man himself, gave me no help in this matter. When he reached the top of Ben Nevis in 1931, he found the ruins of both an observatory and an inn. Who erected Keats's mound and why remains among several walking tour mysteries for me.

[10] I too was reduced to an embarrassing, infantile posture as I climbed Ben Nevis. The first stretch of the ascent was very discouraging. The path was muddy, and if I advanced five feet I would fall back two, finally resorting to locomotion on all fours. Just as I was ready to give up, I encountered some children, quite upright, who told me I'd taken the harder route.

[11] Two points should be made here about the Mrs. Cameron story, which has no foundation in fact that I can discover. First, the name *Cameron* is an ancient Highlands clan name; indeed, the old burial ground of the Camerons of Glen Nevis lies below the mountain in what is called the Old Graveyard. The name figures prominently in the travel literature of Keats's time about this area. Stoddart writes about calling upon a Captain Cameron, "the proprietor of this estate," to take him about the glen. Leyden returned from the top of Ben Nevis with Camerons. "The gentlemen whom I returned with were Camerons of Glen Nevis, his brother, and cousin, Captain Cameron (*Tour in the Highlands*, 188). Second, no one who accomplishes the Ben Nevis climb (six miles up, six miles down) comes away without an anecdote to tell, usually at the expense of someone who had a hard time making it. Leyden, for example, tells of a Mr. Grant, who made it up the hill long after the others, "almost exhausted," and began the descent with help from the others and the local bottled cure: "He plied the whiskey bottle with considerable alacrity, but notwithstanding, he found the descent more perilous and difficult

[8] Keats must have been uncommonly lucky in the weather. He had good views, saw blue sky, observed changes of cloud formations, and grasped the prospect well enough to try to describe it to Tom. I had not the same fortune. There's a saying among the climbers: "The sun shines here every summer." You ask, *When* in the summer?" The climbers tell you, "Last Wednesday!" The word is also (and more seriously) that the sun shines five days out of the year up here, but when it does, you can see all the way to the Isle of Skye.

[9] To my enormous satisfaction I found at the top of Ben Nevis some small mounds of rocks, and one large one. One mound was a memorial to World War II dead, with a red wreath atop it. There were several plaques on it, most of them peace plaques from youth groups (scouts, etc.) from all over the world. One must have come much later than 1945, for it was from a Japanese scout group.

Later in the evening, after I'd rested, I returned to the mouth of Glen Nevis below the mountain and found a plaque which explained the mound at the top:

"The war memorial cairn at the summit of Ben Nevis was originally built by young men from Dudley (Worcs.), on V.J. Day, 15th August 1945. It was rebuilt 7th July 1957 by young men of Fort William under the leadership of Clifford T. C. Beacham. Fort William and Dudley have united in this remembrance of the Glorious dead. At the going down of the sun and in the morning we will remember them. This latest unveiled by Provost M.I.D. Murphie M.A. on Thursday

than the ascent." Grant's group stopped to drink at a well, and "here Mr. Grant's courage entirely failed; and he protested that he would move no further, exclaiming that it was utterly impossible to conceive what could have induced him to ascend Ben Nevis had he not been entirely forsaken by Providence, and imprecating every curse on his head if he was ever again found on this mountain." Leyden and Captain Cameron offered to "whisk him to the bottom, but he assured us he preferred being on his *own parole*" (188–189). Even those who don't make it, like Mrs. Murray, have a tale to tell: "I learnt . . . another instance of the great love a Highland man has for whisky. A lady of fashion, having conquered that ascent, before she quitted it, left on purpose a bottle of whisky on the summit: when she returned to the fort, she laughingly mentioned that circumstance before some Highland men, as a piece of carelessness; one of whom slipped away, and mounted to the pinnacle of 4370 feet, above the level of the fort, to gain the prize of the bottle of whisky, and brought it down in triumph" (*Companion*, 1, 292).

inverness shire who got up this Mountain some few years ago—true she had her servants but then she had her self—She ought to have hired Sysiphus—"Up the high hill he heaves a huge round—Mrs Cameron." 'T is said a little conversation took place between the mountain and the Lady—After taking a glass of Wiskey as she was tolerably seated at ease she thus begun—

M^rs C——

Upon my life, Sir Nevis, I am piqu'd
That I have so far panted, tugg'd, and reek'd
To do an honor to your old bald pate
And now am sitting on you just to bate,
Without your paying me one compliment.
Alas, 'tis so with all, when our intent
Is plain, and in the eye of all mankind
We fair ones show a preference, too blind!
You gentlemen immediately turn tail—
O let me then my hapless fate bewail!
Ungrateful baldpate, have I not disdain'd
The pleasant valleys—have I not, mad brain'd,
Deserted all my pickles and preserves,
My china closet too—with wretched nerves
To boot—say, wretched ingrate, have I not
Left my soft cushion chair and caudle pot?
'Tis true I had no corns—no! thank the fates,
My shoemaker was always Mr. Bates.
And if not Mr. Bates, why I'm not old!
Still dumb, ungrateful Nevis—still so cold!

(Here the lady took some more wiskey and was putting even more to her lips when she dashed it to the ground, for the mountain began to grumble which continued for a few minutes before he thus began,)

BEN NEVIS

What whining bit of tongue and mouth thus dares
Disturb my slumber of a thousand years?
Even so long my sleep has been secure,
And to be so awaked I'll not endure.
Oh pain—for since the eagle's earliest scream

I've had a damn'd confounded ugly dream,
A nightmare sure—What, madam, was it you?
It cannot be! My old eyes are not true!
Red-Crag,* my spectacles! Now let me see!
Good heavens, lady, how the gemini
Did you get here? O I shall split my sides!
I shall earthquake——

MRS. C——

Sweet Nevis, do not quake, for though I love
Your honest countenance all things above,
Truly I should not like to be convey'd
So far into your bosom—gentle maid
Loves not too rough a treatment, gentle sir;
Pray thee be calm and do not quake nor stir,
No, not a stone, or I shall go in fits—

BEN NEVIS

I must—I shall—I meet not such tit bits,
I meet not such sweet creatures every day.
By my old night cap, night cap night and day,
I must have one sweet buss—I must and shall!
Red-Crag!—What, madam, can you then repent
Of all the toil and vigour you have spent
To see Ben Nevis and to touch his nose?
Red-Crag, I say! O I must have you close!
Red-Crag, there lies beneath my farthest toe
A vein of sulphur—go, dear Red-Crag, go—
And rub your flinty back against it—budge!
Dear madam, I must kiss you, faith I must!
I must embrace you with my dearest gust!
Blockhead,* d'ye hear—Blockhead, I'll make her feel.
There lies beneath my east leg's northern heel
A cave of young earth dragons—well, my boy,
Go thither quick and so complete my joy.
Take you a bundle of the largest pines,
And where the sun on fiercest phosphor shines
Fire them and ram them in the dragon's nest;

* A domestic of Ben's.
* Another domestic of Ben's.

[12] Bushnell, hearty though he was, "slid over the six miles down the mountain on my heels all the way; and whoever the god of pedestrians is, he alone saved my shoes and feet from being cut to pieces" (*Walk*, 243). As for myself, an urban woman with a backpack filled with camera equipment, the descent was part magical, part frightening. The temperature dropped suddenly, and the mist got very heavy. My eyelashes were leaded with white drops, and on my fingers the finest hair stood up straight in a strange frosting. I passed a man with a woollen sweater. The fibre held heavy mist, and he had a ring of luminous vapour about his upper body. I have seen a Wordsworthian glory, I thought. But the world about me looked as if it had been shot through one of those terrible starburst filters I would never have put on my own camera lens. I was lost and could neither see nor hear anything around me. The mist had become a baffler and a screen. I had never climbed a mountain before, and the only survival strategy that carried over from my big-city sojourns was the one that told me to stay put. Without warning two figures stepped out of the gloom and stood before me reading a map. I followed them down the slope, zig-zagged through the tall, fernlike growth in the glen, getting soaked from the knees down, crossed a wooden bridge, thanked my bright British guides, blessed their large-scale Bartholomew map, and succumbed to fatigue on level turf.

[13] The typical guidebook route for a traveller was from Fort William to Fort Augustus (stopping at the inn at Letterfinlay and observing the Locks at Loch Lochy), then up along the east side of Loch Ness, following General Wade's road, to Inverness, stopping to see and exclaim over the Falls of Foyers (which Keats does mention) and the General's Hut, in what is now called Dores (which Keats does not note). No doubt if Keats had not been ill, he would have remarked on the Caledonian Canal, which he would have seen being built as he walked up General Wade's road to Inverness. He might have acknowledged the local bitterness prevalent over the Battle of Culloden, which had taken place so close to Inverness. And his sense of the gothic must certainly have seized upon the Loch Ness monster as ripe material for a letter home.

Then will the dragons fry and fizz their best,
Until ten thousand now no bigger than
Poor alligators, poor things of one span,
Will each one swell to twice ten times the size
Of northern whale; then for the tender prize—
The moment then—for then will Red-Crag rub
His flinty back, and I shall kiss and snub
And press my dainty morsel to my breast.
Blockhead, make haste!

O Muses, weep the rest—
The lady fainted and he thought her dead,
So pulled the clouds again about his head
And went to sleep again. Soon she was rous'd
By her affrighted servants. Next day, hous'd
Safe on the lowly ground, she bless'd her fate
That fainting fit was not delayed too late.

But what surprises me above all is how this Lady got down again—I felt it horribly—'T was the most vile descent—shook me all to pieces[12]—

[Inverness]

—Over leaf you will find a Sonnet I wrote on the top of Ben Nevis—We have just entered Inverness.[13] I have three Letters from you and one from Fanny—and one from Dilke. I would set about crossing this all over for you but I will first write to Fanny and Mrs Wylie then I will begin another to you and not before because I think it better you should have this as soon as possible—My Sore throat is not quite well and I intend stopping here a few days.

Read me a lesson, Muse, and speak it loud
    Upon the top of Nevis, blind in mist!
I look into the chasms, and a shroud
    Vaprous doth hide them; just so much I wist
Mankind do know of hell: I look o'erhead,
    And there is sullen mist; even so much
Mankind can tell of heaven: mist is spread
    Before the earth beneath me; even such,
Even so vague is man's sight of himself.
    Here are the craggy stones beneath my feet;
Thus much I know, that, a poor witless elf,

I tread on them; that all my eye doth meet
Is mist and crag—not only on this height,
But in the world of thought and mental might.

Good bye till tomorrow

Your most affectionate Brother
John—

Letter 12 is based on a copy of the original manuscript transcribed by John Jeffrey. Keats is addressing Mrs. James Wylie, the mother of his new sister-in-law, Georgiana. His concern for Mrs. Wylie's loss of her only daughter (she had two sons, Charles and Henry), who was now bound for America, must have been at least in part a projection of his own sense of loss.

[1] William Haslam (see Letter 5, n.20) was Keats's intimate friend and one of the circle of people by whom news of the Keatses regularly passed. Earlier editors (the Formans and Milnes) interpret the transcript to read "Mrs Haslam," but William was not yet married, and there is no evidence he was living with his mother, although it does seem more likely that Mrs. Wylie would call on a woman than on a young man.

[2] Keats draws on the proverb "He that is born to be hanged will never be drowned."

Letter 12

TO MRS. JAMES WYLIE

[6 August 1818]

Inverness 6th August 1818

My dear Madam—

It was a great regret to me that I should leave all my friends, just at the moment when I might have helped to soften away the time for them. I wanted not to leave my Brother Tom, but more especially, believe me, I should like to have remained near you, were it but for an atom of consolation, after parting with so dear a daughter. My brother George has ever been more than a brother to me, he has been my greatest friend, & I can never forget the sacrifice you have made for his happiness. As I walk along the Mountains here, I am full of these things, & lay in wait, as it were, for the pleasure of seeing you, immediately on my return to town. I wish above all things, to say a word of Comfort to you, but I know not how. It is impossible to prove that black is white, It is impossible to make out, that sorrow is joy or joy is sorrow——

Tom tells me that you called on Mr Haslam[1] with a Newspaper giving an account of a Gentleman in a Fur cap, falling over a precipice in Kirkudbrightshire. If it was me, I did it in a dream, or in some magic interval between the first & second cup of tea; which is nothing extraordinary, when we hear that Mahomet, in getting out of Bed, upset a jug of water, & whilst it was falling, took a fortnight's trip as it seemed to Heaven: yet was back in time to save one drop of water being spilt. As for Fur caps I do not remember one beside my own, except at Carlisle—this was a very good Fur cap, I met in the High Street, & I daresay was the unfortunate one. I daresay that the fates seeing but two Fur caps in the North, thought it too extraordinary, & so threw the Dies which of them should be drowned. The lot fell upon Jonas—I daresay his name was Jonas. All I hope is, that the gaunt Ladies said not a word about hanging, if they did, I shall one day regret that I was not half drowned in Kirkudbright.[2] Stop! let me see!—being half drowned by falling from a precipice is a very romantic affair—Why should I not take it to myself? Keep my secret & I will. How glorious to be introduced in a drawing room to a Lady who reads Novels, with—"M^r so & so—Miss so & so—Miss so & so, this is M^r so & so, who fell off a precipice, & was half drowned. Now I refer it to you whether I should loose so fine an opportunity of making my fortune—

No romance lady could resist me—None—Being run under a Waggon; side lamed at a playhouse; Apoplectic, through Brandy; & a thousand other tolerably decent things for badness would be nothing; but being tumbled over a precipice into the sea—Oh it would make my fortune—especially if you could continue to hint, from this bulletins authority, that I was not upset on my own account, but that I dashed into the waves after Jessy of Dumblane—& pulled her out by the hair—But that, Alas! she was dead or she would have made me happy with her hand—however in this you may use your own discretion—But I must leave joking & seriously aver, that I have been *merry* romantic indeed, among these Mountains & Lakes. I have got wet through day after day, eaten oat cake, & drank whiskey, walked up to my knees in Bog, got a sore throat, gone to see Icolmkill & Staffa, met with wholesome food, just here & there as it happened; went up Ben Nevis, & N.B. came down again. Sometimes when I am rather tired, I lean rather languishingly on a Rock, & long for some famous Beauty to get down from her Palfrey in passing; approach me with—her saddle bags—& give me—a dozen or two capital roast beef sandwiches—

When I come into a large town, you know there is no putting ones Knapsack into ones fob; so the people stare—We have been taken for Spectacle venders, Razor sellers, Jewellers, travelling linnen drapers, Spies, Excisemen, & many things else, I have no idea of—When I asked for letters at the Post Office, Port Patrick; the man asked what Regiment? I have had a peep also at little Ireland. Tell Henry[3] I have not Camped quite on the bare Earth yet; but nearly as bad, in walking through Mull—for the Shepherds huts you can scarcely breathe in, for the smoke which they seem to endeavour to preserve for smoking on a large scale. Besides riding about 400, we have walked above 600 Miles, & may therefore reckon ourselves as set out.

I wish my dear Madam, that one of the greatest pleasures I shall have on my return, will be seeing you & that I shall ever be

Yours with the greatest Respect & sincerity

John Keats—

[3] Henry, one of her two sons, lived with his aunt Mrs. Millar and her daughter Mary on Henrietta Street in London. Mrs. Wylie lived on Romney Street.

Letter 13 is incomplete; the manuscript is part of the Dilke Collection in the Keats Museum. Judging by the date, the letter must have gone out of Inverness with the same mail carrying Keats's Letters 11 and 12. Jack Stillinger, in his edition of Brown's letters, indicates that this letter was addressed to Dilke's father, who was retired (from a job in the Navy Pay Office) and lived in Chichester. Another was sent to the C. W. Dilke who was Brown's contemporary (see Letter 5, n.1; Letter 7, n.1), probably in the same mail, but it has been lost. This letter to Dilke, Sr., is important because it contains the physician's report and the decision that Keats should return.

While Brown was sending his letters with news of Keats's illness south, correspondence with other bad news was being sent north to Keats concerning his brother. Tom's tuberculosis had taken a critical turn, and the attending physician had urged that John be sent for. Mrs. Dilke, Jr., of Wentworth Place wrote to her father-in-law on August 16: "John Keats' brother is extremely ill, and the doctor begged that his brother might be sent for. Dilke accordingly wrote off to him, which was a very unpleasant task. However, from the journal received from Brown last Friday, he says Keats has been so long ill with his sore throat, that he is obliged to give up. I am rather glad of it, as he will not receive the letter, which might have frightened him very much, as he is extremely fond of his brother. How poor Brown will get on alone I know not, as he loses a cheerful, good-tempered, clever companion (*Papers of a Critic*, 1, 5).

It was this Mrs. Dilke who on August 19 wrote the disturbing impression of a somewhat ravaged traveller: "John Keats arrived here last night, as brown and as shabby as you can imagine; scarcely any shoes left, his jacket all torn at the back, a fur cap, a great plaid, and his knapsack. I cannot tell what he looked like" (1, 5).

[1] Brown's weight loss grows colourfully comic as he draws from Falstaff's response to Hal in *Henry IV, Part I* (2.4.362–364): "How long is't ago, Jack, since thou sawest thine own knee?" Falstaff quips: "My own knee! When I was about thy years, Hal, I was not an eagle's talon in the waist, I could have crept into any alderman's thumb ring."

Letter 13

CHARLES BROWN TO C. W. DILKE, SR.

[7 August 1818]

Inverness. 7th August 1818.

My dear Sir,

What shall I write about? I am resolved to send you a letter, but where is the subject? I have already stumped away on my ten toes 642 miles, and seen many fine sights, but I am puzzled to know what to make choice of. Suppose I begin with myself,—there must be a pleasure in that,—and, by way of variety, I must bring in Mr Keats. Then, be it known, in the first place, we are in as continued a bustle as an old Dowager at Home. Always moving—moving from one place to another, like Dante's inhabitants of the Sulphur Kingdom in search of cold ground,—prosing over the Map,—calculating distances,—packing up knapsacks,—and paying bills. There's so much for yourself, my dear. "Thank, 'ye, Sir." How many miles to the next Town? "Seventeen lucky miles, Sir." That must be at least twenty; come along, Keats; here's your stick; why, we forgot the map!—now for it; seventeen lucky miles! I must have another hole taken up in the strap of my Knapsack. Oh, the misery of coming to the meeting of three roads without a finger post! There's an old woman coming,—God bless her! she'll tell us all about it. Eh! she can't speak English! Repeat the name of the town over in all ways, but the true spelling way, and possibly she may understand. No, we have not got the brogue. Then toss up heads or tails for right or left, and fortune send us the right road! Here's a soaking shower coming! ecod! it rolls between the mountains as if it would drown us. At last we come wet and weary to the long wished for Inn. What have you for Dinner? "Truly nothing." No Eggs. "We have two." Any loaf bread? "No, Sir, but we've nice oat-cakes." Any bacon? any dried fish? "No, no, no, Sir!" But you've plenty of Whiskey? "O yes, Sir, plenty of Whiskey!" This is melancholy. Why should so beautiful a Country be poor? Why can't craggy mountains, and granite rocks, bear corn, wine, and oil? These are our misfortunes,—these are what make me "an Eagle's talon in the waist."[1] But I am well repaid for my sufferings. We came out to endure, and to be gratified with scenery, and lo! we have not been disappointed either way. As for the Oat-cakes,[2] I was once in despair about them. I was not only too dainty, but they absolutely made me sick. With a little gulping, I can manage them now. Mr Keats however is too unwell for fatigue and privation. I am waiting here to see him off in the Smack for London.[3] He caught a violent cold in the Island of Mull, which far from leaving him, has become worse, and the Physician here[4] thinks him too thin and fevered to proceed on our journey. It is a cruel disappointment. We have been as happy as possible together. Alas! I shall have to travel thro' Perthshire and all the Counties round in solitude![5] But my disappointment is nothing to his; he not only loses my company (and that's a great loss,) but he loses the Country. Poor Charles Brown will have to trudge by himself,—an odd fellow, and moreover an odd figure;—imagine me with a thick stick in my hand, the knapsack on my back, "with spectacles on nose," a white hat, a tartan coat and trowsers, and a Highland plaid thrown over my shoulders! Don't laugh at me, there's a good fellow,—altho' Mr Keats calls me the Red Cross Knight, and declares my own shadow is ready to split its sides as it follows me. This dress is the best possible dress, as Dr Pangloss[6] would say. It is light and not easily penetrated by the wet, and when it is, it is not cold,—it has little more than a kind of heavy smoky sensation about it.

I must not think of the wind, and the sun, and the rain, after my journey thro' the island of Mull. There's a wild place! Thirty seven miles of jumping and flinging over great stones along no path at all, up the steep and down the steep and wading thro' rivulets up to the knees, and crossing a bog, a mile long, up to the ancles. I should like to give you a whole and particular account of the many—many wonderful places I have visited,—but why should I ask a man to pay vigentiple postage? In one word then,—that is to the end of the letter,—let me tell you I have seen one half of the Lakes in Westmoreland & Cumberland,—I have travelled over the whole of the coast of Kirkcudbrightshire, and skudded over to Donaghadee. But I did not like Ireland,—at least that part,—and would go no farther than Belfast. So back came I in a whirligig,—that is in a hurry,—and trotted up to Ayr; where I had the happiness of drinking Whiskey in the very house that Robin Burns was born,—and I saw the banks of the bonny Doon,—and the brigs of Ayr,—and Kirk Alloway,—I saw it all! After this we went to Glasgow, & then to Loch Lomond,—but you can read all about that place in one of the fashionable guide-books. Then to Loch Awe and down to the foot of it,—oh, what a glen we went thro' to get at it! At the top of the glen my Itinerary mentioned a place called "Rest and be thankful" nine miles off; now we had set out without breakfast, intending to take our meal there, when, horror and starvation! "Rest and be thankful" was not an Inn, but a stone seat![7]

[2] By today's standards, the pair had been on an exemplary high-fibre diet, but as the breakfast cereal commercials hasten to point out, unalloyed oats simply don't taste good. Beyond the question of palate was the problem of a balanced diet; Keats's privation must have been at least in part the absence of adequate protein, vegetables, and fresh fruit. To judge from their letters, oat cakes and whiskey were all they were offered by the Scots.

[3] On August 8 Keats sailed from Cromarty harbour on a small boat called *The George* (Walter Strachan, Master, carrying goods to London). He and Brown made their way from Inverness to Cromarty by way of Dingwall so that Keats could catch the only boat sailing for London. Keats had a nine days' passage (he told Fanny in a letter to her on August 18) and landed at London Bridge on August 17.

[4] The physician in Inverness corroborated the warning of another physician whom Keats had seen before arriving in Inverness. Brown writes, in his biography of Keats: "For some time he had been annoyed by a slight inflammation in the throat, occasioned by rainy days, fatigue, privation, and, I am afraid, in one instance, by damp sheets. It was prudently resolved, with the assistance of medical advice, that if, when we reached Inverness, he should not be much better, he should part from me, and proceed from the port of Cromarty to London by sea. He was not recovered, and we parted there" (*Life of Keats*, 52).

[5] Brown continued the walking tour alone and was back in Hampstead by October. Nothing is known about his schedule or his precise itinerary, though it seems likely that he went to John o' Groats as planned and returned by a different route.

[6] The mock-serious tutor of the title character of Voltaire's *Candide*, the philosopher Dr. Pangloss takes to the extreme the theory of Leibnitz that all that happens in the world ultimately does so for good reason. Glossing over atrocities and natural disasters, Dr. Pangloss repeatedly affirms that all is for the best in this best of all possible worlds.

[7] See Letter 8, n.5.

Henry Snook was the elder son of Brown's friends John and Letitia Snook. The uncle referred to in the opening sentence is Charles Wentworth Dilke, brother of Henry's mother, Letitia. Henry was studying at Eton, and Brown wrote to him at the college, in Windsor. Born in 1805, the boy would have been thirteen (or close to this, depending upon his month of birth). The younger brother about whom Brown says he has been thinking is John, referred to as "Jack" at the close of the letter. The "two nephews" Brown has also thought of each day in the same context were the adolescent sons of his own elder brother, John Armitage Brown. The Snook family lived in Bedhampton, Sussex.

Letter 14

CHARLES BROWN TO HENRY SNOOK

[7 August 1818]

Inverness, 7th August 1818

My dear Henry,

Yesterday I had a letter from your Uncle. He told me you had been for a day at Wentworth Place. Why did he not say how you got on at Eton? I am very—very anxious to hear of your success in the Classics. I have thought of you, and your brother, and my two nephews, every day on my walk. To have left you all, after so long having been your companion, sometimes comes across my mind in a painful manner, and the farther I have travelled away the stronger has been the feeling. There may be many who cannot understand why I should think of you so much, but my dear boys know how much I have loved them, and they must likewise know it is not in my nature to be changeable with them. But let the proof of this remain till some future day, that is, the proof of my unchangeablenes for in the meanwhile I can have nothing to offer but assurances of affection. It gives me delight to think I have friends growing round me.

Do you want to hear about my journey? I think you do; and what else can I have to write about? Come,—listen! You shall have an abridgement of the history of Charles Brown's adventures, first part. We set out from Lancaster and went to Windermere Lake, then to Keswick and Derwent Water, and up Mount Skiddaw; these Lakes like all fresh water ones must be in the neighbourhood of great mountains, for they are fed by the springs and rain from the sides of them; it is for this reason they are so beautiful; imagine if you can a large piece of clear, smooth water not round or square like a pond in a Garden but winding about to and fro with parts of the rocks jutting forward in them, and with several little islands peeping up here and there, all wooded with different kinds of trees, while the view upwards rests on grand mountains, one rising above another, with the clouds sailing beneath their summits, and sometimes spreading downwards into the valleys. When we had seen many of these scenes in Cumberland and Westmoreland, we trudged to Carlisle, from which City we took the stage to Dumfries, which was an uninteresting distance of 36 miles. We travelled all over the coast of Kirkcudbright with great pleasure; the country there is very fruitful, and the views delightful. It was our intention to see the Giant's Causeway in Ireland, and we took the packet from Port Patrick to Donaghadee, but did not proceed further than Belfast and returned back again, for the Irish people did not please us, and the expence was enormous. You must follow me, up the coast to Ayr, and I heartily wish I had time to detain you on the road, for it's worth admiring, even at second hand. Near Ayr, we paid a visit to the Cottage in which Burns was born,—thousands go there for no other purpose but the happiness of being under the roof, and I was not the least among them in that happiness; we likewise took a survey of the Ruins of Kirk Alloway, where, you will remember, Tam o'Shanter saw the Witches dancing as he peeped thro' the west window, and we saw the "banks and braes o' bonny Doon," and "auld Brig" and the "new Brig" in the Town; and every thing we could think of that was connected with Burns' poetry. I ought to tell you Burns had as charming a country to live in, as he himself has described,—indeed the sight of it is almost enough to make a man a Poet. In a little time after, we entered the City of Glasgow,—the largest City in all Scotland, and a noble place it is. Then journeying by the banks of the Clyde, we reached Dumbarton, and turned northwards by the side of Loch Lomond, the famous Lake that people go in such crowds to have a sight of. Who shall attempt to describe such scenery? I believe I must pass it over, and take you across the country to the top of Loch Awe, where we had one of our pleasantest days in walking by its side to the south end. We afterwards went to the coast,—a rough and mountainous coast, where the sea breaks in between the hills, twenty and thirty miles up the Country, forming what they call salt water Lakes. At last we arrived at Oban, and took the ferries, first to the Island of Kerrera, and then to the Island of Mull. Here a Guide led us thro' the Country; no stranger could possibly find the road—for in fact *road there was none*, nearly for the whole journey of 37 miles,— sometimes it was over smooth rock, then we had for miles to hop from one stone to another, up hill and down hill, then to cross rivers up to our knees, and, what was worst of all, to walk thro' bogs. At the extremity of Mull, we crossed to the little Island of Iona or Ikolmkill, which is only three miles long, but it was here that Christianity was first taught in Scotland, and for that reason perhaps it was thought a more sacred ground, and it became the burial place of Kings; 48 Scotch Kings have been buried here, 8 Irish, 4 Norwegian, and 1 French; besides there are very interesting ruins of the Cathedral, the College, a Nunnery, Monasteries, and Chapels. We hired a Boat at Iona to take us to Staffa,—that astonishing island of Basaltic Pillars, which you know I so much desired to look at. We went into the cave, nearly to the end, and I shall never forget the solemn impression it made on me;—the pillars on each side, the waves beneath, and the beautiful roof,—all surpassed the work of man,—it seemed like a Cathedral, built by the Almighty to raise the minds of his creatures to the purest and the grandest devotion,—no one could have an evil thought in such a place. We returned to Oban by a different road, and I ought to tell you of the strange sight we had of a swarm of sea gulls attacking a shoal of herrings, with now and then a porpoise heaving about among them for a supper,—I assure you that as our boat passed the spot, the water was literally spangled with herring scales, so great had been the destruction by these Gulls. And now come on with me to Fort William, near Ben Nevis, the highest mountain in Great Britain. We went to the very top of it, and we had to toil up a prodigious steep, chiefly over large loose stones, for eight miles, before we could boast of being above all His Majesty's subjects, and as for the coming down, it was worse than the ascent. It is 4,370 feet above the level of the sea; there is always snow upon it in the hollows of the mountain, where the sun never shines; I walked about on snow, which they said was 100 feet deep; the air is very cold, and there is no vegetation near the top,—not even so much as a little moss on the edges of the stones. I went near,—not *too near* you may be sure,—to some most frightful precipices, they were most tremendous places perhaps 1500 feet deep,—if you holla over them the voice is echoed all the way down till it dies away, and the effect of throwing stones down is extraordinary. I won't trouble you much in my travels to Inverness, along the banks of Loch Lochy and Loch Ness, but I must mention my having seen the grandest fall of water in Europe,—called the Falls of Foyers.[1]—As for the natives,—the Highlanders,—I like them very well; they are very civil, kind, and attentive; I think they are always sincere in what they say; they are much more civilised that I expected to find them in the wild places I have visited. But oh! what a poor Country it is; mountains are fine to look at, but they will not bear corn, and even the valleys afford very scanty crops. We have sometimes been nearly starved; for 3 or 4 days together we have not been able to procure a morsel of meat, and their oat-bread I thought my dainty stomach never would accept of, but I contrive to eat it now;—all this is hard work in such long walks. I have stumped my ten toes over 642 miles, and shall have twice as much more to accomplish if I can, but Mr. Keats will leave me here, and I am full of sorrow about it; he is not well enough to go on; a violent cold and an ulcerated throat make it a matter of prudence that he should go to London in the Packet; he has been unwell for some

[1] The Falls of Foyers, also called Foyers Falls and the Fall of Foyers (or Fyers) was considered one of the great wonders of Great Britain. When Burns visited in September 1787, he produced a poem "written with a pencil on the spot" entitled "Lines on the Fall of Fyers near Loch Ness." Stoddart describes the waterfall at great length, calling it "the great wonder of this country" (*Remarks*, 2, 74), and reports that accounts of its height vary greatly, but "the nearest to the truth is probably that, which makes the fall itself about 200 feet, and the rocks overhanging it nearly 300 more" (2, 78). Brown's mention of the waterfall provided the critical clue to Bushnell in determining on which side of Loch Ness Keats and Brown travelled.

time, and the Physician here is of opinion he will not recover if he journeys on foot, thro' all weathers, and under so many privations. Give my compliments to Mrs. Woods and Mrs. Snook if they will accept of them from one in a tartan dress and with a Highland plaid thrown across my shoulder;—Keats calls me the Red Cross Knight, and declares my own shadow laughs at me! As for cousin John, remember me to him, I have wanted both of you with me, but you are both too young yet, and you must first get learning in wholesale. If you write to me before 20th August, addressed "*Mr Charles Brown, from London, Post Office, Edinburgh,*" I shall receive the letter. When you write to Jack, give my true love to him,—and to your father and mother, my sincere friendship. God keep you well, my dear Boy, and believe me your more than brother-friend.

Chas. Brown.

THIS MORTAL BODY OF A THOUSAND DAYS

This mortal body of a thousand days
   Now fills, O Burns, a space in thine own room,
Where thou didst dream alone on budded bays,
   Happy and thoughtless of thy day of doom!
My pulse is warm with thine old barley-bree,
   My head is light with pledging a great soul,
My eyes are wandering, and I cannot see,
   Fancy is dead and drunken at its goal;
Yet can I stamp my foot upon thy floor,
   Yet can I ope thy window-sash to find
The meadow thou hast tramped o'er and o'er,—
   Yet can I think of thee till thought is blind,—
Yet can I gulp a bumper to thy name,—
O smile among the shades, for this is fame!

ON SOME SKULLS IN BEAULEY ABBEY,
NEAR INVERNESS

"I shed no tears;
Deep thought, or awful vision, I had none;
By thousand petty fancies I was crossed."

Wordsworth

"And mock'd the dead bones that lay scatter'd by."

Shakspeare

1

In silent barren synod met[1]
Within these roofless walls, where yet
The shafted arch and carved fret
   Cling to the ruin,
The brethren's skulls[2] mourn, dewy wet,
   Their creed's undoing.

2

The mitred ones of Nice and Trent[3]
Were not so tongue-tied, —no, they went
Hot to their Councils, scarce content
   With orthodoxy;
But ye, poor tongueless things, were meant
   To speak by proxy.

This poem has a peculiar place among the walking tour pieces because it is not contained in a letter, or the letter in which it was sent has been lost. It was written by Keats and Brown jointly, but it was not published until January 1822, in the *New Monthly Magazine*. The circumstances of the poem tie it to the last few days Keats and Brown were together in Scotland. They left Inverness on August 7 and made their way by coach to Cromarty by way of Beauly and Dingwall. I believe the men crafted the poem while passing time before Keats boarded his smack to London in Cromarty on August 8 and Brown resumed his walk north alone. It would have distracted Keats and sealed their friendship before parting. Jack Stillinger, however, in his definitive edition of Keats's poems, allows that

the poem was written either in early August or "some weeks or even months later" (Keats, *Poems*, 617).

The ruin, alternately called Beauly Priory (with no "e" before the final "y"), is in a village ten miles from Inverness. The priory derives its name from its location, considered a beautiful site, hence, *beau lieu*. The history of the priory must have been well considered by Brown and Keats, since it underlies the meaning of the poem. This was one of three Valliscaulian monasteries built outside of France (all three in the Scottish highlands) in 1206. The Valliscaulians (whose name also derives from their original location, Vallis Caulium, or Val-des-Choux, meaning "valley of cabbages," in Burgundy) based their constitution on Carthusian rule, but they wore

the Cistercian habit, which was gray or white. The Valliscaulian monks lived by an extremely severe code, combining both Cistercian and Carthusian practices. Prayer, vows of silence, and personal deprivation characterized their daily lives. The Cistercian preference for manual labor, including work in the fields, applied to the Valliscaulians of Beauly Priory. Vistors today may learn from a British Department of Environment leaflet that "in 1571 there were still a Prior and four monks in the house. In 1633 the church was described as 'wholly decayed.' The conventual buildings are said to have been demolished by Cromwell to provide materials for his fort at Inverness." But a good sense of what Beauly would have looked like to Keats and Brown comes from Southey, who visited in the fall a year later: "Dined at Beauly, a village near the bridge, which takes its name from Beaulieu Priory, here called a Cathedral. Several huge iron kettles were lying out of doors here—a great deal of salmon being pickled here, for exportation. Some fine elms, sycamores, and ashes are standing by the ruins, and a few fruit trees, the remains of what the Monks had planted; they are now in decay, (reformation having carried ruin with it in all these places!) but the fruits (cherries, apples and pears) are remembered as having been of the very best kind. It is rather an extensive ruin, with some trefoil windows, an uncommon form, which did not deserve imitation. The area, as usual, serves for a cemetary. A few bones and skulls have been collected, and laid decently in some of the recesses of the wall" (*Journal of a Tour*, 117).

[1] "Silent" has a double value, with the vow of silence observed by the Valliscaulians included in the more obvious meaning, and this runs through much of the poem. The paradox of silence or speech-less-ness is central to the problem Keats and Brown examine here and below of the undoing and supplanting of a creed that initially had integrity with a hypocritical religious regime, through church politics and force. The skulls are those of the monks accidentally gathered in a kind of synod, or council meeting.
[2] These are very likely the skulls Southey mentions laid in recesses of a wall of the priory.
[3] The Council of Nicaea, in Asia Minor in 325,

brought over three hundred bishops ("mitred ones") together to establish a creed (now known as the Nicean Creed) declaring the Father, the Son, and the Holy Spirit to be a single substance but three distinct "persons." The Council of Trent, which took place over a period of twenty years, 1545–1563, established reforms and statements of doctrine in the Catholic church and ordered bishops to enforce rules of discipline in their clergy.
[4] John Knox (1505–1572) effected a dramatic, radical reform of the Scottish church. He was one of three to draft the Scottish creed in 1560, in consequence of which the Pope's authority was abolished in Scotland. The Catholic mass could not be practiced there, and a death penalty attended the third violation of this rule. Monasteries were often destroyed in the wake of Knox's preaching. The ramifications of Knox's Presbyterian revolution for a monastery like the Valliscaulian at Beauly were dire, as Keats and Brown recognize in this poem.
[5] The monks who were scribes produced beautiful manuscripts that were also valuable historical documents. Knox destroyed much of this literature.

3

Your chronicles no more exist,
Since Knox, the revolutionist,[4]
Destroy'd the work of every fist
  That scrawl'd black letter;[5]
Well! I'm a craniologist,
  And may do better.

4

This skull-cap wore the cowl from sloth,
Or discontent, perhaps from both;
And yet one day, against his oath,
  He tried escaping,
For men, though idle, may be loth
  To live on gaping.

5

A toper this! he plied his glass
More strictly than he said the mass,
And lov'd to see a tempting lass
  Come to confession,
Letting her absolution pass
  O'er fresh transgression.

6

This crawl'd through life in feebleness,
Boasting he never knew excess,
Cursing those crimes he scarce could guess,
  Or feel but faintly,
With prayers that heaven would cease to bless
  Men so unsaintly.

7

Here's a true churchman! he'd affect
Much charity, and ne'er neglect
To pray for mercy on th' elect,
  But thought no evil
In sending heathen, Turk, and sect
  All to the devil!

8

Poor skull, thy fingers set ablaze,
With silver saint in golden rays,
The holy missal; thou didst craze
    'Mid bead and spangle,
While others pass'd their idle days
    In coil and wrangle.

9

Long time this sconce a helmet wore,
But sickness smites the conscience sore;
He broke his sword, and hither bore
    His gear and plunder,
Took to the cowl,—then rav'd and swore
    At his damn'd blunder!

10

This lily colour'd skull, with all
The teeth complete, so white and small,
Belong'd to one whose early pall
    A lover shaded;
He died ere superstition's gall
    His heart invaded.

11

Ha! here is "undivulged crime"!
Despair forbad his soul to climb
Beyond this world, this mortal time
    Of fever'd sadness,
Until their monkish pantomime
    Dazzled his madness!

12

A younger brother this! a man
Aspiring as a Tartan khan,
But, curb'd and baffled, he began
    The trade of frightening;
It smack'd of power!—and here he ran
    To deal heaven's lightning.

13

This ideot-skull belong'd to one,
A buried miser's only son,
Who, penitent ere he'd begun
    To taste of pleasure,
And hoping heaven's dread wrath to shun,
    Gave hell his treasure.

14

Here is the forehead of an ape,
A robber's mark,—and near the nape
That bone, fie on't, bears just the shape
    Of carnal passion;
Ah! he was one for theft and rape,
    In monkish fashion!

15

This was the porter!—he could sing,
Or dance, or play, do any thing,
And what the friars bade him bring,
    They ne'er were balk'd of;
Matters not worth remembering,
    And seldom talk'd of.

16

Enough! why need I further pore?
This corner holds at least a score,
And yonder twice as many more
    Of reverend brothers;
'Tis the same story o'er and o'er,—
    They're like the others!

CHARLES BROWN'S WALKS IN THE NORTH

Chapter I.   Lancaster to Bowness, 31 Miles.

> The waies thorough which my weary steps I guyde,
> In this delightfull Land * * *
> Are so exceeding spacious and wyde,
> And sprinckled with such sweet variety
> Of all that pleasant is to eare and eye,
> That I, nigh ravisht with rare thoughts delight,
> My tedious travell do forget thereby,
> And when I gin to feele decay of might,
> It strength to me supplies, and chears my dulled spright.
>
> *Faery Queene.*

Without preface—for the one I have written is more tedious than useful—imagine me setting out from Lancaster, accompanied by a dear and lamented friend, each with a knapsack on his back, to enjoy the scenery of Cumberland and Westmoreland, in our way to the Highlands of Scotland.

The early death of that dear friend is not lamented by me alone, but by his countrymen in general; for he was John Keats the poet.

Yet, before entirely taking leave of my rejected preface, it would not be amiss to extract one explanatory passage.

We were not bound on a journey of discovery into "the busy haunts of men." Not that cities, their rise, progress, and increasing prosperity, or the reverse, or their prevailing interests and politics, were objects of indifference; but attention to them, and a love of the beauty and sublimity of nature are so widely distinct in character as not to be harmonized together. Besides, large towns rarely lay in our route. On this account, my pains-taking journal, written at the conclusion of each several stage, though full twenty years old, may serve as an itinerary for a traveller on a similar excursion, equally well as if I had just taken off my knapsack at the end of my northern walks. A score of years will scarcely alter the appearance of a woodland scene; and a thousand years cannot affect the imperishable and unchangeable grandeur of mountain, rock, and torrent. It may be proper, also, to forewarn the reader that I did not go about with a hammer in my hand, to knock off a specimen of every rock in my way. I had no ambition to rival the geologists. Mine is literally a superficial view of nature; which has one recommendation at least—every body can understand it.

"Weather permitting," unless of the bad and excessive kind, was not

These chapters, reconstructed by Brown from the journal he kept on the walking tour with Keats, were published in the *Plymouth and Devonport Weekly Journal* in four installments, October 1, 8, 15, and 22, 1840. A falling out with the proprietor of the newspaper, Daniel May, with whom Brown had had earlier serious differences over tardiness of payment for work he had contributed, resulted in his refusal to continue the weekly series, which was to have included more of Keats's poems. (Only the Meg Merrilies ballad made it into print, in Chapter 4.) Brown thought he might publish the rest of the series in another newspaper but did not. For a fuller account of Brown's difficulties with May, see McCormick, *Friend of Keats,* chapter 13, "Father and Son," in which McCormick links Brown's breach with May to other tensions in his life, especially the instability of his son, Carlino, who turned twenty in July 1840.

of much force in our agreement. But, on the morning of our departure, ready to start at four, a heavy rain detained us till seven. The interim was occupied with Milton, and I particularly preached patience out of Samson Agonistes. When the rain had subsided into a Scotch mist, we chose to consider it as appropriate and complimentary, and we, therefore, felt a pleasure in encountering it. Just out of the town, we overheard a labourer rather sarcastically observe to his companion— "There go a couple of gentlemen!—having nothing to do, they are finding out hard work for themselves!"

True; and those who *must* work may be comforted still further by reflecting that all men, who lead happy lives, labour in some way or another, including the bodily fatigue of field sports and the mental exhaustion of study. Our fellow labourer was in the right. We all work for the means of enjoying life; some one way, some another; some for money, some for the pleasure of excitement, some for health.

Four miles brought us into Bolton to breakfast, when the rain came down heavily again. However, it is always a comfort to have actually begun a long intended journey; and we rejoiced to be out of that city, at the time of a general election, where "the aspiring blood of Lancaster" deprived us of all comfort. There we had to wait two hours for our promised dinner; and were then told—"Not a bed in the house, gentlemen!" Fortunately a private house received us—better than a public one on such roaring occasions.

At mid-day, contrary to the prophecies of country-folks, the clouds cleared off, and we had as pleasant a walk as the muddy state of the road would permit. Near the borders of Westmoreland, two miles from Bolton, there was a fine view, notwithstanding the mistiness of the horizon, and some impeding clouds that the wind had not strength to drive forward over the hills. On our arrival, quite ready for dinner, we turned into the first inn, the Green Dragon, and put up our petition with the usual phrase of—"what we could have?" A voice replied in an instant, and in the gruffest tone, "Nothing! you can have nothing here!" It was the Green Dragon himself, in the shape of a tall, corpulent figure, with the largest face that ever man was blessed with—a face like a target; and none that a starving traveller might be tempted to shoot at. This unfeeling lump went on to tell us his house was full of soldiers, and that he could neither give us food nor a room to sit in. Turning from him into the King's Arms, the landlady there uttered her spleen in a milder strain. She said—"Ah! gentlemen, the soldiers are upon us! The Lowthers had brought 'em here to be in readiness. There'll be sad work at Appleby! There's Mr. Brougham, a great speaker in the house, I understand, comes down to oppose the Lowthers. Dear me! dear me!—at this election time to have soldiers upon us, when we ought to be making a bit of money. Not to be able to entertain any body! There was yesterday—I was forced to turn away two parties in their own carriages; for I have not a room to offer, nor a bed for any one. You can't sleep here, gentlemen; but I can give you a dinner. Dear, dear me! It goes to my heart—my spirits are quite down—to be forced to turn away two such parties! Oh! it's the Lowthers as I suspect—but that's only one's own mind—that brought 'em in."

We truly sympathised with her grievance; for the turmoil of an election was a nuisance to the tranquilly disposed.

After dinner the rain returned. Though compelled to proceed, we gave up all idea of passing the night at Kendal. A little public-house on the road-side was a welcome sight. We entered, and beheld a most uninviting hostess, smoking her pipe in a most formidable style. She informed us her house was quite full, and sent us onward, under the protection of our oilskin capes, to a place called End Moor. There the landlady, eyeing the burthens on our backs, inquired if we provided our own eating; on being answered in the negative, she promised accommodation for the night; though, as she said, she was in a "*squeer*, as all her house was whitewashing." In the room, which served for parlour and kitchen, sat an old soldier—that is, no longer in the service, for he was not above forty. He was shrewd and good tempered—had served in America—in the Peninsula—indeed in the Continental war from the time of Sir John Moore to the battle of Waterloo. He had received but one bullet in his thigh, and a graze on the skull; and now, God bless him! he had a pension of fifteen pence a day. For some time it was difficult to change the conversation from the Appleby election. From a corner in the room came forth, still in a sort of puzzled doze, an old toper, one Richard Radshaw, drunk as a sponge. He staggered forward in an attitude something like a bear, half raising himself on his hind legs, and dangling his fore paws before him. Suddenly he thrust his face forward, made a grasp at my knapsack, and asked if we sold spectacles and razors. Being quietly discouraged he imagined me offended, protesting that nothing was further from his thoughts, and made his apology by assuring me he was always "foolish in his drink." He then whispered in my ear, "I never offend any man—not I!—so if you'll give me something to drink—why—I'll take it!" As this appeal was unavailing, he left the house in a maudlin fit of melancholy, hiccoughing out—"Ah, nobody trusts me with liquor!

Well, I have seen all I ever loved to the grave, and I shall soon go there myself—and there'll be an end!"

While at tea, the attention of our hostess was attracted to our not using sugar, and called the unwilling notice of her loutish son to so economical a fact. Nay, on the following morning, she, the worthy Mrs. Black, almost made it a matter of conscience, on that score, to deduct a something from the reckoning.

During the evening I learnt more of poor Richard Radshaw. He had been once well to do, as a small farmer, with carts and horses, and all he wanted. His wife died; and then, in a short time, he lost both his sons, one in a fever, the other by an accident. No one was near him; for his two daughters were married to tradesmen in Lancaster. He endeavoured to drown his grief in liquor, became reckless, and neglected his farm till he was ruined. Now he was a day labourer, or he made bed mats, spending his money in drink as fast as he earned it.

Sorrow and solitariness may offer some excuse for the desperate remedy of intoxication; scarcely for its becoming an inveterate habit. Yet could not his daughters, by timely tokens of their affection and by their society, have saved him?

Without elevating him to the rank of a Lear in humble life, or degrading his daughters into a Regan and a Goneril, he may be commisserated, and, perhaps, they may be blamed.

One daughter, with a husband whose lordly will was not to be questioned, could not afford filial assistance, while he bluntly declared it was enough for him to support his own wife and family. The other daughter, indeed, ruled her husband; but she gave her father nothing, fearful it might add to his unhappy infirmity, often recurring, with many sighs and a few tears to his "distressing state," expiating on her "hopelessness of his reformation," and protesting it was a subject which "cuts her heart in twain to dwell upon." And thus she had been known to drawlingly speak while taking her share of a pot of ale; but then, as she averred, her constitution was weak, and stood in need of a little help.

Richard Radshaw's case affords scope for a comparison between the evils of selfishness and drunkenness. Not having made up my mind as to which vice is worse than the other, for the present I leave gentlemen over their extra bottle to exclaim against selfishness, and the man who buttons up all the world in his own waistcoat to show no mercy towards the disgusting vice of drunkenness.

On the next morning, after reaching Kendal, we had our first really joyous walk of nine miles towards the lake of Windermere. The country was wild and romantic, the weather fine, though not sunny, while the fresh mountain air, and many larks about us, gave us unbounded delight. As we approached the lake, the scenery became more and more grand and beautiful; and from time to time we stayed our steps, gazing intently on it. Hitherto, Keats had witnessed nothing superior to Devonshire; but, beautiful as that is, he was now tempted to speak of it with indifference. At the first turn from the road, before descending to the hamlet of Bowness, we both simultaneously came to a full stop. The lake lay before us. His bright eyes darted on a mountain-peak, beneath which was gently floating on a silver cloud; thence to a very small island, adorned with the foliage of trees, that lay beneath us, and surrounded by water of a glorious hue, when he exclaimed—"How can I believe in that?—surely it cannot be!" He warmly asserted that no view in the world could equal this—that it must beat all Italy—yet, having moved onward but a hundred yards—catching the further extremity of the lake, he thought it "more and more wonderfully beautiful!" The trees far and near, the grass immediately around us, the fern and the furze in their most luxuriant growth, all added to the charm. Not a mist, but an imperceptible vapour bestowed a mellow, softened tint over the immense mountains on the opposite side and at the further end of the lake. To look on them, with their awful accompaniments, though with the eyes of the most stupid, must bring conviction that there is a God!—however he might half persuade himself to the contrary in a city. It is needless to argue that a single blade of grass—which, by the by, is difficult to be found within a city—its formation, its life, its growth—indicates and even displays the same incomprehensible power—that there can be no degrees in incomprehensibility—and much more that can be easily said. But these mountains stood before us,

> "To elevate the more-than-reasoning mind;"[1]

and the spirit was bowed in reverence.

[1] From Wordsworth's sonnet "Weak Is the Will of Man," l. 7.

Chapter II.   Bowness to Keswick, 22½ Miles.

Every thing at the inn of Bowness was within our beck and call. It was spacious, commodious, and flourishing under the patronage of tourists; for whom the whole conduct was as much after the London fashion as possible. Scarcely had we appeared, when a man was putting off a boat. As we were parties concerned in the operation, he being about to fish for a portion of our dinner, we went with him. Never can fishing be more expeditious, or reduced to a greater certainty. After rowing a short distance on the lake, we came among some pieces of floating cork; they were handles to different ropes; fixing on one, he hauled up a wooden cage, where were salmon trout all jumping alive. We returned; and by the time we had hastily refreshed ourselves with bathing, dinner was announced; experience having taught the landlord that the keen appetites of tourists are not to be trifled with by delay. Nothing could be better than our entertainment; no fault could be found; yet—as man is born never to be perfectly contented in this world—we thought the many luxuries, together with the cold, civil, professional formality attending them, but ill accorded with the view from the window; nay, the curtains, furnished by some gay upholsterer, about that very window, might almost be construed into something like an affront.

A walk or a jaunt by the side of Windermere lake to Ambleside has been so much celebrated, that it is difficult to add any thing in the way of description. Not heeding what others have said—why should I?—let me recur to the words of my journal, written at the close of the walk.

These mountains completely surpassed all our expectations. I had seen those of Wales; Keats had not seen any. Yet even he, with all his imagination, could not, until he beheld them, suggest to himself a true idea of their effect on the mind. You may hear people talk eloquently of these scenes; you may see them portrayed by the best painters—language and art are equally inefficient. The reality must be witnessed before it can be understood. What is it—while moving on, at times unconscious of feet, and incapable of uttering more than sudden tokens of wonder—that so presses on the brain, with such awe, with such intense delight? Can it be that the intellect is then susceptible of the sublimest poetry, is throbbing under its influence while bereaved of the power of clothing it in words? Differ as we may on the cause, all will acknowledge the effect. Our road rambled through a wood, or across open spaces, alternately; sometimes climbing on the hill, at other times close on the margin of the lake. There were a thousand enchanting peeps through the branches of the trees as we journied on. The wind had become fresh, waving the foliage and rippling the water—the sound of which, together with the singing of birds, was perfect. That craggy mountain at the head of Windermere increased in grandeur as we proceeded. We stopped; we strolled; we stopped again. At every third step, something new, some change came upon us. A chasm was more distinctly seen; the woods on the opposite side seemed, now and then, to separate as if to display the torrent they had concealed; a new effect of light and shade was shown by some travelling cloud, shrouding midway a mountain, while its head was dazzling in the sun. But how can a walk—so glorious a walk appear on paper? And what can be said of this romantic Ambleside? Here are the beautiful and the sublime in unison. I am inclined to suspect that this is not a fit place for a descriptive poet's residence—his faculty of ideality might ache in vain amidst these realities. Besides, as Rousseau says, who is good authority on this point—"Would I describe a lovely landscape, I must write within four blank walls." The distance from Bowness is no more than six miles; yet from the multiplicity of objects, of sensations, and, possibly, owing to our unavoidable, pleasant loitering on the way, more days than one, at first thought, must have passed since yesterday. Just before entering the inn, I looked up a richly wooded hill, saw a splendid crag rise high above it, around which—thanks to the viewless mists during the day, now congregated into a large thin cloud—the setting sun shot broad and defined rays of gold through the purple hue of the cloud.

As I rewrite this part of my journal, again is every thing brought before me; yet, those who have not enjoyed a visit to the scene, or who have no such artificial aid to memory, may not, by my description, have more than an indistinct notion of it.

If Ambleside is an unfit spot for the writing of a particular kind of poetry, it is far more so for the speaking of particular town-bred impertinence. A young tourist, habited for the occasion like ourselves, accosted us under pretence of conversation. For the sake of reciprocal information, concerning our common purpose, I was at first glad of the meeting. Not a word could be obtained from him on the subject. He was wholly intent on convincing us that he was a better personage than, according to his own suspicion, he appeared. If he did not mistake us for a brace of pedlers, and his uneasiness was a proof that he did not, why could he not rest satisfied in the belief that we did him equal justice? However, that was not enough; his ambition was to be regarded as an important gentleman in disguise. He complained of the awkwardness he felt in wearing an unaccustomed suit of clothes, and then regretting that he had not brought anything else than fashionable boots. Not giving me proper time to digest these miseries, he went on to talk of his uncle's carriage, of Almack's[2] and of the opera, of the futile attempt at Bowness to ape a London hotel, and of the suppers he used to give at Oxford, interlarding this last account with sundry classic quotations, as evidence of his having been educated there. What could be said to this on the banks of Windermere, unless to ask—what route he had taken? "Oh! really I can hardly tell the names of the places!"

[2] A club on St. James's Street, London, founded before 1763 by William Almack (whose name is an anagram from Macall, or McCaul), noted as a gambling resort. It became Brooks's Club in 1778. Almack also built assembly rooms on King Street, London, in which aristocratic balls were held in the nineteenth century. The reference here might be to either place.

Then, by an extraordinary process of digression, he inveighed against the silly pride of rank and birth, informing me that his lamented father was unhappily gifted with that failing, and that he left, among his papers, a genealogy traced from Edward the First; but he, at the same time, assured me, he thought nothing whatever of it. With his scholarship at Oxford or elsewhere, for certainly he had brought some away from some place, it is a pity he had not learnt how much obtrusive and unsupported attempts to gain distinction are liable to meet with the worst construction. He was very well as he first appeared; but, right or wrong, I soon harboured a suspicion he was a London sharper. Keats wisely walked off the moment he exposed his folly; and, afterwards, I became savage with myself for not having been savage towards him. Yet that was unreasonable; because no provocation ought to ruffle the temper at Ambleside.

Early the next morning, we sallied forth to see the waterfall about a mile off. Descending to a point of the rock, we beheld an almost perpendicular fall of about thirty feet, formed by two streams at the summit, which fell into a basin, from which another fall gushed forth, at the side, into a fan-like shape; after tumbling over huge fragments of rock, it leapt far, far beneath the spot where we stood. The immense chasm of rock in itself was a noble sight. The very grove of trees above our heads, beneath our feet, overhanging every part, so that the branches were interwoven from one side of the torrent to the other, gave it the greatest richness. We went still lower down, till we were on a level with the bottom of the last fall; grasping the trees and edges of rock to prevent our tumbling headlong, when "one false step would be our ruin." Keats scrambled down lightly and quickly; but I never was a sure-footed beast. There we lost the topmost fall, which we had admired, but caught a brother torrent, that tumbled down from an equal height with the other, and they joined together where we stood. After climbing upwards, and at a little distance, we saw the whole in a milder view, from between the branches of the trees, when the water looked like molten silver.

When we returned, in accordance with Keats's desire to pay his respects to Mr. Wordsworth, we went to his house. Unfortunately he had just left Rydale for Lowther Hall. His house had a glorious situation. From the parlour window there was a view of chains of mountains, and of Windermere lake.

An old man escorted us into the park to see the waterfall. On the whole it was not so grand as that at Ambleside. The rocks were inferior; though the water struck us as falling in a more fanciful way.

Perhaps it was better for a picture. It was as well wooded, but had not so great a variety of trees. Viewed from high ground, there was certainly a want of wood near the head fall; but that was not the proper place to look at it; and lower down that want was not discernible. The first, or head fall, was thirty feet perpendicular, so as to plunge without touching the rock. Then from the basin below it sprung forward in different ways, and formed, over rocks of various shapes and sizes, an elegant cascade, that almost appeared artificial. The striking merit in it was the contrast between the lower part and the headlong impetuosity of that above. Our old man then led us to another, which he called— "The beauty of the world!" It had nothing sublime about it, however beautiful it deserves to be called. The fall itself is a trifle. Its effect depends on being viewed through the window of a summer-house, and having a little bridge thrown over it. The date on the summer-house is 1617.

We proceeded by the side of Rydale water. It did not greatly please us; it is small; besides, there is not enough wood about it. A little onward, as we looked from a height, it came admirably into view; and the number of reeds, which I disliked while passing, gave a shadowing in of the banks which had a good effect. Grasmere lake, adjoining it, is far preferable. The opposite shore is beautiful. Mr. Wordsworth formerly had a house there.

His line—

"That ancient woman seated on Helm Crag"

was brought to remembrance as the object itself came in sight. Some whimsically, though naturally disposed stones on the summit of the mountain certainly suggest the idea of a gigantic old woman sitting there. The finest landscape we enjoyed in this stage was when looking back on Grasmere. Thence to Wytheburn, a pretty place, just within Cumberland, we had to walk through a defile of treeless mountains, probably the pass which in former times, served as a protection to either county. Here we were at the foot of Helvellyn, rising "far into the clear blue sky." Begging pardon of Mr. Wordsworth that was not the case just then as it was in the midst of large rolling clouds. It is four miles to the summit; whither we intended to ascend on the morrow, should the weather be favourable—if not, we hoped for better luck with Mount Skiddaw.

During the night there had fallen much rain; many fleas were in the beds; and in the morning, clouds and drizzling rain prevented us from ascending Helvellyn. We passed Hurles Water, a small lake, by no means well wooded; but the water itself was wonderfully transparent. For some little way the country was not interesting; and clouds rested on every mountain around us. As the weather became clearer, we observed that the character of the scenery was different from what we had seen in Westmoreland. The hills were rounder, stretched their bases further, and, in one sense, being less craggy, might be called more graceful. A traveller might be excused for calling the entrance into Keswick vale gorgeous and tremendous; it surpassed that of Windermere, though quite in a different style. A view up Derwent Water, with the nest of mountains there, was the finest part; though Bassenthwaite Water at the right hand, with mighty Skiddaw at its side, was scarcely inferior. It is a profusion of wood that gives Derwent water so much richness.

When wound up to enthusiasm for natural objects, it is like enduring a direct act of hostility to meet with something brought from the depths of sophistication. At the inn here, near mid-day, came a yawning dandy from his bed-room, and sat at his breakfast reading a bouncing novel!

Chapter III.   Keswick to Dalbeattie, 82 miles.

Keswick is not a place to glance at, and then to be quitted, or to be afterwards visited with a mere nod of recognition. Our first jaunt was to walk entirely round Derwent Water, commencing with the east side. The fall of Lodore, however, disappointed us. Its situation is admirable—a mountain with an immense division, both sides nearly perpendicular, where ash trees grow in an inexplicable manner from top to bottom, without apparent nourishment from the earth. In no part is the fall itself of any height, though the water comes from an extraordinary one. That is, it tumbles, it jostles from rock to rock—it turns head over heels, but never once takes a leap. The nest of mountains, at the south end, which had so much attracted our admiration in the morning, still maintained its grandeur on a near view, and we could find none so fine. From the west side, on our return, is the best view of the scenery, though both are enchanting. A walk of only twelve miles completes the circuit.

In the evening we visited the Druidical remains. They are situated a mile and a half off, at the top of the first hill, rising out of the valley, on the road to Penrith, upon circular flat ground, now a field. There are many of them, in the form of a large circle, with others in an oval form touching one part of the inner circumference. Surrounded by a majestic panorama, the spot is suited to render the human mind awestruck, and, possibly, with the ignorant, superstitious.

Nothing was wanting in the town, at least by attempts, to please a London taste. It was full of lures to pass away the time—a circulating library, a fossil museum, an exhibition of Mr. Green's drawings, and a camera obscura. In the last we beheld our mountain scenery in miniature, and were made fully aware of the reason, why the best artist's representation must necessarily be inefficient. Simple magnitude possesses an effect of its own; deprive it of that quality, and, no longer being the same, it cannot possess the same effect. But this is not all: the character and accompaniments of a mountain are utterly destroyed when reduced to an undefinable—nay, an impercessible entity.

A promising morning authorized a guide to call us up at four o'clock, in order to ascend Skiddaw. The distance to the summit from the town is a little more than six miles. Its height, from the level of the sea, is 3,022 feet; but only 1,952 feet above Derwent water—so lofty is all this part of the country. Helvellyn and Skawfell are somewhat higher, but the view from Skiddaw is esteemed the best. In a short time the continued steep became fatiguing; and then, while looking upward to what I thought was no very great distance from the top, it sounded like cruelty to hear from our guide that we were exactly half way! Still, in a colder atmosphere, together with the extraordinary pure air, we climbed merrily; till the guide shook his head, prophesying of clouds and rain, as a cloud passed over the peak, gradually spreading downwards. We went on, till within three quarters of a mile to the summit, when we were enveloped in a hopeless cloud. Not able to see twenty yards around us, it was useless, unless for the sake of saying we had achieved the task, to proceed. It was fortunate we had opportunities of seeing every thing, from the winding road, before the mist came; and the guide confessed that the only advantage we lost was the not having it in our power to see every thing from the same point. After all, I was not much gratified by this sort of bird's-eye view. If you would be delighted with a garden, it is surely better to walk in it, than to stare down upon it from a garret-window. It must be acknowledged there is some thing grand in looking down on a country, as if it were a map; but the strangeness of the sight, more than any thing else, is its attraction. The mountains, which but yesterday I had gazed on with reverence, became comparatively insignificant. People talk of the extensive prospect—it may be too extensive. The hills on the other side of Lancaster appeared to us, and what of that? We had a discernment of Solway Firth, and the coast of Dumfries and Galloway;

but any other Firth, and any other coast would have been the same. The rain came to cool my critical reflections. During the sultry weather below, the winter's snow had not melted; even now, at the end of June, on Helvellyn and Skawfell we saw patches of snow still remaining. It is a sad jolting trot down a mountain—a man's inside seems mixing together like a Scotch haggis. The views of the vale of Keswick, and of other places, from the lower part of Skiddaw, I thought preferable to the loftier ones.

We passed by Bassenthwaite Water, a lake of little repute; it possesses great simplicity of character, and, in some points, its clear and deeply shadowed water had a beautiful effect; it is five or six miles in length. As we approached its north end, we were astonished at the sudden change of scene before us—no mountains, but highly cultivated hills and dales, similar to most parts of Devon, only not so luxuriant.

Without a touch of regret we kept our backs towards the wonders of Cumberland and Westmoreland; for we chalked out a tour in another direction among them, on our return from the Highlands.

Ireby is said to be the oldest market town in the county—with not much of a market. It is a dull, beggarly looking place. Our inn was remarkably clean and neat, and the old host and hostess were very civil and preposessing—but, heyday! what were those obstreperous doings over head? It was a dancing school under the tuition of a travelling master! Folks here were as partial to dancing as their neighbours, the Scotch; and every little farmer sent his young ones to take lessons. We went up stairs to witness the skill of these rustic boys and girls—fine, healthy, clean-dressed, and withal, perfectly orderly, as well as serious in their endeavours. We noticed some among them quite handsome, but the attention of none was drawn aside to notice us. The instant the fiddles struck up, the slouch in the gait was lost, the feet moved, and gracefully, with complete conformity to the notes; and they wove the figure, sometimes extremely complicated to my inexperienced eyes, without an error, or the slightest pause. There was no sauntering, half-asleep country dance among them; all were inspired, yet by

"Nae cotillion brent new frae France;
"But hornpipes, jigs, strathspeys, and reels
"Put life and mettle in their heels."

From time to time, on our way to Carlisle, old Skiddaw raised his head above the hills, as if to watch the progress of his late visitors. We were continually saluted on the road with—"a fine day!—a nice day!"—a voluntary and cheerful thanksgiving. "Merry Carlisle" did not, to our thinking, maintain its epithet—the whole art of yawning might have been learned there. The cathedral is better on the outside than within, where it is poor in size and in architecture; besides being spoiled by whitewash. The Castle, of which we had heard much, is very ancient—they call it 900 years old. It is a massy, ugly building; part is used as Barracks, part as a Magazine. We were displeased with the Court houses, modern buildings, though they give a grandeur to the entrance. They are exactly alike; each consisting of a square Gothic building, to which adjoins a very squab round tower; like a tea-caddy and low sugar-dish placed side by side.

Gretna Green is a sad, ominous place for a young couple—poverty-struck and barren![3] Aware there was nothing interesting in the country between Carlisle and Dumfries, and that, consequently, it would be toil without remuneration, we coached the distance. Till near the end of our ride, there was, indeed, little worth a traveller's regard. Certainly Dumfries stands in a delightful situation. Neither of us expected to remark much difference between English and Scotch towns, generally speaking; but it appeared as if we had stepped into a foreign country. It might be difficult to define in what the distinction lies; for perhaps it consists in numerous small particulars, each unimportant in itself. Without prejudice, however, it did not wear the air of comfort belonging to an English town; but that may have arisen from my not understanding what they possessed for those things which I, as a stranger, missed. The churchyard is the best site near the town for a view. It might be called an enviable place to lie in, and I rejoice that Burns is buried there; for though it may be truly argued that the situation of a grave matters nothing to the dead, yet it matters a great deal to the living—to his family, no doubt; and all Great Britain belongs to the family of a poet like Burns.

His mausoleum is a handsome structure, of red stone, but painted white; surrounded by iron rails, enclosing a flower and shrub garden, rather formally set out, but kept in great neatness. I have since seen a model for an appropriate basso-relievo to adorn this mausoleum. Such memorials to great men in the intellectual world, especially over their graves, should not be neglected. They may excite emulation; they must inspire reverence and gratitude, two feelings of which man is susceptible to the improvement of his nature.

Two miles off are the ruins of Lincluden College. The artist, according to my engraving has done them justice, giving an exact likeness. Praise for great beauty may be honestly bestowed on the

[3] English couples who wanted to be married secretly went to the Scottish border town of Gretna Green, where the marriage could be performed by declaration of banns in the presence of witnesses. The blacksmith usually performed the ceremony.

Chapel. It was once admirable for much fine workmanship about the cornices and capitals, but it is now nearly effaced; the stone being rather soft, and the climate rather hard. There are several vaults beneath, very like the dungeons we read of, for the heretical, the refractory, or the frail.

To our minds the people we had seen and conversed with, both in and out of the town, were more serious and solidly inanimated than necessary. They had a quiet expression and manner, which might be construed into happiness! but why put strangers to the trouble of forming a favourable interpretation? They are, also, in their speech, tedious, slow, and drawling. Except two or three girls, who returned our "speerings"—alias, usual salutations—on the road, with a sort of grin, we did not perceive an approach to a laugh. If laughter, as it is said, proves our distinction from other animals, the line did not seem to be correctly drawn between them and these northerns.

We had been recommended to seek entertainment at the village of Dalbeattie from a Mr. Murray. Besides keeping a *Public,* he kept a shop below, supplying every one in the district with almost every article, from tea down to candles and brick dust, ironmongery of all sorts, whiskey, broad cloth, sheeting, printed cottons, pens, ink and paper. It was a day appointed by the Kirk for a fast in that parish; and, therefore, the shop was shut, and Mrs. Murray only at home. From some unexplained cause, she was at first unwilling to let us enter—she "didna ken what to say!" Such doubts sound cruelly in the ears of hungry travellers, and should be visited with a grievous penalty. A saunter through the village was pleasant, as the cottages were neat, clean, and snug-looking. Then the inhabitants whom we saw were very clean and healthy faced, and every one of the children was dressed tidily—possibly this was partly owing to its being a holiday, but, even then, it was a credit to the village. A chubby urchin stared in alarm at the strangers, and, when called a "fat pig," he cried and screamed till he brought out an "auld wifie" upon us. She was "nae pleased to see bairns made game of." Atonement was made by a sixpence in the child's hand—his plump fingers closed over it with a true Scotch grasp, tight as the claw of a lobster; and off he went to take his place in a formal circle of children, who were amusing themselves by sitting down with their hands before them, in perfect silence—no wonder they grow up to be such staid men and women. Soon after this, a "sonsie lassi" put her head out of a cottage door. "There's a pretty girl!"—out came her shoulders. "A very pretty girl indeed!"—out she came on the threshold; and as we passed on, she stretched her neck out like a goose in a coop, for more of the barley. But, all the time, she maintained an unbecoming gravity.

In the evening Mr. Murray informed us, to our sorrow that we had come by the wrong road for a beautiful country. Had we gone some eight or ten miles round, by what is perversely called the ruins of *New Abbey*, or Sweet-Heart Abbey,[4] and the sea coast, we should have witnessed, he assured us, the finest scenery in the south of Scotland. His description was very enticing, but to return at the cost of the forty miles was out of the question, and we rather hoped that he romanced. He gave us our route for the morrow, six miles astray, to Kirkcudbright, and promised we should be enchanted with it. He boasted of the trade of his shop; and told us he had a better retail trade than any man in Dumfries, and that he had taken as much as sixty three pounds in a day. "This village," said he, "did not exist thirty years ago; at that time it was a bog full of rocky stones. The gentleman who built it died the very day I had my leg cut off."

> "I look down at his feet—but that is a fable,"

thought I with the philosophic Othello.[5] Yet it was true, he had only five inches of thigh on his right side. I might have seen him a thousand times without guessing he had a wooden leg, so admirably was it made, so perfect in the joints—he scarcely walked lame, and was more active than most men with their two natural legs.

Chapter IV.   Dalbeattie to Ballantrae, 92 miles.

Thanks to Mr. Murray's directions, our first stage of eight miles to Auchencairn, a village, was delightful, with noble views on both sides, of wooded hills and craggy mountains to the right, and of a lovely landscape, wherein a lough of the sea appeared like a lake, to the left—a small bush-covered island near the shore added to the charm. For the most part, our track lay through corn-fields, or skirting small forests. I chatted half the way about Guy Mannering, for it happened that Keats had not then read that novel, and I enjoyed the recollection of the events as I described them in their own scenes. There was a little spot, close to our pathway, where, without a shadow of doubt, old Meg Merrilies had often boiled her kettle, and, haply, cooked a chicken. It was among fragments of rock, and brambles, and broom, and most tastefully ornamented with a profusion of honeysuckle, wild roses, and fox-glove, all in the very blush and fullness of blossom. While finishing breakfast, and both employed in writing, I could not

[4] Devorguilla Balliol, founder of this abbey (in 1273), kept the embalmed heart of her dead husband in a silver and ivory casket until she herself died, in 1290, and was buried, with the heart, in front of the altar. "Sweetheart Abbey" is derived from the original Latin name, "Dulce Cor."

[5] Othello, speaking of Iago (*Othello* 5.2.286), refers to the legend that the devil is recognized by his cloven hoofs.

avoid noticing that Keats's letter was not running in regular prose. He told me he was writing to his little sister, and giving a ballad on old Meg for her amusement. Though he called it too much a trifle to be copied, I soon inserted it in my Journal. It struck me as a good description of that mystic link between mortality and the weird sisters; and, at the same time, in appropriate language to the person addressed.

[Here Brown sets the Meg Merrilies poem. See Letter 4]

The road to Kirkcudbright is ten miles; but we chose to add a couple more to them, in order to pass through Dundrennan, and see the Abbey. It is the ruin of a stately building, and must have bordered on the magnificent in its original state. Trees were not only growing about, but on the walls. There was, especially, a flourishing ash, that did not appear to derive any nourishment from earth; the root spreading itself down the wall, curving its branches between the stones, some forty feet from the ground, and feeding, as far as we could judge, on the mortar alone. Probably the mortar was in a nutritious state of decay. With the town not far before us, we were enchanted with the view; the winding bay—the wood-covered hills—the blue mountains beyond them—the island at the mouth of the bay—the sea on each side of it, and in the distance—the extraordinary fertility of the valley, and the surrounding country—all formed a scene that even Keats confessed to be equal and similar to the best parts of his favourite Devon. As we nearer approached the town, through the valley, every thing was in a most luxuriant state; the trees, the corn, the verdure, and even the hedges—nothing could surpass them. We visited the Castle,[6] but were disappointed with those ruins. The date over the door is 1583; which sufficiently explains the ugliness of the architecture.

We began to like the natives much better. That cold, solemn Dumfries is a befitting place wherein to write a libel on the Scotch. For two days we had been admiring the people's neatness of attire, their civility, and their intelligence, both in feature and in speech—for I conversed with all I could. A comparison between them and our labouring classes would be, I am afraid, in these respects, not a little against us. That neatness of attire, however, in the women made me the more object to their not wearing shoes and stockings. Keats was of an opposite opinion, and expiated on the beauty of a human foot, that had grown without an unnatural restraint, and on the beautiful effect of colour when a young lassie's foot was on the green grass. All this I freely acknowledged; but to see the same foot stumping through the dust of the road, or, what is worse, dabbling in the puddles of a town is the reverse of beautiful. It must be owned that, generally speaking,

[6] MacLellan's Castle, built in 1581–1582 by Sir Thomas MacLellan, using stones from the Greyfriars Church. The castle is characterized by local historians today as "a splendid piece of domestic architecture rather than a castle . . . really the town house of the MacLellans" (*Old Kirkcudbright*, 22). The date over the door is 1582 (not, as Brown reports, 1583).

after trudging with bare feet on the road, to save the wear of shoes and stockings, they put them on just before entering a town.

To arrive at Gate House costs four miles to the top of a hill, and four more to the bottom. Fleet bay and its banks might be highly praised by those who have not seen the bay of Kirkcudbright. Taking the sea-side road to Cree Town, four miles longer than the usual road, we became acquainted with a custom which I wish were more general in all countries. We soon met, returning to Gate House, men, women and children, of all ages and descriptions. It looked like an emigration, and we inquired the reason; when "The salt water" was the reply; and truly the greater proportion of the population had taken the opportunity of high tide to wash and be clean, where a jutting rock on the coast separated the sexes; and, morever, they told us it was their daily custom. There was nothing else remarkable in this stage except a deep glen, full of large trees, with a mountain stream running below—a spot that Meg Merrilies must have often frequented. Thence to Newton Stewart (quondam, Newton Douglas) Glenluce, Stranrawer, and Cairn, there was not scenery worth speaking of, though it was pleasant walking.

Our host at Stranrawer told us that, after leaving Cairn, there was a very bad road, either for horses or foot-passengers, being quite mountainous. From this account we promised ourselves a walk of twelve miles full of pleasure; nor were we disappointed. The first mile from Cairn was by the margin of the sea; then the road took a rise on the hill, that sloped, rather awfully, down to the coast. We there, after two miles of ascent, were about midway between the summit and the base. The view above us was grand, and that below both grand and beautiful. We stopped awhile. It was full tide, and the waves were dashing among the rocks, or telling their old tale in the hollow caverns. We proceeded; and, ever and anon, we crossed a little brig, that carried us over some deep, narrow, wooded glen. Yet all this was nothing to the vale of Glenap, through which we had to pass, and which, notwithstanding the length of our day's journey, we should have been sorry to find less than six miles in extent. The entrance to it was like an enchanted region: the mountains so rich with trees, and so various in their shades of green, and the valley itself delightfully wooded, and the silent charm of little cottages at every turn—surely it was another world! For some days we had not met with any scenery fit to inspire raptures; but here our patience was rewarded. Onward as we moved, mountain beyond mountain, all clothed in the liveliest verdure, either of tree or herbage, together with the never ceasing change of prospect

[7] From Burns's "The Cotter's Saturday Night": "And makes him quite forget his labor and his toil" (l. 3).

on all sides, they—"made us quite forget our labour and our toil."[7] A little rain fell; but the clouds were still high, and there was not enough to obscure the atmosphere. At the end of the valley we had to climb a steep ascent, until we looked round on the tops of the neighbouring hills, and often did we cast our eyes beneath on that glen, from which we were loth to part. There, as we strode along, snuffing up the mountain air,—most exhilarating to those who have been long trudging on a plain—a sight of Ailsa rock came upon us like something supernatural. It was seventeen miles distant, rising perpendicularly from the sea nine hundred and forty feet. The strangeness of appearance was occasioned by its seeming to possess an invisible footing above the sea; as the horizon, the sea, was considerably lower than its apparent first rise—that is, the lowest part which, at that distance, could be perceived by us—an optical illusion. This rock is famous, like many others on the coast of Scotland, for sea-foul, and its rental was fifty pounds a year.[8] There is a path-way to its summit; but, at that height, and standing so far off from the shore, there could not be a view from it to afford me much pleasure.

[8] See Letter 7, n.7.

At nearly the close of our day's journey the rain fell in earnest, and we hastened down to Ballantrae, near the sea-shore, taking up our quarters in that little town, at a dirty inn—the first of that description we had entered in Scotland. We had been warned not to go to the Post-chaise-inn, as things might not be quite comfortable there, because the landlord was a little in trouble. A little in trouble!—he had been just taken up for being concerned in robbing the Paisley bank! Coming into the town, a lassie afforded some amusement by mistaking us, with our neat knapsacks, for jewellers, and by her eagerness to inspect the supposed finery.

I asked an old man, who spoke on several subjects with much intelligence, if he had ever seen his countryman Burns, or what he had heard of him. It was soon evident I had not pitched on one with the right intelligence. "I ha' ne'er seen that Burns," quoth he, "but I parfecly approve o' him; for he may ha' had, and so in fac I think, some guid sense; an', what I nae much ken o', he had a clever knack o' rhyming." Alas! a poet, no more than a prophet, is honoured in his own district!

A stormy night followed; "Dan Æolus, in great displeasure sent forth the winds"—[9]

> "They breaking forth with rude unruliment
> "From all four parts of heaven do rage full sore,
> "And toss the deeps and tear the firmament";[10]

[9] Spenser's *Faerie Queene*, book 4, canto 9, stanza 23: As when *Dan Æolus* in great displeasure, / For losse of his deare love by *Neptune* hent, / Sends forth the winds out of his hidden treasure (ll. 1–3).
[10] *Faerie Queene*, book 4, canto 9, stanza 23, ll. 5–7.

and then at the end of every half hour—

> "All suddenly a stormy whirlwind blew
> "Throughout the house, that clapped every door";[11]

so that, after our long walk, when watchfulness should not have been the order of the night, we met each other in the morning with mutual condolence on the want of sleep. Miserable accommodation! How provoking that the master of the good inn should have been so sillily improvident as to be taken up for a robbery, inflicting a bad lodging on us as well as on himself!

C. A. B.

(To be Continued.)

[No more installments were published.]

[11] *Faerie Queene*, book 3, canto 12, stanza 3, ll. 1–2.

SELECT BIBLIOGRAPHY

The works I have listed here are those I found most useful in making this book. The selection represents the range of reading I did in acquiring background and is intended to give the reader direction in pursuing my ideas further. The body of Keats scholarship to date is immense, and only a fraction of it is represented here. I have not listed the several local newspapers of Great Britain I consulted for the period of the walking tour, nor have I included recent guide books, maps, and other sources that would occur obviously to the reader who might actually want to follow Keats's walk to the north.

Baedeker, Karl. *Great Britain: A Handbook for Travellers*. 5th ed. Leipzig: Karl Baedeker, 1901.

Bardon, Jonathan. *Belfast: An Illustrated History*. Belfast: Blackstaff Press, 1983.

Bate, Walter Jackson. *John Keats*. Cambridge, Mass.: Harvard University Press, 1963.

Beattie, William. *Scotland Illustrated*. 2 vols. London: George Virtue, 1838.

Black's Picturesque Guide to the English Lakes. 13th ed. Edinburgh: Adam and Charles Black, 1865.

Black's Picturesque Tourist of Scotland. Edinburgh: Adam and Charles Black, 1869.

Boswell, James. *Boswell's Journal of a Tour to the Hebrides with Samuel Johnson, LL.D.* [1773]. Ed. Frederick A. Pottle and Charles H. Bennett. New York: Viking Press, 1936.

Brown, Charles Armitage. *The Letters of Charles Armitage Brown*. Ed. Jack Stillinger. Cambridge, Mass.: Harvard University Press, 1966.
————. *Life of John Keats*. Ed. Dorothy Hyde Bodurtha and Willard Bissell Pope. London: Oxford University Press, 1937.

Burns, Robert. *The Poetical Works of Burns*. Cambridge Edition. Ed. Raymond Bentman. Boston: Houghton Mifflin, 1974.

Bushnell, Nelson S. *A Walk after John Keats*. New York: Farrar and Rinehart, 1936.

Dilke, Charles Wentworth. *The Papers of a Critic. Selected from the Writings of the Late Charles Wentworth Dilke. With a Biographical Sketch by His Grandson, Sir Charles Wentworth Dilke*. 2 vols. London: J. Murray, 1875.

Gittings, Robert. *John Keats*. Boston: Little, Brown, 1968.

Gray, Thomas. *Journal in the Lakes*. [1775]. In *Works of Thomas Gray*. 4 vols. Ed. Edmund Gosse. New York: A. C. Armstrong and Son, 1885. Vol. 1.

Hazlitt, William. "Mr. Wordsworth's New Poem, *The Excursion*." In *The Complete Works of William Hazlitt*. 21 vols. Ed. P. P. Howe. London: Dent and Sons. 1933. Vol. 19.

Heron, Robert. *Observations Made in a Journey through the Western Counties of Scotland in the Autumn of 1773*. 2 vols. R. Morrison and Son, 1893.

Hewlett, Dorothy. *A Life of John Keats*. London: Barnes and Noble, 1950.

Jones, Leonidas. *The Life of John Hamilton Reynolds*. Hanover, N.H.: University Press of New England, 1984.

Keats, John. *John Keats: Complete Poems*. Ed. Jack Stillinger. Cambridge, Mass.: Harvard University Press, 1982.
————. *The Keats Circle: Letters and Papers, 1816–1878*. 2 vols. Ed. Hyder Edward Rollins. Cambridge, Mass.: Harvard University Press, 1948.
————. *The Letters of John Keats, 1814–1821*. 2 vols. Ed. Hyder Edward Rollins. Cambridge, Mass.: Harvard University Press, 1948.
————. *The Poems of John Keats*. Ed. Jack Stillinger. Cambridge, Mass.: Harvard University Press, 1978.
————. *The Poetical Works and Other Writings of John Keats*. Ed. H. Buxton Forman, rev. Maurice Buxton Forman. 8 vols. New York: Charles Scribner's Sons, 1938–39.

Leslie, Lionel. *The Drover's Inn*. Isle of Mull: L. Leslie, n.d.

Leyden, John. *Journal of a Tour in the Highlands and Western Islands of Scotland in 1800*. Ed. James Sinton. Edinburgh: William Blackwood and Sons, 1903.

Lowell, Amy. *John Keats*. 2 vols. Boston: Houghton Mifflin, 1925.

McCormick, E. H. *The Friend of Keats: A Life of Charles Armitage Brown*. Wellington, N.Z.: Victoria University Press, 1989.

Milnes, Richard Monckton. *Life, Letters, and Literary Remains, of John Keats*. 2 vols. London: Edward Moxon, 1848.

————. (Lord Houghton). *The Life and Letters of John Keats*. 1867. Reprint. London: Dent; New York: Dutton, 1969.

Moorman, Mary. *William Wordsworth: The Later Years, 1803–1850*. London: Oxford University Press, 1968.

Murray, Sarah (Aust). *A Companion and Useful Guide to the Beauties of Scotland, and the Hebrides, to the Lakes of Westmoreland, Cumberland, and Lancashire; and to the Curiosities in the District of Craven, in the West Riding of Yorkshire. Also a Description of Part of Scotland, Particularly of the Highlands; and of the Isles of Mull, Ulva, Staffa, I-Columbkill, Tirii, Coll, Eigg, Rum, Skye, Raza, and Scalpa. To Which Is Now Added, An Account of the New Roads in Scotland, and of a Beautiful Cavern Lately Discovered in the Isle of Skye*. 2 vols., 3rd ed. London, 1810. Published by the author.

Old Kirkcudbright. Ed. I. F. Macleod. Old Galloway Papers no. 1. Glasgow, 1975.

Pennant, Thomas. *Pennant's Second Tour in Scotland* in *A General Collection of the Best and Most Interesting Voyages and Travels in All Parts of the World. . . .* Vol. 3. Ed. John Pinkerton. London: Longman . . . , 1809.

Phillips, Richard. *Journal of a Tour in Ireland, &tc &tc Performed in August 1804*. London: Barnard and Sultzer, 1806.

Radcliffe, Ann. *A Journey through Holland and the Western Frontier of Germany, with a Return down the Rhine: to which Are Added, Observations during a Tour to the Lakes of Lancashire, Westmoreland, and Cumberland*. Dublin: P. Wogan, 1795. Reprint. Hildesheim, Germany: Georg Olms Verlag, 1975.

Robinson, Howard. *The British Post Office, a History*. Westport, Conn.: Greenwood, 1970.

St. Fond, Faujas. *Travels through England and Scotland, to the Hebrides*. In *The British Tourist's Pocket Companion*. 6 vols. Ed. William Mavor. London, 1809.

Semple, John MacKenzie. *The Nunnery and the Tombs of the Kings: The Pilgrim's Way to the Abbey, Iona*. Glasgow: Iona Community Publishing, n.d.

Southey, Robert. *Journal of a Tour in Scotland in 1819*. Ed. C. H. Herford. London: John Murray, 1929.

Stoddart, Sir John. *Remarks on Local Scenery and Manners of Scotland during the Years 1799 and 1800*. 2 vols. London: W. Miller, 1801.

Topographical Dictionary of Scotland. 2nd ed., 2 vols. London: S. Lewis, 1851.

The Traveller's Guide through Scotland. 6th ed., 2 vols. Edinburgh: John Thompson, 1814.

Ward, Aileen. *John Keats: The Making of a Poet*. New York: Viking, 1963.

Wordsworth, Dorothy. *Recollections of a Tour Made in Scotland, A.D. 1803*. 3rd ed. Ed. J. C. Shairp. Edinburgh: David Douglas, 1894.

Wordsworth, William. *Guide to the Lakes* (Original title: *A Guide through the District of the Lakes*). 1810, 1835. Reprint. 5th ed. Ed. Ernest de Selincourt. Oxford: Oxford University Press, 1982.

INDEX OF NAMES AND PLACES

Variants and location of inns are in parentheses. Illustration numbers are in italics.